Biologically Inspired Artificial Intelligence for Computer Games

Darryl Charles
University of Ulster, Ireland

Colin Fyfe
University of Paisley, UK

Daniel Livingstone
University of Paisley, UK

Stephen McGlinchey
University of Paisley, UK

MEDICAL INFORMATION SCIENCE REFERENCE

Hershey · New York

Acquisition Editor:	Kristin Klinger
Senior Managing Editor:	Jennifer Neidig
Managing Editor:	Sara Reed
Development Editor:	Kristin Roth
Copy Editor:	Ashlee Kunkel
Typesetter:	Jamie Snavely
Cover Design:	Lisa Tosheff
Printed at:	Yurchak Printing Inc.

Published in the United States of America by
    IGI Publishing (an imprint of IGI Global)
    701 E. Chocolate Avenue
    Hershey PA 17033
    Tel: 717-533-8845
    Fax: 717-533-8661
    E-mail: cust@igi-global.com
    Web site: http://www.igi-global.com

and in the United Kingdom by
    IGI Publishing (an imprint of IGI Global)
    3 Henrietta Street
    Covent Garden
    London WC2E 8LU
    Tel: 44 20 7240 0856
    Fax: 44 20 7379 0609
    Web site: http://www.eurospanonline.com

Library of Congress Cataloging-in-Publication Data

Biologically inspired artificial intelligence for computer games / Darryl Charles, Colin Fyfe, Daniel Livingstone, & Stephen McGlinchey, editors.
    p. cm.
  Summary: "This book examines modern artificial intelligence to display how it may be applied to computer games. It spans the divide that exists between the academic research community working with advanced artificial intelligence and the games programming community which must create and release new and interesting games, creating an invaluable collection supporting both technological research and the gaming industry"--Provided by publisher.
  Includes bibliographical references and index.
  ISBN-13: 978-1-59140-646-4 (hardcover)
  ISBN-13: 978-1-59140-648-8 (ebook)
  1. Artificial intelligence--Computer games. 2. Artificial intelligence--Biological applications. 3. Research--Computer games. I. Charles, Darryl.
  Q336.B415 2008
  794.8'163--dc22
                    2007024492

British Cataloguing in Publication Data
A Cataloguing in Publication record for this book is available from the British Library.

All work contributed to this book is original material. The views expressed in this book are those of the authors, but not necessarily of the publisher.

Biologically Inspired Artificial Intelligence for Computer Games

Table of Contents

Foreword

As game developers a few years from now, we may look back at current generation AI with astonishment and possibly with a hint of nostalgia. We will notice the extreme simplicity of the systems and behaviours we created, asking ourselves whether it was in fact by design or more by necessity. More importantly, we will be surprised by the amount of time taken to prototype such AI. These classical game AI techniques (such as finite-state machines or scripts) appeal to us game developers because they can be easily controlled, but they suffer from this very same property; the content creators must craft each behaviour manually. Any progress in game AI necessarily involves finding a solution to this bottleneck without our designers loosing control over their creations.

This book provides an overview of modern AI techniques that can alleviate the burden. Biologically inspired AI techniques—and machine learning in general—provide us with methods and tools for creating complex in-game behaviours in a manageable way. Not only does this allow designers to prototype simple tasks quickly, but it also means that additional resources can be directed to improving the believability of our characters. While such AI techniques enable the creation of behavioural content in a much more scalable fashion, they are also broadly applicable across the many disciplines of game programming, particularly in off-line tools, as they are already used in parts of the games industry.

In general, the next generation of games is relying increasingly on third-party software, rather than home grown systems. These solutions provide strong toolsets and standardised algorithm that empower the game developer to create game content with indirect support from the programmer. Biologically inspired AI techniques fit into this paradigm since they are available as a set of algorithms that process data. However, these techniques are no longer just loading the designers' data directly from disk, but they are in essence assisting the creation process. For example, the AI can provide statistics about our gameplay prototypes, and find patterns in playtests to detect possible anomalies. Such powerful computational tools help produce higher quality behaviours and increase the scalability of the development process.

The role of us AI programmers in this environment is to provide a framework for the content creators. The designers decide what they want out of the machine learning, and we use our knowledge and experience to get the best results. Of course, there will always be a need for the classical AI techniques (Chapter X shows how they can successfully be combined with modern ones), but developers will increasingly default to modern approaches. This book is a great opportunity for game programmers to extend their skill set with modern AI techniques. It may take a bit of time for biologically inspired AI techniques to become commonplace in the industry, but there is certainly a need for them. Most players dream of playing against highly believable adaptive opponents, and with developers that can leverage modern technology to solve any problem at hand, this goal is certainly attainable.

Alex Champandard

Alex J. Champandard has worked in the entertainment industry as an AI programmer for many years, notably for Rockstar Games. With a strong academic background in artificial intelligence, he authored the book AI Game Development: Synthetic Creatures with Learning and Reactive Behaviors *and often speaks about his research, notably at the Game Developer Conference. Champandard is currently a freelance consultant at games companies in central Europe, helping developers integrate state of the art techniques into commercial games. He also maintains open source AI engines at http://AiGameDev. com where he writes tutorials for game programmers.*

Preface

Why would anyone want to make a computer game intelligent? What motivation is there for putting **intelligence** into perfectly good games? After all, humans have played games since prehistory and we have never had the ability to create intelligence in our games until now. This, of course, overlooks the fact that we typically played games against other human beings (most board games and sports) or against ourselves (often memory based games), sometimes with a statistical element involved (such as the solo card games of 'patience'). Most people would agree that the most satisfying is playing games against other people, particularly when the other people are of the same standard as ourselves. There is something inherently satisfying about competition with our peers. We do not get the same satisfaction competing against, for example, children who do not yet have our capabilities. Similarly we get no fun at all playing against an opponent who is perceived to be much better than us at a particular game. Thus we want to create games in which the opponent is, in some way, a worthy opponent for us. The computer promises to liberate us from the need to find such opponents by providing us with artificial opponents of a suitable ability. Thus our computer games commonly come not just with the game itself but with built-in artificial opponents who aspire to being worthy opponents for us.

Even in the realm of online multiplayer gaming, nonplayer characters (NPCs) are a required staple of many games, such as in most massively-multiplayer online games (MMOG), where NPCs may be required to provide missions or combat encounters. Here the contrast between intelligent players and nonintelligent computer controlled characters is even sharper, and clearly an area where more machine intelligence could be applied to improve the game for all the players.

This book is concerned with the application of modern artificial intelligence (AI) techniques to computer games. We suggest that the current generation of computer games is largely free of this technology. You may well protest that AI is already well established in such games; after all the computer opponent in such games not always known as the 'AI.' But we highlight the use of the word 'modern.' Most, though by no means all, games of recent and current generations use fairly old and certainly rather standard forms of artificial intelligence. In this book we will concentrate on technologies which are still the subject of large scale effort in the research field, such as artificial neural networks, genetic algorithms, or artificial immune systems. We shall not discuss, for example, case based reasoning since we concentrate solely on techniques which are based on those thought to dominate in real life.

So what is it that these technologies bring to computer games that finite state machines, expert systems, and the rest do not bring? The unifying theme of these techniques is adaptation, whether as a means to learn how to play a game or even while the game is being played. In artificial neural networks we are changing the network weights—corresponding to the synaptic efficiencies—so that the response from the artificial neural network changes from game to game. In evolutionary algorithms, the artificial chromosomes are being selected base on their fitness so that better solutions are being found as the game proceeds; in artificial immune systems, our artificial antibodies are being produced in response to attacks by artificial antigens which allows the artificial immune system to adapt to varying threats.

Why do we consider adaptation to be so central to creating intelligence in computer games? We feel that most people playing against an AI wish to feel that they are playing against another intelligent person. When two people play a competitive game, each uses a continually changing strategy: if you know your opponent's strategy in advance, you can prepare a defence specific to such a strategy. Even in completely nonrandom games such as chess, no player will use exactly the same opening or defence in each game. To do so would leave an opponent with a very simplified problem and would certainly result in long-term defeat. This is not to say that we will not have a set of preferred strategies in a game but the emphasis must be on having a nonsingular set, not just a single strategy.

There is one other point which may be made with respect to these biologically inspired AI techniques. Competition (for food, for shelter, for mates) is built into life itself and so we consider that using analogies in software of real biological processes means that we are basing our techniques on methodologies which have already proved successful in real life. Thus we may anticipate that the resulting techniques match in some way the experiences we already have as human beings in our existing environments.

By focussing on biologically-inspired AI techniques, rather than just those methods commonly used in the games industry, some sections of this book may appear to be more theoretical than applied. A number of case-studies are scattered throughout—either as chapters in their own right, or included into larger chapters—to offset this. These vary from simple illustrative examples, to case studies in contemporary action and racing games.

Origin of this Book

This book arose from our experience of teaching on a range of modules related to computer game development, including modules specifically focussed on game AI. We found that there was no existing text which satisfied our desired pedagogical aims. Many textbooks on game AI tend to be devoted to state space methods and efficient searches. Most present algorithms and solutions, but in concentrating on showing how to achieve results, they provide little in the way of theoretical underpinnings. A notable exception is that field which is devoted to evolutionary game theory; however, this field is much more based on mathematical game theory which is outside the interests of most programmers who are investigating computer games.

The research background of several of the authors is in the broad area of artificial neural networks (ANN), and this accordingly features in several of the chapters. It was our intention, however, to present a book which presented a more complete, yet still academic, view of game AI. We have also been able to draw upon our experience from research in a range of related areas, from artificial life and genetic algorithms to artificial immune systems and ant-colony optimisation.

Composition of this Book

In Chapter I, we present a brief review the history of computer games, from the 1950s to the present day. Needless to say the rate of change over the last decade has been much greater than that seen in earlier times and this acceleration seems likely to continue but we have tried to do justice to the major trends in existence today. The goal of this chapter is to more clearly set out what the common goals of game AI are, and to explain why much of modern game AI is not of academic interest.

In Chapter II, we provide a broad introduction to natural and artificial neural networks, including notes on the history of the development of modern artificial neural networks. Then, in Chapter III, we introduce the technique which, to many people, *is* artificial neural networks, the multilayered perceptron, or MLP. This well known technique uses the back-propagation of errors to learn. We give the theory behind the learning and some heuristics about its performance before illustrating its use on some general data problems. We then illustrate how it may be used in a game context. In Chapter IV, we provide a short case study on the use of artificial neural networks—particularly the multilayered perceptron—in digital games, using the Robocode competition framework as a suitable example.

The artificial neural networks in Chapters III and IV use supervised learning to adapt; the training set must include a set of answers appropriate to the problems in hand. However, a lot of human and animal learning occurs without a teacher. In particular, when playing a game we may learn by creating internal models of the game as it is being played, without a teacher taking on the role of a 'learning supervisor.' Thus in Chapter V, we discuss two types of artificial neural networks which organise according to unsupervised learning principles. We differentiate between competitive learning, a variation of which leads to self-organising maps, and Hebbian learning; the former tends to be used for clustering a data set while the latter leads to low dimensional projections of a data set. The self-organising map is used to develop AI opponents in the rather old game of Pong while the projection methods are illustrated in a high dimensional hide-and-seek game.

We stated that, for many people, artificial neural networks are equated with the multilayered perceptron, however the multilayered perceptron is actually only one network in a rather large field of supervised learning methods. Therefore in Chapter VI, we introduce a further alternative which can be used instead of the multilayered perceptron. We pay particular emphasis on the radial basis network since its speed of learning makes it extremely attractive in the context of computer games. Returning to Pong, we are then able to compare the in-game performance of different artificial neural networks in creating players for this simple game.

In Chapter VII, we switch to evolutionary algorithms, the most famous of which is the genetic algorithm. We spend some time examining issues of representation before illustrating its use on a computer game. The case study presented in this chapter, a motocross game with realistic physics, is a particularly challenging problem for AI to solve; the solution presented combining the power of both evolutionary and artificial neural net approaches. The games industry's traditional solution to this problem has been to use designer intelligence rather than machine intelligence and have the developers implement the paths to be followed. This work clearly demonstrates that contemporary games can potentially benefit from biologically inspired AI.

In Chapter VIII we explore just some of the many ways in which the standard genetic algorithm can be extended, and look at a few alternative evolutionary methods. Deceptive problems are introduced before we consider the first extension of the structured GA. Other alternatives introduced include probability based incremental learning (PBIL), which is also demonstrated through an example of the N-Persons Iterated Prisoners' Dilemma.

Chapter XI introduces the basic concept of multiobjective problems, with particular relation to the genetic algorithm. It then considers how genetic algorithms and evolutionary methods might be applied in the real-time strategy genre of computer games. In such games, AI has to work at a number of distinct levels, roughly speaking covering the strategic goals and the low level tactics. Exploring the full set of strategies and finding all the good solutions in such situations is far from straightforward, and this chapter illustrates some of the issues.

In Chapter X, we discuss artificial immune systems and show how our resulting models can be used in a variety of computer games. Since this topic is rather newer than the other AI techniques, we spend some time developing the artificial immune systems in a variety of game situations.

Two further, very distinct, biologically inspired AI techniques are introduced in the following two chapters. In Chapter XI ant-colony optimisation (ACO) is demonstrated as an alternative method of path-planning. An example application, the classic game of Combat is presented.

The following chapter, Chapter XII, outlines the methods used in reinforcement learning. Although the term 'reinforcement learning' can be used more generally to describe the learning methods used in a variety of AI techniques, it is also the name of a particular approach and set of algorithms for AI learning. The reinforcement learning approach is one based on the payment of rewards for actions leading to good results, such as winning a game. This simple notion forms the basis for a group of methods which at their core resemble human game playing approaches in a number of ways, although which have yet to be used to any extent in the commercial world of game development.

We close with two chapters which focus less on particular AI methods, but on issues relating to their use and misuse. Chapter XIII discusses adaptivity in games more generally. Current approaches to adaptivity in commercial games are discussed, along with issues facing developers wishing to introduce and develop adaptive solutions. It is our feeling that most attempts to include adaptivity in games have been (often deliberately) limited, and that there is a great deal of potential in making games more adaptive in a range of areas.

Finally in Chapter XIV, we assess how successful our attempt to install human-like intelligence in computer games has been using methods suggested by the famous Turing Test. It is of interest that Turing expected computers to pass his test by the year 2000. We believe that success in the game version of the Turing Test is more reachable in the near future than success in the standard Turing Test.

The book need not be read in any particular order and the chapters are intended to be self-contained, the exception being that Chapter III should be read before any of the other chapters on artificial neural networks. Thus we have also provided references at the end of each separate chapter rather than a single section at the end of the book. We hope that you will enjoy the book, that it will stimulate you to experiment with the AI techniques discussed, and that you will have as much fun playing with these techniques in your games as we have had while writing this book.

Trademarks

Naturally, in a book which discusses game AI, mention is made of a large number of commercial computer games, as well as a few films and other media outputs. All such trademarks and copyrights are property of their respective owners.

Acknowledgment

The authors would like to thank first of all Kristen Roth, and all at IGI Global, for much understanding and a vast reservoir of patience with the repeated delays in the delivery of this manuscript. Apologies, and thanks.

Thanks also to the two anonymous reviewers for their perceptive comments and suggestions, which have greatly benefited this volume.

Benoit Chaperot participated in many fruitful discussions and shared his research findings with us, for which we are very grateful.

We would also like to thank the students of the Paisley University Game AI class for their comments, which have helped us greatly in revising this text.

And finally we would all like to thank our respective wives, families, and friends for all the help and support over the long period that we have been working on this.

Chapter I

Contemporary Video Game AI

Introduction

This chapter provides a brief outline of the history of video game AI, and hence by extension, an extremely brief outline of some of the key points in the history of video games themselves.

The objectives of this chapter are to provide an overview of this broad topic, to outline those areas which this book will focus on, and to explain why other areas of game AI will not concern us.

The Dawn of the Computer Video Game

Those who were in their teenage years or older in the 1980s got their first exposure to videogames in the home of these machines, the amusement arcade. Many of the games that were played in the arcades during this period have left an indelible, nostalgic imprint in our memories and are now considered classic games. Computer and videogames have thoroughly invaded our homes so we now have a vast array of games that can be played on a range of formats. In this section we take a brief look at some of the classic games from a gaming period known as the golden age of videogames and discuss the rudimentary AI used in these early games.

The first videogame was actually created by William Higinbotham who worked to the U.S. government at the Brookhaven National Laboratory (Hunter, 1998). For an open day he put together a rudimentary two-player tennis game made by wiring an oscilloscope up to an analogue computer. Thus, this not only was the first computer/videogame game but also the first **multiplayer computer/videogame**. The game more usually quoted as the first computer game is Space War. Perhaps this is understandable as this was written on a digital computer that has a strong relationship with computers as we know them today. This game was written by Stephen Russell and colleagues during 1960 on a PDP-1 computer at MIT. Two spaceships controlled by separate players battled against each other in the void of space, firing missiles at each other, and trying to avoid being pulled towards a central sun. Asteroids is perhaps a game that bears most resemblance to this granddaddy of games.

It is noticeable that these early games had no semblance of AI in them. This was in part because noncomputer games are all played between individuals and the concept of playing against a computer had yet to really mature in the minds of programmers. Of course, resources were very much more limited on early computers and programs were cumbersome to code, enter, and debug on these machines. As computers become more powerful over the following decades, then AI in games became more important and elaborate.

Mainframe programmers continued to show off their prowess throughout the 60s with pioneering games like Lunar Lander in which two players took turns to control rocket-thrusters via a text interface during a landing, and Hammurabi which could be described as a precursor to the more recent Civilisation. However, it was possibly another **tennis-inspired game** that truly began the videogame revolution. In 1972 the first arcade version of Pong was created by an Atari engineer, Al Alcorn (and Nolan Bushnell). The game consisted of a hypnotic 'blip' sound, white dot ball, and white line paddles for rackets on a black background court; simple, but people could not get enough of it. According to Poole (2000), its popularity could be explained by the fact that 'players had only to use one hand to rotate the paddle control, thus facilitating simultaneous beer consumption!' Later to appear on home consoles (1975), this game was very influential in the evolution of videogames.

With games such as Pong the mechanics are such that early versions of the game were primarily multiplayer orientated. Single player versions of the game can use very rudimentary 'game AI' such as tracking AI. With tracking, typically the AI computer opponent follows and hones in on the player character's position. In the case of Pong the computer controlled paddle would move in response to the position of the ball, and would be limited by a maximum speed. To implement a more elaborate form of AI in this game, another common (and somewhat controversial) form of AI may be employed—'cheating AI.' The term cheating AI is used if the computer uses complete information about the current game state to inform its strategy or behaviour. In the example of Pong, complete information about the position and velocity of the player and ball can be used to decide its parameters of movement through an accurate look up table or predictive algorithm. This relates to the central issue for AI within games: irrespective of the technology that is used to implement the game AI, it should be designed to maximise the interactive experience for the player and it always should provide an appropriate level of **challenge**; the computer opponent should not always win nor always lose. This is actually more difficult than it may sound and is the focus for some recent game AI research. Of course, the AI that we use in computer controlled opponents may be more complex. For example, later in this book you will see an implementation of a Pong AI opponent where the AI has been modelled on an actual player and therefore it contains much of the quirky actions of that player. That is, the behaviour is more believable and it may be more difficult to distinguish the AI opponent from a real opponent. This is a second important aspect of any game AI: the computer controlled behaviour is believable so as to suspend our disbelief for the period of the game. Note that **believability** is generally a more important goal in game AI than simulated reality.

In 1978 Space Invaders was released and it has gone on to be one of the most well known and liked games in computer game history. It has grossed over $500 million dollars in its lifetime, and is still played on the Internet and emulators of arcade hardware. This was the beginning of the 'golden age of videogames' (Kent, 2001) which lasted from 1979 to 1983. Many of the classic games that are familiar to millions of gamers were released during this period. Games like Asteroids, Pac Man, and Donkey Kong are now household names and continue to influence game design today. The 'shoot'em up' genre was particularly important during this period and as well as Space Invaders we were treated to classics such as Asteroids, Robotron, Defender, Galaxian, Scramble, and Tempest.

Where present, much of the AI in these early 80s games still included simple tracking (or evading) and cheating AI but new forms of AI were evolving. Space Invaders used an elementary form of 'pattern' AI, which simply means that the computer controlled space ships were designed to follow a preset pattern of movement down the screen; this was the alien's 'not so clever' intelligent behaviour. The pattern of behaviour implemented as the AI in games such as Galaxian or Scramble may be a little more complex but often we find that the virtual intelligence that our imagination embellishes on the computer AI's behaviour is often more powerful than that implemented actually in the technology. Aspects of random behaviour can often be as effective as any other technique by creating 'AI in the mind of the player,' another crucial but fairly intangible aspect of designing a game AI. Pac Man is a very interesting case-in-point in relation to this sort of virtual game AI. A significant subculture has evolved around Pac Man and working out how the ghosts AI have been designed. A complete understanding of the AI of the 'ghosts' in the game seems illusive and at times players may feel that there is a complex and collective strategy being executed by the ghosts using realistic intelligence. In reality the complexity and effectiveness of the AI is largely down to the designer's diligence, Toru Iwatani, in tuning the AI to the gameplay experience by using a mixture of patterns, randomness, and tracking behaviours (and perhaps some cheating) in different measures for each ghost AI. The power of creating 'AI in the mind of the user' can be illustrated by the fact that each of the ghosts in this game have been given a name, for example, Red (Shadow/Blinky), Pink (Speedy), Blue (Bashful), Orange (Clyde), and these names are reflective of the ghosts 'personalities.' One illustration of the designer's tuning in this game is the change from the 'search and destroy' mode for all ghosts to 'scatter mode' where the ghosts move much more randomly thus very deliberately occasionally relieving some of the tension of gameplay on the player and introducing further possibilities in the gameplay.

The first **racing games** with a driver's view point were developed during this classic period, the prime examples being Atari's Night Driver and Namco's Pole Position (1982). These were linear games in which used simple tricks to give the visual impression of a curving racetrack. Sprint (in various versions from 1976 on) presented a top-down view of a race-track featuring AI cars to race against. AI in early racing games could be constructed simply using a combination of patterns to make a computer controlled car follow the race track, way point following, evasive or simple collision detection to avoid the player's vehicle, and perhaps some collision detection on the edges of the track (though collision detection may also be thought of as part of the physics of a game). Realism or believability in the racing may have been enhanced by giving cars different racing attributes (speed, etc.) and perhaps introduction elements of randomness and individual behaviours. Modern games like Mario Kart can still adhere to many of the early principles governing a car AI but often also use significant cheating AI to keep the race even and competitive, that is, if the player is winning easily it is possible to speed up the computer controlled cars or to penalise the leading car with harsher penalties. There is evidence to suggest that players do not mind being handicapped or helped by the game, so long as they do not know about it!

In 1981, Donkey Kong was born and began a minirevolution with a new genre, the **platform-game**. Its creator, Shigeru Miyamoto, went on to design such as Mario Bros. (1983), and later Zelda: Ocarina of Time (1998). The Mario Bros. series of games have been renowned for innovating on the platform genre, culminating in Super Mario 64 (1996), which many people believe to be the definitive 3D platform computer game. The 'pure' platform game may now be gone forever, replaced now with 3D adventure games and similar ones that include platform-like levels, for example, Tomb Raider. We can think about another aspect of game AI as beginning in this genre: player-character AI. Although the player controls the character, for example, Mario, this character is still required to behave reasonably as we control it in context of its environment. For example, in the one of the earlier Mario games, jumping by pressing the 'A' button can have several effects depending on the context: if there is no one or nothing close by he will simply jump into the air and fall back down, if a platform is present he will land on that, whereas if an enemy is below him and he falls then this enemy is stunned or destroyed. In a modern game, this sort of character behaviour is now implemented commonly by finite state machines in games.

The real-time strategy game genre can also trace its roots back to this period with Atari's Missile Command (1980). The essence of this type of game is in table top war game simulations. Troops and resources are managed and controlled as efficiently as possible and strategies developed to overcome artificially intelligent or real opponents. AI in the modern form of this genre is a little bit different from other games in that it heavily relies on strategic planning and management of resources. Path finding is also a very important AI technology in this genre in that the game units spend a lot of their time negotiating the game environment and either moving towards the player's units or away from them. Although, early examples of games from this genre used little AI, perhaps simple way-point mechanisms, now the A* path-finding algorithm is a consistent component of these and many other games.

Between the end of the 'golden age' of videogames, through the 'PlayStation generation,' and on to current games, there have been many changes in gaming platforms and games. As gaming console and PC hardware have become much more powerful and as games have become increasingly visually realistic, there is a greater demand for more advanced AI within games to enhance the immersive experience. With this in mind we will now present an overview of both current standard AI approaches now used in commercial games and go on to outline some of the current innovative methods.

Contemporary Video Game AI

Games have clearly come some way in the decades since they first appeared to the public at large; from simplistic two-dimensional worlds presented using monochrome or simple palettes of primary and secondary colours, to complex, interactive 3D worlds presented with near-photo realism. Over the same time, the progress made by game AI has been significant but game AI still has far to go before the degree of realism it presents matches that of current graphics. In the remainder of this book we focus on a range of biologically inspired techniques which might prove useful in future game AI, but first we will present the briefest of reviews of contemporary game AI. Other, extended reviews can be found in a variety of texts that include works by Rabin (2002c, 2004).

Searching With A*

A* has already been mentioned, and it is certainly a core AI technique found in a vast number of games. Search is a fundamental problem, one that was an early target of AI researchers. Searches might be attempts to find the shortest (or any) route between two points on a map. More generally, a search might be an attempt to find a solution in some more abstract problem space, perhaps modelled using graphs of connected points, each point being some distance from other points where one point represents the desired solution and another the start of our search. Being generally useful, many algorithms were developed for search problems. Depth-first searches pick one direction and follow that until the goal is found or no more progress could be made. Breadth-first searches take a single step in each and every possible direction before extending the search by taking a second step in each direction. The A* algorithm (and its very many variants) is in most cases a vastly better performer than either of these, using a heuristic in an attempt to guide the search towards the goal destination. Search algorithms (including A*) are discussed widely, for example, by Ginsberg (1993) and Stout (1996), and an entire section by Rabin (2002c) is devoted to this area. One recent alternative, good where it is possible to precompute searches, is the fast-march method (Sethian, 1998; Stout, 1996), which has some advantages over alternative methods (principally in its ability to approximate continuous solutions using a discrete search space). A game application of this is presented by Livingstone and MacDowell (2003).

Minimax

One of the first AI algorithms applied specifically to playing games was **Minimax** (Schaeffer and Plaat, [1996] have more recent work in this area), used in checkers and chess games for many decades. The basic idea here is for a computer player to evaluate all of its possible moves and to select the one which generates the largest score according to some evaluation metric. The min-part of this is to assume that the opponent will make a move to minimise the computer's score, and the computer will again respond by attempting to maximise, and so on. This is a form of search, but with chess the search space is huge and only relatively recently did it become possible to use brute force to allow a computer to consider a huge number of possible moves. Instead, min-max may search through a set (possibly quite small) number of moves and responses before selecting the one which appears is predicted to lead to the best possible result.

A combination of brute-force computer power, plus many refinements and developments to the AI techniques used, has allowed chess computers to successfully compete against human grand masters and world champions of the game (see also Chapter X where there is some discussion of the significance of this).

Finite-State-Machines

One area where the academic view of what AI is differs greatly from that of the commercial game-developer is where **finite-state-machines** (FSM) are considered. Another core components in the game-developers AI toolbox, academically FSM are not thought of as AI at all, although they are sometimes used within AI systems. FSM consider some thing to consist of a number of possible states, with a number of possible transitions between states and a collection of triggers which cause state transitions to occur. These are commonly used to have game characters switch between different preprogrammed behaviours, such as patrolling guards who leave their patrol routes when the investigate mode is triggered by nearby sounds, and return to patrolling after some time when triggered by a timeout event. The use of FSM in games is detailed by Rabin (2002a, 2002b) and Champandard (2003). Perhaps the most significant use of FSM (or similar) as a component of more 'academic' AI is when triggering changes in robot behaviours using Brooks' (1991) subsumption architecture, and in similar approaches.

Flocks, Agents, and Artificial Life

A seminal work which has had a major effect on AI used in games, and in film CGI, is Craig Reynolds' (1987) **flocking** algorithm. Using a small set of simple rules governing the behaviour of each individual in a large group, it was possible to simulate the behaviour of a whole flock of, for example, birds. This distributed approach to AI demonstrates how simple rules implemented by individuals can give rise **emergent behaviour**, interesting behaviour at the group level which is not explicitly programmed. These ideas of placing simple AI in each individual and of modeling large numbers of such individuals have also given rise to one modern branch of academic AI, one which looks out to biology and other sciences for inspiration and interesting problems: **artificial life** (e.g., Langton, 1989). Agent-based approaches to AI are common outside of these areas also, but definitions of agents are now very varied and broad.

Considering moving vehicles more generally, Craig Reynolds also extended his work to present a model of autonomous steering behaviours (Reynolds, 1999), and this more recent work is also proving influential in current game AI.

While we do not focus particularly on these areas within this book, there is a clear relation to ant-colony optimisation which we do cover in one of the later chapters.

Artificial Neural Networks

Artificial neural networks (ANN) have been a growing area of biologically-inspired academic AI research over the past few decades, yet to date there have been very few commercial games which have made use of them. Interest is rising, however, and ANN have had some coverage in games development books of late, with some material by Rabin (2002c, 2004) and Champandard (2003), for example. Such coverage has only scratched the surface of what ANN can do and of the myriad forms ANN can take. Reviews of ANN with example game applications form a major part of this book, and the reader is referred forward to learn about these in significantly more detail.

Artificial Evolution

Evolution has proven to be a highly effective problem solver, and has inspired a number of AI techniques, most famously genetic algorithms (GA) (Holland, 1975). Like ANN, few games have used GA. Those games that have used GA or ANN, have—with few exceptions—used them to learn good solutions to, for example, find the optimal driving line in a racing game during game development then fix the parameters once the game is ready for sale. Thus, most uses to date of these learning, adaptive AI techniques have disabled the learning, adaptive portion in the finished product.

Other evolution inspired techniques include evolutionary strategies and genetic programming. From quite different inspiration, artificial immune systems (AIS) have, in practice, many similarities to GA, and in this book we will look at both of these approaches, comparing results on particular test problems, alongside those using related methods.

Artificial Biochemistry

Almost ten years ago, the computer game Creatures introduced virtual play-pals complete with a basic artificial biochemistry (Grand & Cliff, 1998). Creatures successfully combined ANN 'brains' with a biochemistry with needs which could be met by the creatures eating the various substances in their play-world. Over time, it became possible for creatures to breed, creating eggs containing genetic-material from both parents which would be used in helping to develop offspring creatures.

Thus, the Creatures series of games combined a variety of different biologically inspired AI techniques in creating a new digitally-based life form. Many of these ideas have survived in some form in The Sims, where simulated humans need to satisfy a range of basic biological needs as part of their daily routines. It is notable that a decade after Creatures first emergence, there is still no commercial game AI around that has advanced on it. In this book we do not look at artificial biochemistry, but note that it can help add a touch of realism to a game when the characters within it needs to eat once in a while.

Other AI Methods

The focus of this book is quite deliberately on biologically inspired AI techniques for computer games, but we need to note that a large number of other techniques are currently in use. Many classical AI architectures and methods—blackboard systems, rule-based systems, constraint-satisfaction, and more—are in use. Blackboard and rule-based systems might be used, for example, in complex strategy games, where the rule-base is used to determine what actions a computer player should opt for, while the blackboard allows different AI components to share information. For more information on these, refer to a general AI textbook, such as that written by Ginsberg (1993), or to those books which provide an overview of current game AI methods (e.g., Rabin, 2002c, 2004; Champandard, 2003).

Future of Game AI

It is interesting to consider what future game AI systems might look like. There are certainly a number of interesting current developments. First, game-AI is establishing itself firmly in academic research, with an ever increasing number of conferences and workshops dedicated to it, often within larger AI conferences dedicated to specific fields of AI (such as ANN or case-based reasoning). In part this is also being driven by the development of new multicore processor architectures which promise to allow developers more processor time dedicated to AI without adversely affecting the graphical quality of games, something which until now has been a severely limiting factor in the development of game AI.

A committee of the International Game Developers' Association (IGDA) has been working to establish a set of AI standards, and is symptomatic of the increasing attention that has been given to AI within the industry over recent years.

One particular topic which is slow to develop, however, is the inclusion of learning AI systems in game, such systems forming the majority of this text. While there is increased interest in learning AI, commercial considerations require predictable products without the possibility of nasty surprises. Learning AI will have to prove itself before it comes as standard.

There are a number of interesting topics that are not touched on at all in this book, such as using AI for emergent story-telling (e.g., Young, Riedl, Branly, Jhala, Martin, & Saretto, 2004). Going beyond emergent behaviour, can AI systems adapt the interactions between players and game characters to produce novel, interesting, and compelling plots (Fairclough & Cunningham, 2004)? This is just one of the interesting directions AI methods are being applied to. Some others are mentioned with this text, others will surprise us all. The one thing we can predict with confidence is that there will be a lot more interesting AI in the games of tomorrow.

Conclusion

We have provided a short background to the history of computer games, and of AI for games, along with a round-up of some current techniques and some brief thoughts on the future of game AI. The following chapters detail some of the biologically-inspired techniques which might form a significant part of that future.

References

Brooks, R.A. (1991). Intelligence without representation. *Artificial Intelligence Journal, 47*, 139-159.

Champandard, A. (2003). *AI game development*. New Riders.

Fairclough, C., & Cunningham, P. (2004, November). AI structuralist storytelling in computer games. In *Proceedings of the CGAIDE International Conference on Computer Games: Artificial Intelligence, Design and Education*, Reading (pp. 8-10).

Ginsberg, M. (1993). *Essentials of artificial intelligence*. Morgan Kaufmann.

Grand, S., & Cliff, D. (1998). Creatures: Artificial life autonomous software agents for home entertainment. *Autonomous Agents and Multi-Agent Systems, 1*(1), 39-57.

Holland, J.H. (1975). *Adaptation in natural and artificial systems*. Ann Arbor, MI: University of Michigan Press.

Hunter, W. (1998). *The dot eaters: Classic video game history.* Retrieved October 12, 2006, from http://www.emuunlim.com/doteaters/

Kent, S. (2001). *The ultimate history of videogames.* Prima Life.

Langton, C.G. (1989). Artificial life. *SFI studies in the sciences of complexity.* Addison-Wesley.

Livingstone, D., & McDowell, R. (2003). *Fast marching and fast driving: Combining off-line search and reactive A.I.* Paper presented at the Game-On 2003, 4th International Conference on Intelligent Games and Simulation, London.

Poole, S. (2000). *Trigger happy: Videogames and the entertainment revolution.* Arcade Publishing.

Rabin, S. (2002a). Implementing a state machine language. In S. Rabin (Ed.), *AI game programming wisdom* (pp. 314-320). Hingham, MA: Charles River Media, Inc.

Rabin, S. (2002b). Enhancing a state machine language through messaging. In S. Rabin (Ed.), *AI game programming wisdom* (pp. 321-329). Hingham, MA: Charles River Media, Inc.

Rabin, S. (Ed.). (2002c). *AI game programming wisdom.* Hingham, MA: Charles River Media.

Rabin, S. (Ed.). (2004). *AI game programming wisdom II.* Hingham, MA: Charles River Media.

Reynolds, C.W. (1987). Flocks, herds and schools: A distributed behavioural model. *Computer Graphics, 21*(4).

Reynolds, C.W. (1999). *Steering behaviours for autonomous characters.* Paper presented at the Game Developers Conference, San Jose, California. San Francisco: Miller Freeman Game Group.

Schaeffer, J., & Plaat, A.. (1996). New advances in Alpha-Beta searching. In *Proceedings of the ACM 24th Conference on Computer Science* (pp. 124-130).

Sethian, J.A. (1998). *Level set methods and fast marching methods: Evolving interfaces in computational geometry, fluid mechanics, computer vision and materials sciences.* Cambridge University Press.

Stout, B. (1996, October). *Smart moves: Intelligent pathfinding.* Game Developer.

Young, R.M., Riedl, M.O., Branly, M., Jhala, A., Martin, R.J., & Saretto, C.J. (2004). An architecture for integrating plan-based behaviour generation with interactive game environments. *Journal of Game Development, 1*(1).

Chapter II

An Introduction to Artificial Neural Networks

Introduction

The design of the first computers were influenced by the power of the human brain and attempts to create **artificial intelligence**, yet modern day digital computers are very different from what we understand about human neural processing. Most computers today are sequential (or only partially parallel) and have no (or very limited) learning capability. We have succeeded in building machines that can reliably store and quickly access information from large databases of data but we have only recently been able to create control mechanisms that enable robots to walk on two legs on flat surfaces. However, as far as image recognition is concerned, and in particular face recognition, our attempts to replicate the power of our own visual systems have been very limited. Our own biological visual systems are still much more advanced than current artificial models. For example, human visual systems are able to recognise people's faces from various distances and angles, or when we are shown a picture of a person when they were much younger, and even when someone is in disguise. If we could artificially recreate even some of the most powerful parallel processing or learning capabilities of the brain then it would be very worthwhile. Whether for learning, generalisation, modelling complex nonlinear functions, or intelligent data compression, artificial neural networks can be also be useful in game design and development.

In the next chapters we discuss the two main forms of neural network learning in detail: supervised and unsupervised learning. This will then be used as a base for us to outline a number of practical applied examples for digital games. First we will explain the background and basic ideas surrounding artificial neural networks.

Biological Neural Networks

The first neural cells were discovered in 1873 by Italian scientist Camillo Golgi who found when brain tissue was stained in Silver Chromate solution that a small percentage of neurons became darkly stained. The **human brain** contains approximately 95-100 billion of these neurons (grey matter), each between 0.01 and 0.05 mm in size, and each neuron may have up 10 000 connections (white matter). The following diagram illustrates the structure and main components of a typical biological neuron.

In a real neuron, signals are transmitted between neurons by electrical pulses (action-potentials or "spike" trains) travelling along the axon. Information is received by the neuron at synapses on its dendrites. Each **synapse** represents the junction of an incoming axon from another neuron with a dendrite of the neuron represented

Figure 1. The structure of a biological neuron

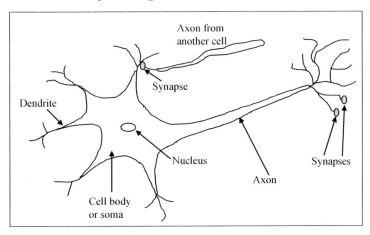

information to be transmitted from one neuron to the next. The information is then transmitted along the dendrites until it reaches the cell body where a summation of the electrical impulses reaching the body takes place and some function of this sum is performed. If this function is greater than a particular threshold the neuron will fire. This means that it will send a signal (in the form of a wave of ionisation) along its axon in order to communicate with other neurons. In this way, information is passed from one part of the network of neurons to another. It is crucial to recognise that synapses are thought to have different efficiencies and that these efficiencies change during the neuron's lifetime. We will return to this feature when we discuss learning.

It is an interesting observation that neurons respond slowly, 10^{-3} s compared to 10^{-9} s for electrical circuits, but that the brain gains its power through massively **parallel computation**, around 10^{10} neurons in the brain and 10^{4} connections per neuron. It is through the massively parallel nature of neural networks that they have the capability to learn and derive meaning from a complex, imprecise, or noisy data, and generalise well for unseen data. The ability for neural networks to solve complex (large-scale) and seemingly intractable problems is one of the key reasons that there has been considerable interest for many decades now in harnessing this power through computational models.

Artificial Neural Networks

Although some models of a neuron are very complex and attempt to accurately reproduce the full functionality of a real neuron, the **artificial neural networks** that we will discuss and use in this book are designed to model the way in which our brain performs in more general ways. That is, the models that we discuss are more biologically relevant with regard to the learning mechanisms than the underlying physical structure or mechanisms. The most complete textbook we know of in this area is that of Haykin (1994).

One of the earliest models of the neuron is called the threshold logic unit (TLU) originally proposed by McCulloch and Pitts in 1943. A general representation of this model is shown below:

The inputs to the neuron, as illustrated in the figure above, are represented by the input vector $\mathbf{x}_m$ and the synapses' efficiencies are modelled by a weight vector $\mathbf{w}_m$. Each of the individual data inputs are multiplied by the value of its connecting weight and all of these resulting multiplications are added together to give, a, at the summing junction. The final output, y, from the neuron is obtained by applying a function $f(.)$ to this summation. This function typically falls into one of three categories:

Figure 2. A simple artificial neuron. The weights model the synaptic efficiencies and the activation function models a form of processing within the cell body

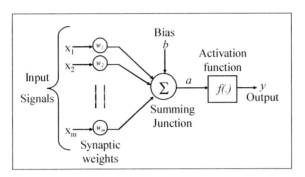

- Threshold.
- Linear (or ramp – the example shown below is semi-linear).
- Sigmoid. $f(x) = 1/(1 + e^{-s(z-T)})$ where z is the input activity, T is a threshold, and 's' is a measure of the slope of $f(x)$.). The function $tanh()$ is sometimes used as an alternative.

Mathematically, a single output value of this neuron is given by,

$$y = f\left(\sum_i w_i x_i \right) = f(\mathbf{w}.\mathbf{x}) = f(\mathbf{w}^T \mathbf{x})$$

You will meet all three ways of representing the operation of summing the weighted inputs. Sometimes $f()$ will be the identity function that is, $f(\mathbf{x}){=}\mathbf{x}$. Notice that if the weight between two neurons is positive, the input neuron's effect may be described as excitatory; if the weight between two neurons is negative, the input neuron's effect may be described as inhibitory.

To consider an example for the single neuron case, as illustrated above, let 1234 and let the activation function, $f()$, be the Heaviside (threshold) function such that,

$$f(t) = \begin{cases} 1 & \text{if } t > 0 \\ 0 & \text{if } t \leq 0 \end{cases}$$

Now if the input vector,

$$\mathbf{x} = x_1 x_2 x_3 x_4 = (1, 2, 1, 2).$$

Then the activation of the neuron is,

$$\mathbf{w.x} = \Sigma_j w_j x_j = 1*1 + 2*2 + 1*(-3) + 2*3 = 8$$

and so,

$$y = f(8) = 1.$$

However if the input vector,

$$\mathbf{x} = x_1 x_2 x_3 x_4 = (3, 1, 2, 0),$$

then the activation is

$$\mathbf{w.x} = \Sigma_j w_j x_j = 3*1 + 1*2 + 2*(-3) + 0*3 = -1$$

and so,

$$y = f(-1) = 0.$$

Therefore we can see that the single neuron is an extremely simple processing unit. The power of neural networks is believed to come from the accumulated power of adding many of these simple processing units together, that is, we throw lots of simple and robust power at a problem.

In a neural network, the neurons are grouped in layers and generally each neuron from one layer is connected to all neurons of the adjoining layers. The data provided to the neural network are propagated through the layers from input layer to output layer often through one or more hidden layers. As you will see with the Backpropagation neural network later in this chapter, sometimes information is propagated backwards through the network as well. The following figure illustrates a typical three layer neural network.

Figure 3. A typical artificial neural network consisting of 3 layers of neurons and 2 connecting layers of weights

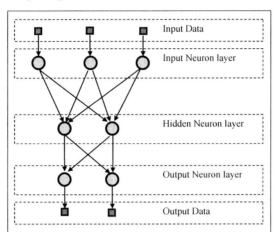

In Figure 3, we have a set of inputs entering the network from the top and being propagated through the network via the weights until the activation reaches the output layer. The middle layer is known as the hidden layer as it is invisible from out with the net: we may not affect its activation directly.

Neural Networks Classification

Neural networks can be trained to solve logical problems. For example, let us say that we want to train a neural network to decide whether I should have a curry or a pizza on the basis of the following table.

If we encode weekend = 1, hungry = 1, and curry = 1, then we can encode the table using binary numbers (of course we are assuming that all I eat is curry and pizza,

Table 1. A simple classification example

Condition 1	Condition 2	Outcome
It is the weekend	I am hungry	Buy a curry
It is a weekday	I am hungry	Buy a pizza
It is the weekend	I am not hungry	Buy a pizza
It is a weekday	I am not hungry	Buy a pizza

Table 2. Encoding of the simple classification problem

Weekday or weekend?	Am I hungry?	Conclusion
1	1	1
0	1	0
1	0	0
0	0	0

which is not far from the truth). The numerical encoding of a problem is often one of the most difficult aspects but it is not so difficult in this case.

If you are eagle-eyed you will have noticed that this is the truth table for a logical AND, and that we do not need to train a neural network to do this! Never mind, it still provides a nice example. Notice also that in this case all possible binary input combinations are represented by input-output mappings and that this example of a neural network will not be required to generalise unseen input data (normally one of reasons to use a neural network).

We can build this simple neuron circuitry without actually training by using a neural activation function which 'fires' an output equal to 1 if the sum of the inputs is greater than 1.5 (i.e., a hard limiter function with a threshold of 1.5). If it is the weekend and I am hungry I will have curry, otherwise I will have pizza (Seems to be nothing wrong with that logic!).

We can look at this neural processing another way, in terms of classification. We can say that we are using neural processing to distinguish curry eating circumstances from pizza ones. Graphically this classification can be illustrated by the following diagram.

This problem is solvable by a single neuron because the classes within the problem are linearly separable. As can been seen from the diagram above, a single line can be drawn between the numerical coordinates of the inputs that lead to pizza eating nights and those that lead to curry nights.

If I decide to have curry on every occasion except on a weekday when I am not hungry, we now have a logic OR problem, but it is still a linearly separable problem that can be solved by a single neuron (or single layer of neurons).

Figure 4. A simple neuron activation function

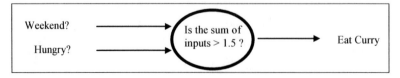

Figure 5. Logic AND problem

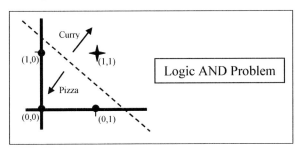

Figure 6. Logic OR problem

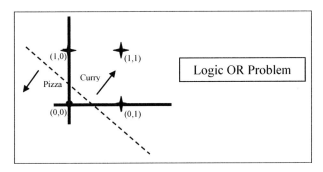

Figure 7. Logic XOR problem

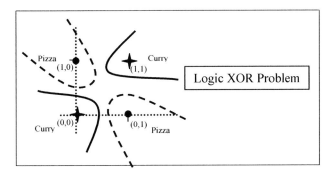

Let us say for the sake of argument that I am an odd sort of person and that I only want to have curry when I am hungry at the weekends or on weekdays when I am not hungry (strange, I agree). This is more easily illustrated in the following diagram.

Not only is this an odd way to choose what to eat, but as you can see it is also impossible to draw a straight line between the curry night and the pizza night outcomes. XOR-type problems are not solvable by a single trainable neuron (or single layer of neurons) because the classes are not linearly separable. In 1969, Marvin Minsky and Seymour Papert published a book which pointed out this limitation within **perceptron** neurons. After this, research on neurons and neural networks slowed down significantly until the early 1980s when several multilayered algorithms were shown to overcome this limitation. We will look at the XOR problem again shortly.

The following diagram illustrates how adding more neurons and in particular how adding more layers of neurons allows us to solve more complex problems and classify patterns that are more nonlinear.

In Figure 8 it can be seen that a one or two layered neural network is unable to perform the classification correctly, although a three layered mapping can potentially do so.

Figure 8. Diagram showing the effect that adding further neuron layers can have to the classification of data

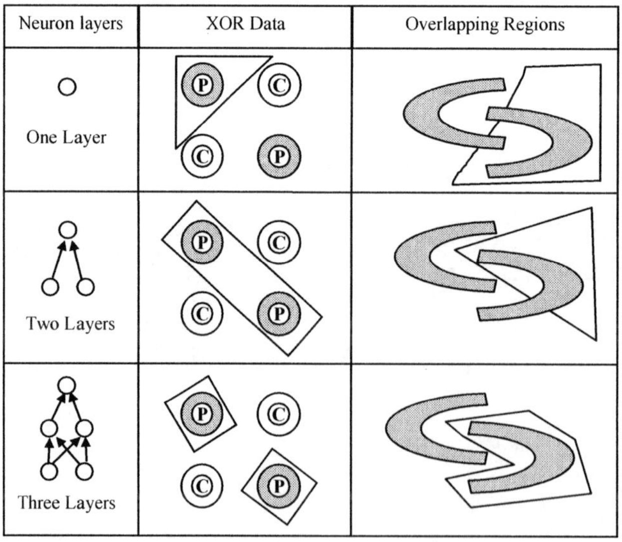

Learning in Artificial Neural Networks

There are two modes in artificial neural networks:

1. **Activation transfer mode:** When activation is transmitted throughout the network.
2. **Learning mode:** When the network organises usually on the basis of the most recent activation transfer.

We stated earlier that neural networks need not be programmed when they encounter novel environments, yet their behaviour changes in order to adapt to the new environment. Such behavioural changes are due to changes in the values associated with the weights in the network. The change of weight values in a neural network is called learning, and these changes in an artificial neural network are intended to model the varying synaptic efficiencies in real neural networks. It is believed that our learning is due to changes in the efficiency with which synapses pass information between neurons.

Neural network learning methods may be classified into three major categories: supervised, unsupervised, and reinforcement learning (though we will concentrate on the first two in this book).

Supervised Learning

With this type of learning, we provide the network with input data and the correct answer, that is, what output we wish to receive given that input data. The input data are propagated forward through the network until activation reaches the output neurons. We can then compare the answer which the network has calculated with that which we wished to get. If the answers agree, we do not need to make changes to the network; if, however, the answer which the network is giving is different from that which we wished then we adjust the weights to ensure that the network is more likely to give the correct answer in the future if it is again presented with the same (or similar) input data. This weight adjustment scheme is known as supervised learning or learning with a teacher.

For example, if a neural network were to be taught to recognise hand written characters, then several examples of each letter ('A,' 'B,' 'C,' etc.) written by different people could be given to the network. With each of these examples we know what the response of the network should be; for example, the first output neuron should 'fire' with an activation of 1 when the network is presented with a letter 'A' and the second neuron should 'fire' when a 'B' is presented and so on through the alphabet.

Initially because the weights are untrained, the responses on the output neurons are seemingly quite random and incorrect, but as the weights are updated on the basis of the how close or far the outputs are from the correct classification of the letters then the network gradually becomes more accurate. Through a number of iterations of this process and by providing thousands of examples, the neural network will eventually learn to classify all characters it has seen, as long the data are not too complex for the neural network. When trained, the network should ideally also be able to classify previously unseen letters accurately; this of course is the main point of the training—the ability of the network to generalise—as it is not actually that difficult to train the network to recognise characters when we know a priori what the answer should be.

The following chapter is dedicated to supervised learning, and Chapter IV provides a game-based case-study application of supervised learning.

Unsupervised Learning

With this type of neural network learning there is no external teacher and learning is generally based only on information that is local to each neuron. This is also often referred to as **self-organisation**, in the sense that the network self-organises in response to data presented to the network and detects the emergent collective properties within the data. Amongst the earliest works on self-organising maps is the work by Willshaw and von der Malsburg (1976), taking their cue from topological maps in biological neural networks. Unsupervised neural methods are often used in an exploratory manner; we use statistical relationships between data variables in order to establish an understanding of the nature of the data. Unlike supervised learning, we do not know the answers before we begin training.

Unsupervised learning will be revisited in Chapter V.

Reinforcement Learning

A third less commonly used from of neural learning is **reinforcement learning**, which gained prominence from Barto, Sutton, and Anderson's (1983) publication. This learning relates to maximising a numerical reward signal through a sort of trial-and-error search. In order to learn, the network is not told which actions to take but instead must discover which actions yield the most reward by trying them. If an action has been successful then the weights are altered to reinforce that behaviour otherwise that action is discouraged in the modification of the weights.

Reinforcement learning is different from supervised learning in that with supervised methods, learning is from examples provided by some knowledgeable external supervisor. With interactive sorts of problems it is quite often unrealistic to expect to be able to provide examples of desired behaviour that are both correct and representative for all scenarios which an agent may encounter. Yet this is perhaps where we would expect learning to be most beneficial, particularly with agent technology where an agent can learn from experience.

References

Barto, A.G., Sutton, R.S., & Anderson, C.W. (1983). Neuronlike adaptive elements that can solve difficult learning control problems. *IEEE Transactions on Systems, Man, and Cybernetics, 13*, 834-846.

Haykin, S. (1994). *Neural networks: A comprehensive foundation*. MacMillan.

McCulloch, W.S., & Pitts, W. (1943). A logical calculus of the ideas immanent in nervous activity. *Bulletin of Mathematical Biophysics, 5*, 115-133.

Minsky, M.L., & Papert, S.A. (1969). *Perceptrons*. Cambridge, MA: MIT Press.

Willshaw, D.J., & von der Malsburg, C. (1976). How patterned neural connections can be set up by self-organization. *Proceedings of the Royal Society of London Series B, 194*, 431-445.

Chapter III

Supervised Learning with Artificial Neural Networks

Introduction

In this chapter we will look at supervised learning in more detail, beginning with one of the simplest (and earliest) **supervised neural learning** algorithms: the Delta Rule. The objectives of this chapter are to provide a solid grounding in the theory and practice of problem solving with artificial neural networks, and an appreciation of some of the challenges and practicalities involved in their use.

The Delta Rule

An important early network was the Adaline (ADAptive LINear Element) (Widrow & Hoff, 1960). The **Adaline** calculates its output as $o = \Sigma_j w_j x_j + \theta$, with the same notation as before. You will immediately note the difference between this network and the perceptron is the lack of thresholding. The interest in the network was partly due to the fact that it has an easily implementation as a set of resistors and switches.

The Learning Rule: Error Descent

For a particular input pattern, x^P, we have an output o^P and target t^P. Then the sum squared error from using the Adaline on all training patterns is given by,

$$E = \sum_P E^P = \frac{1}{2} \sum_P (t^P - o^P)^2$$

where the fraction is included due to inspired hindsight. Now, if our Adaline is to be as accurate as possible, we wish to minimise the **squared error**. To minimise the error, we can find the **gradient** of the error with respect to the weights and move the weights in the opposite direction. If the gradient is positive, the error would be increased by changing the weights in a positive direction and therefore we change the weights in a negative direction. If the gradient is negative, in order to decrease the error we must change the weights in a positive direction. This is shown diagrammatically in Figure 1. Formally:

Figure 1. A schematic diagram showing error descent

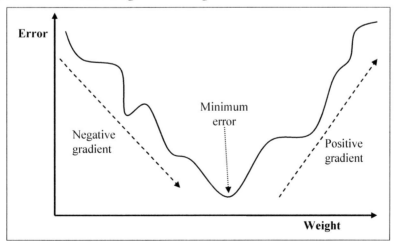

Note. In the negative gradient section, we wish to increase the weight; in the positive gradient section, we wish to decrease the weight

$$\Delta P w_{ij} = -\gamma \frac{\partial E^{P}}{\partial w_{j}}$$

We say that we are searching for the **least mean square** (LMS) error and so the rule is called the LMS or Delta rule or Widrow-Hoff rule. Now, for an Adaline with a single output, o,

$$\frac{\partial E^{P}}{\partial w_{j}} = \frac{\partial E^{P}}{\partial o^{P}} \cdot \frac{\partial o^{P}}{\partial w_{j}}$$

and because of the linearity of the Adaline units, $\dfrac{\partial o^{P}}{\partial w_{j}} = x^{P}$. Also, $\dfrac{\partial E^{P}}{\partial o^{P}} = -(t^{P} - o^{P})$, and so $\Delta P w_{j} = \gamma (t^{P} - o^{P}).x_{j}^{P}$. Notice the similarity between this rule and the perceptron learning rule; however, this rule has far greater applicability in that it can be used for both continuous and binary neurons. This has proved to be a most powerful rule and is at the core of almost all current supervised learning methods. But it should be emphasised that the conditions for guaranteed convergence which we used in proving the perceptron learning theorem do not now pertain. Therefore there is nothing to prevent learning in principle never converging.

However, since it is so central we will, consider two variations of the basic rule in the sections below.

Nonlinear Neurons

The extension to nonlinear neurons is straightforward. The firing of an output neuron is given by $o = f(\Sigma_{j} w_{j} x_{j})$, where $f()$ is some nonlinear function of the neuron's activation. Then we have,

$$E = \sum_{P} E^{P} = \frac{1}{2} \sum_{P} (t^{P} - o^{P})^{2} = \frac{1}{2} \sum_{P} \left(t^{P} - f\left(\sum_{j} w_{j} x_{j}^{P} \right) \right)^{2}$$

and so

$$\frac{\partial E}{\partial w_{j}} = \frac{\partial E}{\partial o} \cdot \frac{\partial o}{\partial act} \cdot \frac{\partial act}{\partial w_{j}}$$

$$\frac{\partial E}{\partial w_{j}} = -\sum_{P} \left(t^{P} - f\left(\sum_{j} w_{j} x_{j}^{P} \right) \right).f'\left(\sum_{j} w_{j} x_{j}^{P} \right).x_{j}^{P}$$

So using the error descent rule, $\Delta w_j = -\gamma \dfrac{\partial E}{\partial w_j}$, we get the weight update rule

$$Dw_j = gdx_j$$

where $\delta = \sum_P \left(t^P - f\left(\sum_j w_j x_j^{\ P} \right) \right) . f'\left(\sum_j w_j x_j^{\ P} \right)$

The sole difference between this rule and that presented in the last section is the f' term. Its effect is to increase the rate of change of the weights in regions of the weight space where f' is large, that is, where a small change in the activation makes a large change in the value of the function. You can see from the diagrams of the activation functions given earlier that such regions tend to be in the centre of the function's range rather than at its extreme values.

This learning rule is a **batch** learning rule, that is, the whole set of training patterns are presented to the network and the total error (over all patterns) is calculated and only then is there any weight update. A more usual form is to have **online** learning where the weights are updated after the presentation of each pattern in turn. This issue will be met again in the next chapter. The online version of the learning rule is,

$$\Delta Pw_j = \gamma \delta^P x_j^P$$

where $\delta^P = \left(t^P - f\left(\sum_j w_j x_j^{\ P} \right) \right) . f'\left(\sum_j w_j x_j^{\ P} \right)$

Typical activation functions are the logistic function and the *tanh*() function both of which are differentiable. Further, their derivatives can be easily calculated:

- If $f(x) = tanh(bx)$, then $f'(a) = b(1 - f(a)*f(a))$; that is, the derivative of the function at a point a is an easily calculable function of its value at a.
- Similarly, if $f(x) = 1/(1+exp(-bx))$ then $f'(a)=bf(a)(1 - f(a))$.

As noted earlier, these functions have the further important property that they asymptote for very large values.

Multilayered Perceptrons

The Adaline proved to be a powerful learning machine but there were certain map-pings which were (and are) simply impossible using these networks. Such mappings are characterised by being **linearly inseparable**. Now it is possible to show that many linearly inseparable mappings may be modelled by **multilayered perceptrons**; this indeed was known in the 1960s, but what was not known was a rule which would allow such networks to learn the mapping. Such a rule appears to have been discovered independently several times (Werbos, 1974) but has been spectacularly popularised by the Parallel Distributed Processing (PDP) Group (Rummelhart & McClelland, 1986) under the name backpropagation. An alternative, multilayer neural network was presented the previous year—the *Boltzman machine* (Ackley, Hinton, & Sejnowski 1985)—though the backpropagation rule proved more efficient.

An example of a multilayered perceptron (MLP) was shown in the last chapter in Figure 3. Activity in the network is propagated forwards via weights from the input layer to the hidden layer where some function of the net activation is calculated. Then the activity is propagated via more weights to the output neurons. Now two sets of weights must be updated: those between the hidden and output layers and those between the input and hidden layers. The error due to the first set of weights is clearly calculable by the previously described LMS rule; however, now we re-quire propagating backwards that part of the error due to the errors which exist in the second set of weights and assign the error proportionately to the weights which cause it. You may see that we have a problem—the **credit assignment problem** (a term first used in by Marvin Minsky in 1961)—in that we must decide how much effect each weight in the first layer of weights has on the final output of the network. This assignment is the core result of the **backprop (backpropagation of errors)** method.

We may have any number of hidden layers we wish since the method is quite gen-eral, however, the limiting factor is usually training time which can be excessive for many-layered networks. In addition, it has been shown that networks with a single hidden layer are sufficient to approximate any continuous function (or indeed any function with only a finite number of discontinuities) provided we use nonlinear (differentiable) activation functions in the hidden layer.

The Backpropagation Algorithm

Because it is so important, we will repeat the whole algorithm in a 'how-to-do-it' form and then give a simple walk through for the algorithm when it is trained on the XOR problem:

1. Initialise the weights to small random numbers.

2. Choose an input pattern, **x**, and apply it to the input layer.

3. Propagate the activation forward through the weights until the activation reaches the output neurons.

4. Calculate the δs for the output layer $\delta_i^P = (t_i^P - o_i^P) f'(Act_i^P)$ using the desired target values for the selected input pattern.

5. Calculate the δs for the hidden layer using $\delta_i^P = \sum_{j=1}^{N} \delta_j^P w_{ji}.f'(Act_i^P)$.

6. Update all weights according to $\Delta P w_{ij} = \gamma.\delta_i^P.o_j^P$

7. Repeat Steps 2 through 6 for all patterns.

A final point is worth noting: the actual update rule after the errors have been back-propagated is local. This makes the backpropagation rule a candidate for parallel implementation.

The XOR Problem

You can use the net shown in Figure 2 to solve the XOR problem. The procedure is:

Initialisation

*   Initialise the W-weights and V-weights to small random numbers.
*   Initialise the learning rate η to a small value, for example, 0.001.
*   Choose the activation function, for example, *tanh*().

Select Pattern

It will be one of only four patterns for this problem.

Note that the pattern chosen determines not only the inputs but also the target pattern.

Feedforward to the hidden units first, labelled 1 and 2.

$$act_1 = w_{10} + w_{11}x_1 + w_{12}x_2$$
$$act_2 = w_{20} + w_{21}x_1 + w_{22}x_2$$
$$o_1 = tanh(act_1)$$
$$o_2 = tanh(act_2)$$

Figure 2. The net which can be used for the solution of the XOR problem using backpropagation

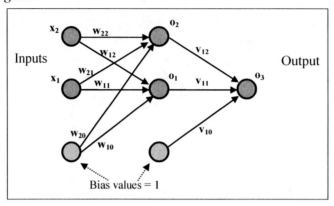

Now feedforward to the output unit which we will label 3,

$$act_3 = v_{10} + v_{11}o_1 + v_{12}o_2$$
$$o_3 = tanh(act_3)$$

Feedback errors calculate error at output,

$$d_3 = (t-o_3)*f'(o_3) = (t-o_3)(1-o^{2;3})$$

and feedback error to hidden neurons,

$$d_1 = d_3v_{11}f'(o_1) = d_3v_{11}(1-o^{2;1})$$
$$d_2 = d_3v_{12}f'(o_2) = d_3v_{12}(1-o^{2;2})$$

Change weights

$$Dv_{11} = h.d_3.o_1$$
$$Dv_{12} = h.d_3.o_2$$
$$Dv_{10} = h.d_3.1$$
$$Dw_{11} = h.d_1.x_1$$
$$Dw_{12} = h.d_1.x_2$$

$Dw_{10} = h.d_1.1$

$Dw_{21} = h.d_2.x_1$

$Dw_{22} = h.d_2.x_2$

$Dw_{20} = h.d_2.1$

Go back to Select Pattern

Issues in Backpropagation

Batch vs. Online Learning

The backpropagation algorithm is only theoretically guaranteed to converge if used in **batch** mode, that is, if all patterns in turn are presented to the network, the total error calculated, and the weights updated in a separate stage at the end of each training epoch. However, it is more common to use the **online** (or pattern) version where the weights are updated after the presentation of each individual pattern. It has been found empirically that this leads to faster convergence though there is the theoretical possibility of entering a cycle of repeated changes. Thus in online mode, we usually ensure that the patterns are presented to the network in a random and changing order.

The online algorithm has the advantage that it requires less storage space than the batch method. On the other hand the use of the batch mode is more accurate. The online algorithm will zig-zag its way to the final solution. It can be shown that the expected change (where the expectation is taken over all patterns) in weights using the online algorithm is equal to the batch change in weights.

Activation Functions

The most popular **activation functions** are the **logistic function** and the *tanh()* function. Both of these functions satisfy the basic criterion that they are differentiable. In addition, they are both monotonic and have the important property that their rate of change is greatest at an intermediate values and least at extreme values. This makes it possible to saturate a neuron's output at one or other of their extreme values. The final point worth noting is the ease with which their derivatives can be calculated:

- If $f(x) = tanh(bx)$, then $f'(a) = b(1 - f(a)*f(a))$

- Similarly, if $f(x) = 1/(1+\exp(-bx))$ then $f'(a)=bf(a)(1 - f(a))$

There is some evidence to suggest that convergence is faster when *tanh*() is used rather than the logistic function. Note that in each case the target function must be within the output range of the respective functions. If you have a wide spread of values which you wish to approximate, you must use a linear output layer.

Initialisation of the Weights

The initial values of the weights will in many cases determine the final converged network's values. Consider an energy surface with a number of energy wells; then, if we are using a batch training method, the initial values of the weights constitute the only stochastic element within the training regime. Thus the network will converge to a particular value depending on the basin in which the original vector lies. There is a danger that, if the initial network values are sufficiently large, the network will initially lie in a basin with a small basin of attraction and a high **local minimum**; this will appear to the observer as a network with all weights at saturation points (typically 0 and 1 or +1 and -1). It is usual therefore to begin with small weights uniformly distributed inside a small range. Haykin (1994, p. 162) recommends the range:

$$\left(-\frac{2.4}{F_i}, +\frac{2.4}{F_i} \right)$$

where i is the fan-in of the ith unit.

Momentum and Speed of Convergence

The basic backprop method described above is not known for its fast speed of convergence. Note that though we could simply increase the learning rate, this tends to introduce instability into the learning rule causing wild oscillations in the learned weights. It is possible to speed up the basic method in a number of ways. The simplest is to add a **momentum** term to the change of weights. The basic idea is to make the new change of weights large if it is in the direction of the previous changes of weights, while if it is in a different direction, make it smaller. Thus we use $Dw_{ij}(t + 1) = (1- a).d_j.o_i + aDw_{ij}(t)$, where the α determines the influence of the momentum. Clearly the momentum parameter α must be between 0 and 1. The second term is sometimes known as the 'flat spot avoidance' term since them momentum has the additional property that helps to slide the learning rule over local minima (see below).

Stopping Criteria

We must have a stopping criterion to decide when our network has solved the problem in hand. It is possible to stop when:

1. The **Euclidean norm** of the gradient vector reaches a sufficiently small value since we know that at the minimum value, the rate of change of the error surface with respect to the weight vector is zero. There are two disadvantages with this method:
    *   It may lead to excessively long training times.
    *   It requires calculating the gradient vector of the error surface with respect to the weights.
2. The rate of change of the mean squared error is sufficiently small.
3. The mean squared error is sufficiently small.
4. A mixture of the last two criteria.

Typically we will stop the learning before each pattern has been perfectly learned (see later) so that learning will stop when outputs are greater than 0.9 or less than 0.1.

Local Minima

Error descent is bedevilled with **local minima**. You may read that local minima are not much problem to ANNs, in that a network's weights will typically converge to solutions which, even if they are not globally optimal, are good enough. There is as yet little analytical evidence to support this belief. A heuristic often quoted is to ensure that the initial (random) weights are such that the average input to each neuron is approximately unity (or just below it). This suggests randomising the initial weights of neuron j around the value $\frac{1}{\sqrt{N}}$, where N is the number of weights into the neuron. A second heuristic is to introduce a little random noise into the network either on the inputs or with respect to the weight changes. Such noise is typically decreased during the course of the simulation. This acts like an annealing schedule.

Weight Decay and Generalisation

While we wish to see as good a performance as possible on the training set, we are even more interested in the network's performance on the test set since this is a measure of how well the network **generalises**. Remember the training set is composed of instances for which we already have the answer. We wish that the network gives accurate results on data for which we do not already know the answer. There is a trade-off between accuracy on the training set and accuracy on the test set.

Note also that perfect memory of the patterns which are met during training is essentially a look-up table. Look-up tables are discontinuous in that the item looked-up is either found to correspond to a particular result or not. Also generalisation is important not only because we wish that a network performs on new data which it has not been seen during learning but also because we are liable to have data which are noisy, distorted, or incomplete. Consider the set of five training points in Figure 3. We have shown two possible models for these data points: a linear model (perhaps the line minimising the squared error) and a polynomial fit which models the five given points exactly.

The problem with the more explicit representation given by the curve is that it may be misleading in positions other than those directly on the curve. If a neural network has a large number of weights (each weight represents a degree of freedom), we may be in danger of **overfitting** the network to the training data which will lead to poor performance on the test data. To avoid this danger we may either remove connections explicitly or we may give each weight a tendency to decay towards zero. The simplest method is $w_{ij}^{new} = (1 - \varepsilon)w_{ij}^{old}$ after each update of the weights. This does have the disadvantage that it discourages the use of large weights in that a single

Figure 3. A set of data points may be approximated by either the straight line or the curve.

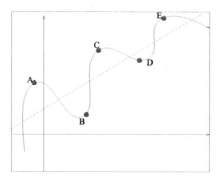

Note. Either would seem to fit the data; however, the line may give a better generalisation performance (on the test set) than the curve which is actually producing a lower mse on the training data.

large weight may be decayed more than a lot of small weights. More complex decay routines can be found which will encourage small weights to disappear.

Adaptive Parameters

A heuristic sometimes used in practice is to assign learning rates to neurons in output layers a smaller value than those for hidden layers. The last layers usually have larger local gradients than the early layers and we wish all neurons to learn at the same rate.

Since it is not easy to choose the parameter values, a priori one approach is to change them dynamically. For example, if we are using too small a learning rate, we will find that the error E is decreasing consistently but by too little each time. If our learning rate is too large, we will find that the error is decreasing and increasing haphazardly. This suggests adapting the learning rate according to a schedule such as:

$$\Delta\eta = +a, \qquad \text{if } \Delta E < 0 \text{ consistently}$$
$$\Delta\eta \quad = -b\eta, \quad \text{if } \Delta E > 0$$

This schedule may be thought of as increasing the learning rate if it seems that we are consistently going in the correct direction but decreasing the learning rate if we have to change direction sometimes. Notice however that such a method implicitly requires a separate learning parameter for each weight.

The Number of Hidden Neurons

The number of hidden nodes has a particularly large effect on the generalisation capability of the network: networks with too many weights (too many degrees of freedom) will tend to memorise the data; networks with too few will be unable to perform the task allocated to it. Therefore many algorithms have been derived to create neural networks with a smaller number of hidden neurons. Two obvious methods present themselves:

1. Prune weights which are small in magnitude. Such weights can only be refining classifications which have already been made and are in danger of modelling the finest features of the input data.
2. Grow networks until their performance is sufficiently good on the test set.

An Example

Using the Stuttgart neural network simulator (Zell, 2006), a network was trained to identify all of the 26 roman letters, *a* through *z* presented on a 5*7 display. Training was stopped sufficiently early that some degree of generalisation was possible.

Figure 4 shows the network's response during training to the letter *B* while Figure 5 shows the network's response to a noisy *B*.

*Figure 4. The Stuttgart neural network simulator trained on the 26 letters. Note. Here we show the response of the network to the presentation on the 5*7 display of the letter B.*

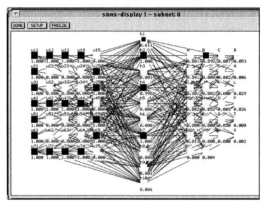

Figure 5. The input pattern B has been changed in just one pixel yet the effect on the network's response is fairly large. The network is responding maximally to the pattern as both B and D yet an observer could not be sure that it was seeing either.

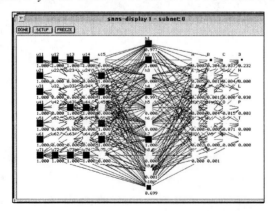

Notice how large the effect of just one 'pixel' change is on the network's output: the network is 'hedging its bets' between classifying the letter as a *B* or a *D*. The single 'pixel' was specifically chosen because it has just this effect. Other 'pixels' have a much smaller effect. This 'pixel' was chosen for this demonstration precisely because it is so important to the classification process particularly to the differentiation of *B*s and *D*s. Of interest in this example also is the effect on the hidden neurons of the single pixel change in the input layer. Clearly this pixel was inhibiting pixels 1 and 10 in the hidden layer; in this case we can see quite explicitly how the network is differentiating between the two patterns of *B* and *D*.

A Prediction Problem

We are going to use a network such as shown in Figure 6 to predict the outcome of the next day's trading on the Stock Market. Our inputs to the network correspond to the closing prices of day $(t-1)$, day $(t-2)$, day $(t-3)$, and so forth, and we wish to output the closing price on day t. We have arbitrarily chosen to input five days' information here and only used a training set of 100 days. (We will not make our fortune out of this network).

For this problem we choose a network which has a nonlinearity (actually *tanh*()) at the hidden layer and linear output neurons. We chose to make the output neuron linear since we hope that it takes values in the range 0 - 3800 or whatever value the stock market might achieve. It would have been possible to have sigmoids in the output layer but we would then have had to scale the target values accordingly so that the network outputs could approximate the target values.

Figure 6. A prectication neural network: The inputs to the neural network comprise the last 5 day's closing prices and the network must predict the next day's closing prices.

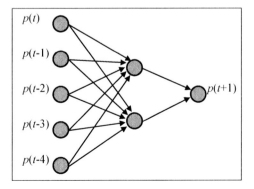

Figure 7. An MLP with a single nonlinear hidden neuron is attempting to predict the closing price of the stock market on 100 days.

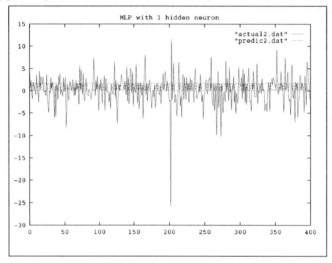

In practice, we find it easiest to take out the trend information from the raw data before feeding it to a network and so we adopt a very simple procedure of subtracting the previous days' data from the current days' data. Similarly with the outputs and targets. So what we are actually predicting is whether the market will go up or down and by how much.

We show in Figure 7 the results of using a single hidden neuron (plus a bias term at the hidden layer) on the financial data. The results are clearly not good since the network is only finding out that in general the market is going up.

Figure 8. With 5 hidden neurons (plus a bias) the prediction properties of the network have vastly improved but with 15 hidden neurons the ntwork's powers of prediction have deteriorated again.

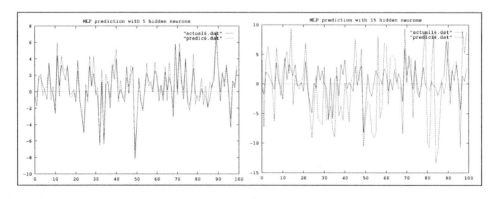

As we might expect, the results are very much dependent on the size of network chosen and so we show in Figure 8 a network with five hidden neurons. The results are clearly much better but again we must take care about adding neurons since with 15 neurons the results are very much worse.

Practical Issues

If you were asked to create an artificial neural network to perform prediction on the FTSE index, what factors must you take into account? Some of the obvious ones are:

- Number of inputs: We cannot specify in advance the number of days of inputs which are valuable in training the network optimally. So we would have to try different lengths of input vectors under the criteria below and find the best.

- Number of hidden neurons: The smaller the better, but depends on the number of inputs and so forth. We wish to use the least possible number of neurons which gives us a good predictor since if we add too many hidden neurons (which equals too many degrees of freedom), we will have an over-powerful neural network which will model the noise as well as any underlying series. We should probably stick with a single hidden layer.

- Number of outputs is not an issue since we only wish one step look ahead.

- Output activation function will probably be linear since financial data is up to 4000 and so forth. Another possibility is to normalise the data between 0 and 1 and use a logistic function.

- Learning rate is usually determined by trial and error but is almost often small (<0.1). It may be annealed to 0 during the course of the experiment, something which seems to give better accuracy.

- We must split the historical data into test set/training set. We could experiment with division under a number of different regimes, that is, not just train on first 1000 samples, test on last 100. For a stopping criterion, we should probably use the least mean square error or least mean absolute error on the test set.

- We could experiment with a momentum term to see if we get better results.

References

Ackley, D.H., Hinton, G.E., & Sejnowski, T.J. (1985). A learning algorithm for Boltzmann machines. *Cognitive Science*, *9*, 147-169.

Haykin, S. (1994). *Neural networks: A comprehensive foundation*. MacMillan

Rummelhart, D. E., & McClelland, J.L. (Eds). (1986). *Parallel distributed processing* (Vols. 1-2). MIT Press.

Zell, A., et. al. (2006). *Stuttgart neural network simulator.* Retrieved December 5, 2006, from http://www-ra.informatik.uni-tuebingen.de/SNNS/

Werbos, P. (1974). *Beyond regression: New tools for prediction and analysis in the behavioural sciences*. Unpublished doctoral thesis, Harvard University.

Widrow, B. J., & Hoff, M.E. (1960). *Adaptive switching circuits*. Paper presented at the IRE WESCON Convention Record (pp. 96-104).

Chapter IV

Case Study:
Supervised Neural Networks in
Digital Games

Introduction

In this short chapter we present a case study of the use of ANN in a video game type situation. The example is one of duelling robots, a problem which, as we will see, lends itself to a range of different solutions and where we can demonstrate the efficacy of a biologically inspired AI approach.

Robocode

For this case study we discuss the use of **Robocode** (Nelson, 2001) to explore the use of neural networks as an AI state selector within a game (Stewart, 2004). Robocode may be thought of a special case of a computer game in which the player is responsible for creating programs that operate their own derivation of Java 'robots' to compete with other stock robots or against other player-created robots. The competitions occur in real-time in a 2D plain square arena with four walls containing the competing robots. Gameplay is relatively straightforward; the **robots** move autonomously around the arena shooting bullets attempting to hit other robots while also trying to avoid being shot. Competitions may be one-on-one or against multiple opponents, and team play is also supported, though we do not use this aspect in our case study. The autonomous nature of the robots, the ease with which the robots may be created, and the restriction of resources—particularly with the time restrictions for the AI of each robot—make Robocode a very interesting and suitable medium for testing a variety of AI mechanisms for real-time computer games.

The Robocode Web community has been very active and enthusiastic since the release of the product in 2001, but most of the focus in the development of new bots has been placed on bullet dodging algorithms and/or geometric or statistical approaches for predicting opponent movement. A few attempts have been made to utilise neural networks but most have been relatively unsuccessful against the best bot examples on the Robocode repository. This illustrates one of the difficulties of using neural networks in a real-time, constrained, and dynamic game environment. It is difficult to set up and train a neural network based AI bot that generalises well to new situations and that is successful in performing in a dynamic environment.

Let us start with a simple example that uses a more traditional form of game AI: the **state machine**. The finite state machine has been one of the most common and effective means for realising an AI within computer games, particularly for the implementation of a behavioural AI. A large part of the reason for its use being that the underlying principles are easy to understand, that it is a straightforward tech-

Figure 1. An example of a state machine that may be used to define the behaviour for a computer controlled opponent in a game

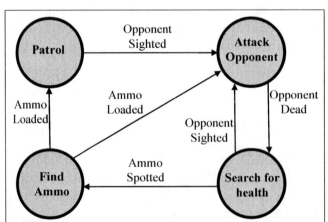

nology to implement—often written as a multidimensional array or a tree structure (Penton, 2003)—and it is a relatively fast method to use in-game.

The following diagram (Figure 1) illustrates a typical (but simplified) example of a state machine for a computer opponent in an action based game. The circles are used to signify the possible states for a **nonplayer character** (NPC) and the lines indicate scenarios that trigger transitions from one state to another. So a finite state machine defines a form of high level AI for a game character and we must predict all necessary state and transitions that the character may need in-game a priori and build the state machine accordingly; that is, generally the character does not adapt its behaviour within the game and so all game scenarios must be accounted for in the game design and development.

After testing a variety of stock and showcase robots (see Table 1) in Robocode, it becomes clear that even the most successful robots may be defeated by a few other robots whose key strategies so happen to focus on the weakest aspect of the champion robot's strategy. It therefore seems reasonable to develop an approach for a robot that allows it to identify its opponent and coupled with its current state then change to a strategy that maximises its possibility of increasing its advantage over the next short period of time. This is quite easy to achieve using a state-machine approach as Figure 2 illustrates.

So it is a matter of pairing off a winning strategy for our own robot that is known to be successful, on average, against its opponent (we focus on one vs. one competition for simplicity in this example). The top level strategy is quite simple; the robot may evade or attack depending on its current health and opponent. Evading can be very effective in this game because a robot will lose health/energy not only by being hit but also by firing shots, thus it is generally not a sensible strategy for a robot to shoot bullets continually as fast as possible. Note that the lower level strategy state switching operates on the basis of recognising the current opponent,

Table 1. Stock robot strategies

Stock Robot	Typical Behaviour
Corners	Moves to a corner and its gun back and forth.
Avoider	Moves around in an unpredictable pattern.
Fire	Sits still unless hit. When still, spins around to find enemy.
Ramfire	Charges at robots to damage them, then fires.
SpinBot	Moves around in a circle and will fire rapidly when enemy sighted.
Tracker	Locks on to a robot and moves close before firing.
TrackFire	Tracks and fires at the nearest robot.
Walls	Moves around the outer walls will gun facing inwards.

Figure 2. Robocode state-machine robot architecture

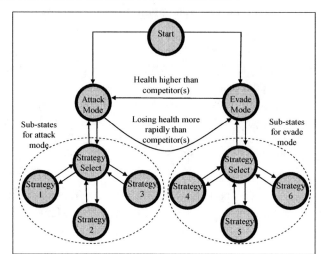

which is quite easy with Robocode because each of the robots have a name, but of course the robot must previously have been known and tested for us to code the appropriate strategy to combat it. A comprehensive set of tests were performed (Stewart, 2004) (100 battles between each pairing of robots) to discover which strategy worked best against each of the known stock robots (see Table 2 below). As it turned out, the simple strategy as executed by Walls is effective against most of the stock robots (though importantly not against all); this is perhaps not that surprising as Walls keeps its back to the wall and so it may only be hit from the front. A fairly complex motion predictive robot may combat Walls quite well, but it is more straightforward to employ the simple combination of evasion and use of its

Table 2. Table showing mapping of most likely robot to succeed in a battle against the key stock robots in Robocode

Stock Robot	Loses against	Toughest Opponent
Corners	SpinBot, Tracker, and TrackFire	TrackFire
Crazy	Tracker, Walls	Walls
Fire	SpinBot, Tracker, TrackFire and Walls	Tracker
Ramfire	Fire, and TrackFire	TrackFire
SpinBot	Walls	Walls
Tracker	SpinBot, Trackfire, and Walls	Walls
TrackFire	SpinBot, and Walls	Walls
Walls	Avoider	Avoider

toughest opponent against it as utilised in our model. In tests of 100 battles against each of the stock robots, the state-machine robot was approximately 95% effective in defeating its opponent.

The state-machine robot can be made more adaptive by storing the outcomes of battles with the other robots in a text file and using this information to inform strategy selection in future battles. Also, a previously unencountered robot may be dealt with by using this technique paired with trial-and-error strategy selection and storing the outcomes in file so that future battles with the new robots may be more successful. In fact, game developers have employed a wide range of techniques to improve and make the basic state-machine architecture more effective. However, as we hope the example above serves to illustrate, there are considerable limitations with the use of state machines and similar techniques for next generation game AIs. State machines are very much ruled-based and although the mainstream AI research community on a whole has moved away from rule-based approaches to agent and learning, the game development community is still quite reliant on rule-based techniques. The main issue with rule-based approaches is that as the complexity of the AI behavioural system being modelled increases, it becomes exponentially more difficult to predict all of the necessary states and state changes, and so it becomes much more difficult to design and test effective models in this manner.

A neural network is a more scalable technology to use for a state selector and it can also be used in an adaptive manner more easily because we can retrain the network when we receive new data (there are issues within online adaptation [Charles, 2003] but we will not dwell on that here). Using the **backpropagation** algorithm that we explained in the previous chapter we can implement similar state-selector functionality to that of the state machine but with increased flexibility. The first two issues to deal with in setting up a neural network involve getting appropriate data and choosing the most effective variables for training. We set the neural network as illustrated below (Figure 3). In this case the data were generated in real battles by saving values from the battlefield every minute and the recording the most appropriate state for the robot given the current position of the battle. Allowing the player to select a state for the robot in the game is a little tricky in Robocode because robots are really intended to operate autonomously. Basically, this is achieved by running another Java program in parallel to the Robocode contest so that a player may select a state via this program which writes the desired robot state to file and this may be read in by the robot with the Robocode environment (Stewart, 2004). This seems a little convoluted, but it works well and it essentially allows us to record desired (or target) values for the outputs of the neural network that we wish to train that correspond to battlefield data at the same point in time, which are the inputs to the neural network.

Figure 3. Setup of backpropagation neural network state selector

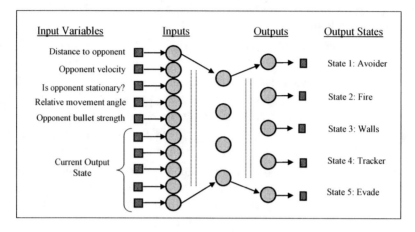

Conclusion

Conclusions on the experiment are as follows:

1. The ANN could be used to classify robot opponents in a more flexible and reliable manner than with the previous method. We did not have to rely on knowing the opponent robot names or having to retrain for each new robot.

2. The trained ANN could be used to classify new but similar robots to those used in training. This is useful because robots with similar behaviour often have very similar characteristics.

3. Retraining of the robot is possible in-game.

The results using this method proved very successful, and the performance improved on the previous state-machine model.

References

Charles, D. (2003, November). Enhancing gameplay: Challenges for artificial intelligence in digital games. In *Proceedings of the 1ˢᵗ World Conference on Digital Games, University of Utrecht, The Netherlands.*

Penton, R. (2003). *Data structures for game programmers.* Premier Press.

Nelson, M. (2001). Robocode. Retrieved February 5, 2007, from http://www.alpha-works.ibm.com/tech/robocode

Stewart , D. (2004, May). *Java robocode AI investigation* (honours computing project). University of Ulster.

Chapter V

Unsupervised Learning in Artificial Neural Networks

Unsupervised Learning

With the artificial neural networks we have met so far, we must have a training set on which we already have the answers to the questions we are going to pose to the network. Yet humans appear to be able to learn (indeed some would say can only learn) without explicit supervision. The aim of **unsupervised learning** is to mimic this aspect of human capabilities and hence this type of learning tends to use more biologically plausible methods than those using the error descent methods of the last two chapters. The network must self-organise and to do so, it must react to some aspect of the input data, typically either **redundancy** in the input data or **clusters** in the data; for example, there must be some structure in the data to which it can respond. There are two major methods used,

1. **Hebbian learning**
2. **Competitive learning**

We shall examine each of these in turn.

Hebbian Learning

Hebbian learning is so-called after Donald Hebb who in 1949 conjectured:

*When an axon of a cell A is near enough to excite a cell B and repeatedly or persis-
tently takes part in firing it, some growth process or metabolic change takes place
in one or both cells such that A's efficiency as one of the cells firing B, is increased.*
(Hebb, 1949)

In the sort of feedforward neural networks we have been considering, this would
be interpreted as the weight between an input neuron and an output neuron is very
much strengthened when the input neuron's activation passes forward to the output
neuron and causes the output neuron to fire strongly. We can see that the rule favours
the strong: if the weights between inputs and outputs are already large (and so an
input will have a strong effect on the outputs) the chances of the weights growing
is large.

More formally, consider the simplest feedforward neural network which has a set
of input neurons with associated input vector, $\mathbf{x}$, and a set of output neurons with
associated output vector, $\mathbf{y}$. Then we have, as before, $y_i = \sum_j w_{ij} x_j$, where now the
(Hebbian) learning rule is defined by $\Delta w_{ij} = \eta x_j y_i$. That is, the weight between each
input and output neuron is increased proportional to the magnitude of the simultaneous firing of these neurons.

Now we can substitute into the learning rule the value of $\mathbf{y}$ calculated by the feeding
forward of the activity to get,

$$\Delta w_{ij} = \eta x_j \sum_k w_{ki} x_k = \eta \sum_k w_{ki} x_k x_j.$$

Writing the learning rule in this way emphasises the statistical properties of the
learning rule, for example, that the learning rule depends on the correlation between
different parts of the input data's vector components. It does however also show
that we have difficulty with the basic rule as it stands which is that we have a positive feedback rule which has an associated difficulty with lack of stability. If the
input and output neurons are tending to fire strongly together, the weight between
them will tend to grow strongly; if the weight grows strongly, the output neuron
will fire more strongly the next time the input neuron fires and this will cause an
increased value in the rate of change of the weights which will.... If we do not take
some preventative measure, the weights will grow without bound. Such preventative measures include:

1. Clipping the weights, for example, insisting that there is a maximum, *max* and minimum *min* within which the weights must remain.

2. Specifically normalising the weights after each update. For example, $\Delta w_{ij} = \eta x_j y_i$ is followed by $\Delta w_{ij} = \eta x_j y_i - \gamma(w_{ij})$ which ensures that the weights into each output neuron have length 1.

3. Having a weight decay term within the learning rule to stop it growing too large, that is, $\Delta w_{ij} = \eta x_j y_i - \gamma(w_{ij})$, where the decay function $\gamma(w_{ij})$ represents a monotonically increasing function of the weights, for example, if the weights grow large so does the weight decay term. Create a negative feedback topology for the network so that, if the weights grow large and positive a strong inhibitory (turn-off) message is being given to the input neurons.

4. Creating a network containing a negative feedback of activation.

The Stability of the Hebbian Learning Rule

Recall first that a matrix A has an **eigenvector x** with a corresponding eigenvalue λ if $Ax=\lambda x$.

In other words, multiplying the vector **x** or any of its multiples by A is equivalent to multiplying the whole vector by a scalar λ. Thus the direction of **x** is unchanged, only its magnitude is affected.

Consider a one output-neuron network and assume that the Hebb learning process does cause convergence to a stable direction, **w***; then if w_k is the weight vector linking x_k to y,

$$0 = \left\langle \Delta w_i^* \right\rangle = \left\langle yx_i \right\rangle = \left\langle \sum_j w_j x_j x_i \right\rangle = \sum_j R_{ij} w_j \tag{1}$$

where the angled brackets indicate the expected value taken over the whole distribution and R is the correlation matrix of the distribution. Now this happens for all i, so $Rw^* = 0$.

Now the correlation matrix, R, is a symmetric, positive semidefinite matrix and so all its eigenvalues are non-negative. But the above formulation shows that **w*** must have eigenvalue 0. Now consider a small disturbance, ε, in the weights in a direction with a nonzero (i.e., positive) eigenvalue. Then,

$$\left\langle \Delta w^* \right\rangle = R(w^* + \varepsilon) = R_\varepsilon > 0 \tag{2}$$

for example, the weights will grow in any direction with nonzero eigenvalue (and such directions must exist). Thus there exists a fixed point at $W = 0$ but this is an unstable fixed point. In fact, in time, the weights of nets which use simple Hebbian learning tend to be dominated by the direction corresponding to the largest eigenvalue.

Hebbian Learning and Information Theory

Quantification of Information

Shannon (1948) devised a measure of the **information** content of an event in terms of the probability of the event happening. He wished to make precise the intuitive concept that the occurrence of an unlikely event tells you more than that of a likely event. He defined the information in an event i, to be $-\log(p_i)$ where p_i is the probability that the event labelled i occurs.

Using this, we define the entropy (or uncertainty or average information content) of a set of N events to be,

$$H = -\sum_{i=1}^{N} p_i \log(p_i) \tag{3}$$

That is, the entropy is the information we would expect to get from one event happening where this expectation is taken over the ensemble of possible outcomes.

The basic facts in which we will take an interest are:

- Because the occurrence of an unlikely event has more information than that of a likely event, it has a higher information content.
- Hence, a data set with high variance is liable to contain more information than one with small variance.

Principal Component Analysis

Inputs to a neural net generally exhibit high dimensionality, for example, the N input lines can each be viewed as one dimension so that each pattern will be represented as a coordinate in N dimensional space.

A major problem in analysing data of high dimensionality is identifying patterns which exist across dimensional boundaries. Such patterns may become visible when a change of basis of the space is made, however an *a priori* decision as to which basis will reveal most patterns requires foreknowledge of the unknown patterns.

A potential solution to this impasse is found in **principal component analysis** (PCA) which aims to find that orthogonal basis which maximises the data's variance for a given dimensionality of basis. A useful tactic is to find that direction which accounts for most of the data's variance; this becomes the first basis vector. One then finds that direction which accounts for most of the remaining variance; this is the second basis vector, and so on. If one then projects data onto the principal component directions, we perform a dimensionality reduction which will be accompanied by the retention of as much variance in the data as possible.

In general, it can be shown that the kth basis vector from this process is the same as the eigenvector of the co-variance matrix, C defined by $c_{ij} = \langle (x_i - \langle x \rangle)(x_j - \langle x \rangle) \rangle$ where the angled brackets indicate an ensemble average. For zero-mean data, the covariance matrix is equivalent to a simple correlation matrix.

Now, if we have a set of weights which are the eigenvectors of the input data's co-variance matrix, C, then these weights will transmit the largest values to the outputs when an item of input data is in the direction of the largest correlations which corresponds to those eigenvectors with the largest eigenvalues. Thus, if we can create a situation in an artificial neural network (ANN) where one set of weights (into a particular output neuron) converges to the first eigenvector (corresponding to the largest eigenvalue), the next set of weights converges to the second eigenvector and so on, we will be in a position to maximally recreate at the outputs the directions with the largest variance in the input data.

Figure 1. A cloud of data points and the corresponding first principal component

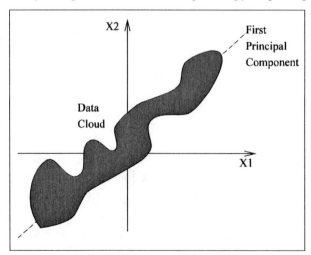

Figure 1 shows a simple example of a principal component analysis. The original data are two dimensional (in the X1, X2 plane). If you wished to know the position of each data point as accurately as possible using only a single coordinate, you would be best to give each point's position in terms of the first principal component (PC) shown in the diagram. We can see that the first PC is the direction of greatest spread (variance) of the input data.

Note that representing data as coordinates using the basis found by a PCA means that the data will have greatest variance along the first principal component, the next greatest variance along the second, and so on. While it is strictly only true to say that information and variance may be equated in Gaussian distributions, it is a good rule-of-thumb that a direction with more variance contains more information than one with less variance. Thus PCA provides a means of compressing the data while retaining as much information within the data as possible. It can be shown that if a set of input data have eigenvalues $\lambda_1, \lambda_2, ..., \lambda_N$ and if we represent the data in coordinates on a basis spanned by the first m eigenvectors, the loss of information due to the compression is $\sum_{i=m+1}^{N} \lambda_i$.

Weight Decay in Hebbian Learning

As noted earlier, if there are no constraints placed on the growth of weights under Hebbian learning, there is a tendency for the weights to grow without bounds.

Hence, interest has grown in the use of decay terms embedded in the learning rule itself. Ideally such a rule should ensure that no single weight should grow too large while keeping the total weights on connections into a particular output neuron fairly constant. One of the simplest forms of **weight decay** was developed as early as 1968 by Grossberg (1991) and was of the form,

$$\frac{dw_{ij}}{dt} = \eta y_i x_j - w_{ij} \qquad (4)$$

It is clear that the weights will be stable (when $\frac{dw_{ij}}{dt} = 0$) at the points where $w_{ij} = \eta \langle y_i x_j \rangle$ where the angled brackets indicate an ensemble average. Using a similar type of argument to that employed for simple Hebbian learning, we see that at convergence we must have $\lambda C w = w$. Thus **w** would have to be an eigenvector of the correlation matrix of the input data with corresponding eigenvalue $\frac{1}{\eta}$. (In fact, $w = 0$ is a possible solution, but, as before, we can show that this is an unstable solution).

Ojay's One Neuron Model

Oja (1982) developed a model of Hebbian learning with weight decay which not only stopped the weights growing without bound, it also caused the weights to converge to the **principal components** of the input data. In other words, the weight decay had the amazing effect of not only causing the weight increase to stabilise, it also caused the convergence of the weights to values that extracted the maximum information from the input data.

He used a single output neuron which sums the inputs in the usual fashion,

$$y = \sum_{i=1}^{m} w_i x_i,$$

but used a Hebbian learning neuron with weight decay,

$$\Delta w_i = \alpha(x_i y - y^2 w_i).$$

However, this rule will find only the first eigenvector (that direction corresponding to the largest eigenvalue) of the data. It is not sufficient to simply throw clusters of neurons at the data since all will find the same (first) principal component; in order to find other PCs, there must be some interaction between the neurons. Other rules which find other principal components have been identified by subsequent research, an example of which is shown in the next section.

Oja's Subspace Algorithm

The one neuron network reviewed in the last section is capable of finding only the first principal component. While it is possible to use this network iteratively by creating a new neuron and allowing it to learn on the data provided by the residuals left by subtracting out previous principal components, this involves several extra stages of processing for each new neuron.

Therefore Oja's subspace algorithm (Oja, 1989) provided a major step forward. The network has N output neurons each of which learns using a Hebb-type rule with weight decay. Note however that it does not guarantee to find the actual directions of the principal components; the weights *do* however converge to an orthonormal basis of the principal component space. We will call the space spanned by this basis the principal subspace. The learning rule is,

$$\Delta w_{ij} = \alpha \left(x_i y_j - y_j \sum_k w_{ik} y_k \right) \tag{5}$$

which has been shown to force the weights to converge to a basis of the principal subspace. In other words, this network will act so that, depending on the number of output neurons, the network weights will converge on all the major information filters possible.

One advantage of this model is that it is completely homogeneous, for example, the operations carried out at each neuron are identical. This is essential if we are to take full advantage of parallel processing.

The major disadvantage of this algorithm is that it finds only the principal subspace of the eigenvectors not the actual eigenvectors themselves. This need not be a disadvantage for biological networks, but for engineering applications it is preferable to be able to find the actual principal components themselves.

Oja's Weighted Subspace Algorithm

The final stage is the creation of algorithms which finds the actual principal components of the input data. In 1992, Oja recognised the importance of introducing asymmetry into the weight decay process in order to force weights to converge to the principal components (Oja, Ogawa, & Wangviwattana 1992). The algorithm is defined by the equations,

$$y_j = \sum_{i=1}^{n} w_{ij} x_i,$$

where a Hebb-type rule with weight decay modifies the weights according to,

$$\Delta w_{ij} = \eta y_j \left(x_i - \theta_j \sum_{k=1}^{N} y_k w_{kj} \right).$$

Ensuring that 123 allows the neuron whose weight decays proportional to 1 (i.e., whose weight decays least quickly) to learn the principal values of the correlation in the input data. That is, this neuron will respond maximally to directions parallel to the principal eigenvector, for example, to patterns closest to the main correlations within the data. The neuron whose weight decays proportional to 2 cannot compete with the first but it is in a better position than all of the others and so can learn the next largest chunk of the correlation, and so on.

It can be shown that the weight vectors will converge to the principal eigenvectors in the order of their eigenvalues. Now we have a network which will extract the direction with maximum information using output neuron 1, the direction of second greatest information using output neuron 2, and so on.

Sanger's Generalized Hebbian Algorithm

Sanger (1989) has developed a different algorithm (which he calls the 'Generalized Hebbian Algorithm') which also finds the actual principal components. He also introduces asymmetry in the decay term of his learning rule:

$$\Delta w_{ij} = \alpha \left(x_i y_j - y_j \sum_{k=1}^{j} w_{ik} y_k \right) \tag{6}$$

Note that the crucial difference between this rule and Oja's subspace algorithm is that the decay term for the weights into the neuron is a weighted sum of the first j neurons' activations. Sanger's algorithm can be viewed as a repeated application of Oja's One Neuron Algorithm by writing it as,

$$\Delta w_{ij} = \alpha \left(x_i y_j - y_j \sum_{k=1}^{j-1} w_{ik} y_k - y_j w_{ij} y_j \right)$$

$$= \alpha \left([x_i y_j - y_j \sum_{k=1}^{j-1} w_{ik} y_k] - y_j^2 w_{ij} \right)$$

$$= \alpha \left([x_i - \sum_{k=1}^{j-1} w_{ik} y_k] y_j - y_j^2 w_{ij} \right) \tag{7}$$

Now the term inside brackets is the projection of the output neurons' values onto the first $i-1$ principal components; it is basically stating that the first neurons have captured those $(i-1)$ directions with most information. We can look at the effect on the weights into the first output neuron (Neuron 1):

$$\Delta w_{1i} = \alpha (x_i y_1 - y_1 \sum_{k=1}^{1} w_{ki} y_k)$$

$$= \alpha (x_i y_1 - y_1 w_{1i} y_1)$$

$$= \alpha (x_i y_1 - w_{1i} y_1^2) \tag{8}$$

So the first principal component will be grabbed by the first output neuron's weights since this is exactly Oja's One Neuron Rule.

Now the second output neuron is using the rule,

$$\Delta w_{2i} = \alpha(x_i y_2 - y_2 \sum_{k=1}^{2} w_{ki} y_k)$$

$$= \alpha(x_i y_2 - y_2 w_{1i} y_1 - y_2 w_{2i} y_2)$$

$$= \alpha([x_i - w_{1i} y_1] y_2 - w_{2i} y_2^2)$$

$$= \alpha(x_i' y_2 - w_{2i} y_2^2)$$

Now the bit inside the square brackets is the original x-value minus the projection of the first y (output) neuron on the first principal component. This subtracts out the direction of greatest information (the first principal component) and leaves the second neuron performing Oja's One Neuron Rule on the subspace left after the first principal component has been removed, for example, the x' space. It will then converge to the second principal component.

The same argument holds for the third output neuron:

$$\Delta w_{3i} = \alpha(x_i y_3 - y_3 \sum_{k=1}^{3} w_{ki} y_k)$$

$$= \alpha(x_i y_3 - y_3 w_{1i} y_1 - y_3 w_{2i} y_2 - y_3 w_{3i} y_3)$$

$$= \alpha([x_i - w_{1i} y_1 - w_{2i} y_2] y_3 - w_{3i} y_3^2)$$

$$= \alpha(x_i'' y_3 - w_{3i} y_3^2)$$

where x'' is the remainder after the first two directions of most information are subtracted.

In general, we see that the central term comprises the residuals after the first $j - 1$ principal components have been found, and therefore the rule is performing the equivalent of One Neuron learning on subsequent residual spaces. However, note that the asymmetry which is necessary to ensure convergence to the actual principal components is bought at the expense of requiring the neuron to 'know' that it is the neuron by subtracting only j terms in its decay. It is Sanger's contention that all true PCA rules are based on some measure of deflation such as shown in this rule.

Summary of Hebbian Learning

Hebbian learning is rarely used in its simple form; typically a **weight decay** term is included in the learning rule which has the property of stopping the weights from growing indefinitely. If the decay term is of the correct form, it also causes the weights to converge to the principal component directions. In other words, we now have a very simple neural network which is extracting as much information as possible from a set of raw data in an unsupervised manner. The network is responding solely to the redundancy in the input data to find an optimal compression of the input data which retains as much information in the data as possible in as few dimensions as possible. This is an important property for any information processing machine —carbon or silicon—to have.

Applications

Principal component networks are primarily useful when we wish to compress data by losing as little of the information in the data as possible. Then by projecting the individual items of raw data onto the principal components (of the ensemble of input data), we will on average be able to represent the data most accurately in as concise a form as possible. A second use for such networks is in exploratory data investigations. If we have to search for structure in data in a high-dimensional space it cannot be done by eye and the automatic identification of structure may be inhibited by the high-dimensionality of the data. By projecting the data onto the lower dimensional subspace spanned by the principal components we hope to retain as much structure in the data as possible while making it easier to spot the structure. Finally, principal component networks are finding uses in preprocessing data for other networks (such as the backprop network of the last chapter) and since the principal components directions are orthogonal to one another we do not have interference between the sets of patterns in each direction. Thus projecting inputs onto the principal component directions and then using a standard multilayer perceptron can greatly speed the perceptron's learning.

A typical application of principal component networks has been in the area of image coding in which a set of images can require an extremely high bandwidth channel in order to be transmitted perfectly. However the human eye does not require (nor can it handle) infinite precision and so we may transmit images over a lossy channel. The optimal linear compression of the image data is determined by the projection of the data onto their principal components. We may then receive image data which are good enough for human recognition though it has lost some of its precision in the transmission.

Anti-Hebbian Learning

All the ANNs we have so far met have been feedforward networks; activation has been propagated only in one direction. However, many real biological networks are characterised by a plethora of recurrent connections. This has led to increasing interest in networks which, while still strongly directional, allow activation to be transmitted in more than one direction, for example, either laterally or in the reverse direction from the usual flow of activation. One interesting idea is to associate this change in direction of motion of activation with a minor modification to the usual Hebbian learning rule called **anti-Hebbian** learning.

If inputs to a neural net are correlated, then each contains information about the other. In information theoretical terms, there is redundancy in the inputs ($I(x;y) > 0$).

Anti-Hebbian learning is designed to **decorrelate** input values. The intuitive idea behind the process is that more information can be passed through a network when the nodes of the network are all dealing with different data. The less correlated the neurons' responses, the less redundancy is in the data transfer. Thus the aim is to produce neurons which respond to different signals. If two neurons respond to the same signal, there is a measure of correlation between them and this is used to affect their responses to future similar data. Anti-Hebbian learning is sometimes known as lateral inhibition as this type of learning is generally used between members of the same layer and not between members of different layers. The basic model is defined by,

$$\Delta w_{ij} = -\alpha y_i y_j$$

Figure 2. Anti-Hebbian weights negative decorrelating weights between neurons in the same layer are learned using an 'anti-Hebbian' learning rule

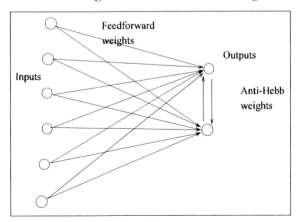

Therefore, if initially *i* and *j* are highly correlated then the weights between them will grow to a large negative value and each will tend to turn the other off.

It is clear that there is no need for weight decay terms or limits on anti-Hebbian weights as they are automatically self-limiting, provided decorrelation can be attained.

$$(\langle y_i.y_j \rangle \to 0) \Rightarrow (w_{ij} \to 0) \tag{9}$$

For example, weight change stops when the outputs are decorrelated. Success in decorrelating the outputs results in weights being stabilised.

It has been shown that not only does anti-Hebbian learning force convergence in the particular case of a deflationary algorithm but that the lateral connections do indeed vanish.

Several authors have developed principal component models using a mixture of one of the above PCA methods (often Oja's One Neuron Rule) and anti-Hebbian weights between the output neurons.

We note a similarity between the aims of PCA and anti-Hebbian learning: the aim of anti-Hebbian learning is to decorrelate neurons. If a set of neurons performs a principal component analysis, their weights form an orthogonal basis of the space of principal eigenvectors. Thus, both methods perform a decorrelation of the neurons' responses.

Further, in information theoretic terms, decorrelation ensures that the maximal amount of information possible for a particular number of output neurons is transferred through the system. This is true only for noise-free information transfer since if there is some noise in the system, some duplication of information may be beneficial to optimal information transfer.

The Novelty Filter

An interesting early model was proposed by Kohonen (1997) who uses negative feedback in a number of models, the most famous of which (at least of the simple models) is the so-called 'novelty filter' (see Figure 3).

Here we have an input vector *x* which generates feedback gain by the vector of weights, M. Each element of M is adapted using anti-Hebbian learning:

$$\frac{dm_{ij}}{dt} = -\alpha x_i' x_j' \tag{10}$$

Figure 3. The system model of the novelty filter

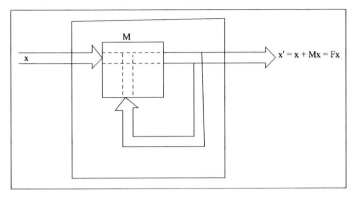

where $\mathbf{x}' = \mathbf{x} + \mathbf{M}\mathbf{x}'$ (11)

$= (\mathbf{I} - \mathbf{M})^{-1}\mathbf{x} = F\mathbf{x}$ (12)

'It is tentatively assumed always exists.' Kohonen shows that, under fairly general conditions on the sequence of **x** and the initial conditions of the matrix M, the values of F always converge to a projection matrix under which the output approaches zero although F does not converge to the zero matrix. For example, F converges to a mapping whose kernel is the subspace spanned by the vectors **x**. Thus any new input vector **1** will cause an output which is solely a function of the novel features in **1**.

Thus the 'novelty filter' knows what patterns it has seen and extracts information from any pattern which is equivalent to patterns which it has seen; the residuals are the 'novelties.'

Independent Component Analysis

Independent component analysis (ICA) is often thought of as an extension of PCA. It is also a projective method which attempts to identify the independent components of a signal. A typical problem is the 'blind separation of sources' such as in the 'cocktail party problem' in which there are a number of simultaneous speakers each of whose conversations we wish to identify separately. The linear problem has been largely solved: let there be n different sources, $s_1, \ldots, s_n$ mixed with a square mixing matrix, A. Then the received signal is an n-dimensional vector $\mathbf{x} = (x_1, \ldots, x_n)$

so that $\mathbf{x} = A\mathbf{s}$. The ICA method finds solutions $y_1,\ldots,y_n$ so that the ys are equal to the original sources, $s_1,\ldots,s_n$ in some order. There is a further ambiguity in that the magnitude of the original signals cannot be determined unless we know something about the mixing matrix A.

In games in which speed is of the essence, we need a fast method for solving this and so we use Hyvarinen's FastICA method to find a separating matrix B. This method is defined as (Hyvarinnen, Karhunen, & Oja, 2001, p. 210):

1.   Centre the data to make them zero mean.
2.   Choose an initial (e.g., random) separating matrix B. Choose initial values of γ_i, $i = 1,\ldots,n$ either randomly or using prior information. Choose the learning rates μ and μ_γ.
3.   Compute $y = B\mathbf{x}$.
4.   If the nonlinearities are not fixed a priori:
     a.   Update $\gamma_i = (1 - \mu_\gamma)\gamma_i + \mu_\gamma E\{-tanh(y_i)y_i + (1 - tanh(y_i)^2)\}$
     b.   If $\gamma_i > 0$, $g_i = -2\ tanh(y_i)$ else $g_i = tanh(y_i) - y_i$
5.   Update the separating matrix by,
     $B \leftarrow B + \mu[I + g(\mathbf{y})\mathbf{y}^T]B$ where $g(\mathbf{y}) = \{g(y_1), g(y_2),\ldots,g(y_n)\}$
6.   If not converged, go back to Step 3.

A Case Study: Independent Component Analysis

Proof of Concept

We may apply this method to identification of a signal in a very noisy environment. We have modelled the situation in which an attacker is approaching within an extremely noisy environment. The method of transport of the attacker is not known *a priori* and the signal which is received by the AI may be disguised by the attacker. The AI must identify the approach of the attacker within this noisy environment. We create a system in which the AI has 10 sensors corresponding to 10 channels with which to identify the attacker, but:

1.   The environment is extremely noisy. We add noise from a zero mean, unit variance Gaussian distribution to each sensor independently at each time instant.

2.   The attacker can choose to disguise the channel which the attacker is using by employing any linear mixing matrix to the signal. So, for example, if the attacker is using channel 1, the signal should be (1,0,…,0), but in practice can appear to the AI as that is (0.37,0.41,0.21,-0.64,0.88,-0.13,0.55,-0.45,-0.76,0.43).

The AI must identify the signal quickly and accurately recovering the sensory inputs.

The sensors and signals can be of any type, however, for the purposes of this chapter, we have created a visual signal. Each sensor operates on a 10×10 grid; the signal should be seen on a single channel. Figure 4 is deemed to be the signal representing a spaceship. Figure 5 shows an example of one of the other nine channels; all are merely noise. However the opponent is allowed to disguise the signal. For the purposes of this demonstration, we randomly mixed the signal and the nine noise inputs to get 10 mixtures which are shown in Figure 6. It is difficult (we believe impossible) to identify the spaceship in any of these.

In Figure 7 we show the recovered spaceship. For example, the method has identified the correct demixing matrix which will reveal the spaceship exactly. We note that it actually appears as a negative. This is an innate ambiguity in the problem. If

Figure 4. The spaceship to be identified

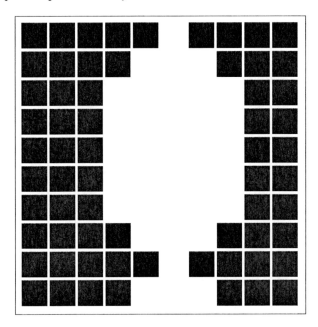

Figure 5. One of the noise signals which were mixed with the spaceship

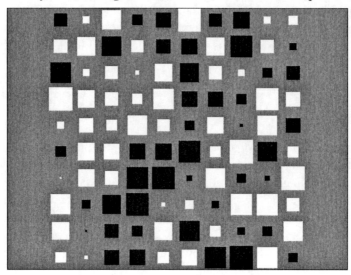

Figure 6. The 10 mixtures containing the spaceship and the 9 noise mixtures

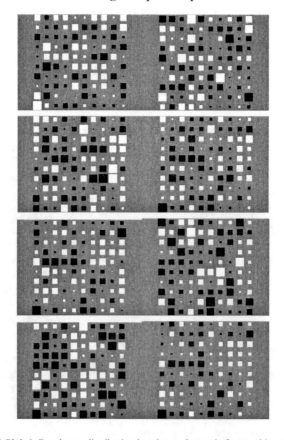

Figure 7. The recovered spaceship

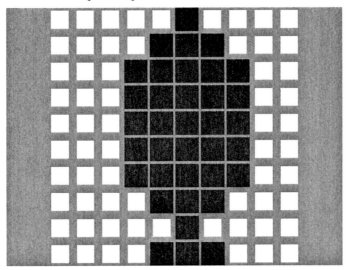

Figure 8. The method has attempted to identify 4 independent components (the top one is the spaceship) before acknowledging that there is no other signal in the mixture

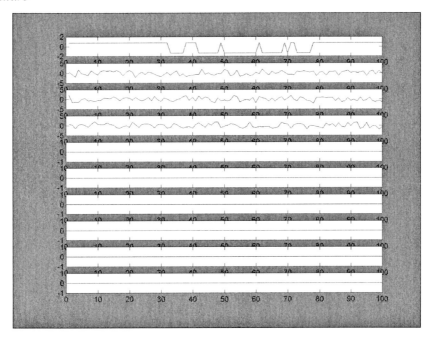

we multiply one signal by -1 and the corresponding column of the mixing matrix A by -1, we get exactly the same mixture; we cannot tell whether we are recovering s_i or -s_i.

The method can be extended to deal with up to the same number of opponents as there are sensors; in the above scenario, we could have up to 10 opponents being identified at any one time. In Figure 8, we show the results of the same experiment (with a single signal) when we allow FastICA to search for 10 signals. The elements of the recovered ys are now spread out as 100 dimensional vector. The top vector corresponds to the signal. The next three are due to FastICA finding some structure in the data which exist purely because of the limited number of samples. We can see that the remaining six attempts remain close to 0 and no structure of any type has been found.

The method is best introduced in a game in which the opponent has the option of changing the camouflage dynamically while the AI (using FastICA) must track the changes. It is possible to seed the FastICA method to use the previous search results as the starting position for the new search; however this gives too much advantage to the AI with the FastICA method. A more entertaining alternative is to start from scratch each time so that the FastICA method has to work harder to find the signal; this results in occasional failures so that its opponent's camouflage gains the upper hand for a short spell which means that the AI is blind for a spell. Occasionally too a less than 100% accurate demixing matrix B is found giving an estimate of the signal, such as shown in Figure 9.

Figure 9. The camouflage is overcome but the demixing is not done perfectly

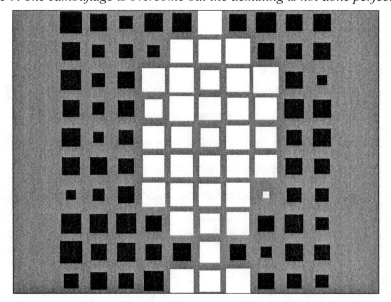

The Game

The game is essentially 10 dimensional hide and seek.

Since 10 dimensions are rather difficult to visualise, we illustrate the basic idea in three dimensions in Figure 9. We split each dimension into two and label the halves 0 and 1. Thus the box in the face closest to the viewer in the top right corner is labelled (across, up, in)=(1,1,0). We are going to allow only movement into adjacent boxes and so from (1,1,0) we can only move to (1,0,0), (1,1,1), or (0,1,0). In our 10 dimensional hide and seek, we may correspondingly move directly from any 10 dimensional box to only 10 of the possible $2^{10}=1024$ boxes.

Various treasures are hidden in eight of the boxes in this 10 dimensional space. This space is guarded by a fierce AI which searches the boxes continually for intruders. However the AI itself is limited by the movement restriction; it too can only move from the box it currently occupies into one of the 10 adjacent boxes. However if it gets to within a Hamming distance of 3 of the intruder, it can smell the intruder and knows that an intruder is near. It will then search the nearby area getting positive and negative feedback as it gets closer or further away from the intruder. The human intruder also has an invisibility cloak—a linear mixing matrix as before—which can be used to try to escape detection, but both this and the AI's FastICA method come with costs. Since the FastICA is not perfect, there is a possibility that even if the AI gets to the human's box, it will not be able to detect the human. The human is given information as to which box the AI is in and which the human is in (both coded in 1s and 0s) at each instant in time.

The game comes with various levels of difficulty. We can increase the dimensionality of the space or we can increase the granularity of the boxes, that is, divide each

Figure 10. A three-dimensional illustration

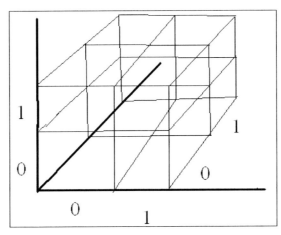

dimension into three boxes but note that $3^{10} = 59049$ and that boxes may be adjacent to up to 20 others. This makes the game more interesting but much more difficult.

Conclusion

We began with the observation that true intelligence requires adaptation. It is impossible in life to determine each situation in advance and so living creatures have to be adaptable if they are to survive. Thus we wish to build this into our AIs with a view to making our computer games more enjoyable. We have illustrated how an unsupervised artificial neural network technique, independent component analysis, can be used in a simple artificial game in which the human player is allowed to disguise the signal while the AI attempts to overcome the camouflage.

We can also state that, with the FastICA method, the AI's responses are real-time responses; the human is aware of very little pausing in the game itself. We note that this is not the case if we use neural network methods.

Competitive Learning

One of the nonbiological aspects of the basic Hebbian learning rule is that there is no limit to the amount of resources which may be given to a synapse. This is at odds with real neural growth in that it is believed that there is a limit on the number and efficiency of synapses per neuron. In other words, there comes a point during learning in which if one synapse is to be strengthened, another must be weakened. This is usually modelled as a competition for resources.

In competitive learning, there is a competition between the output neurons after the activity of each neuron has been calculated and only that neuron which wins the competition is allowed to fire. Such output neurons are often called **winner-take-all** units. The aim of **competitive learning** is to categorise the data by forming **clusters**. However, as with the Hebbian learning networks, we provide no correct answer (i.e., no labelling information) to the network. It must self-organise on the basis of the structure of the input data. The method attempts to ensure that the similarities of instances within a class are as great as possible while the differences between instances of different classes are as great as possible.

It has been pointed out that simple competitive learning leads to the creation of grandmother cells, the proverbial neuron which would fire if and only if your grandmother hove in sight. The major difficulty with such neurons is their lack of robustness: if you lose your grandmother cell, will you never again recognise your granny. In addition, we should note that if we have N grandmother cells we can only recognise N categories whereas if we are using a binary code, we could distinguish between categories.

Simple Competitive Learning

The basic mechanism of simple competitive learning is to find a winning unit and update its weights to make it more likely to win in the future should a similar input be given to the network. We first have the activity transfer equation,

$$y_i = \sum_j w_{ij} x_j, \forall i,$$

which is followed by a competition between the output neurons and then,

$\Delta w_{ij} = \eta(x_j - w_{ij})$, for the winning neuron i.

Note that the change in weights is a function of the *difference* between the weights and the input. This rule will move the weights of the winning neuron directly towards the input. If used over a distribution, the weights will tend to the mean value of the distribution since $\Delta w_{ij} \to 0 \sum_j \Leftrightarrow w_{ij} \to \langle x_j \rangle$, where the angled brackets indicate the ensemble average. We can actually describe this rule as a variant of the Hebb learning rule if we state that $i = 1$ for the winning neuron and $i = 0$ otherwise. Then the learning rule can be written $\Delta w_{ij} = \eta y_i (x_j - w_{ij})$, for example, a Hebbian learning rule with weight decay. A geometric analogy is often given to aid understanding simple competitive learning. Consider Figure 11. We have two groups of points lying on the surface of the sphere and the weights of the network are represented by the two radii. The weights have converged to the mean of each group and will be used to classify any future input to one or other group.

A potential problem with this type of learning is that some neurons can come to dominate the process, for example, the same neuron continues to win all of the time while other neurons (**dead neurons**) never win. While this can be desirable if we wish to preserve some neurons for possible new sets of input patterns it can be undesirable if we wish to develop the most efficient neural network. It pays in this situation to ensure that all weights are normalised at all times (and so already on the surface of the sphere) so that one neuron is not just winning because it happens to be greater in magnitude than the others. Another possibility is **leaky learning** where the winning neuron is updated and so too by a lesser extent are all other neurons. This encourages all neurons to move to the areas where the input vectors are to be found. The amount of the leak can be varied during the course of a simulation.

Figure 11. The input vectors are represented by points on the surface of a sphere and the lines represent the directions to which the weights have converged. Each is pointing to the mean of the group of vectors surrounding it.

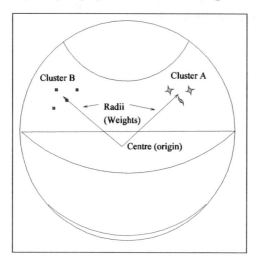

Another possibility is to have a variable threshold so that neurons which have won often in the past have a higher threshold than others. This is sometimes known as learning with a **conscience**. Finally noise in the input vectors can help in the initial approximate weight learning process till we get approximate solutions. As usual an annealing schedule is helpful. We now consider three important variations on competitive learning:

1.   Learning vector quantisation
2.   The ART models
3.   The Kohonen feature map

Learning Vector Quantisation

In **vector quantisation**, we create a codebook of vectors which represent as well as possible the vectors of each class. One obvious way to represent vectors is to use the mean of each class of vectors; competitive learning can be used to find the mean. If we use this method we can be sure that there is no vector codebook of equal length which is better able to represent the input vectors.

Kohonen (1996) has suggested a *supervised* quantisation method called learning vector quantisation (LVQ) which means that the classes must be known in advance (so that we have a set of labelled input data). We feedforward the activation through the weights as before but now we are in a position to tell if the correct unit has won the competition. If it has, we use the same learning rule as before but if neuron i has won the competition erroneously we move its vector of weights away from the input pattern. Formally the learning rule becomes,

$$\Delta w_{ij} = \eta(x_j - w_{ij}), \text{ if class } i \text{ is correct,}$$
$$\Delta w_{ij} = -\eta(x_j - w_{ij}), \text{ if class } i \text{ is wrong.}$$

An improved algorithm called LVQ2 only changes the weights negatively i:

1. The input vector is misclassified.
2. The next nearest neighbour is the correct class.
3. The input vector is reasonably close to the decision boundary between the weights.

Note that this is a supervised learning method but we include it in this chapter since it is a variant of competitive learning.

Art Models

There are a number of **ART** models all developed in response to what Grossberg (1991) calls the **stability-plasticity dilemma**. This refers to the conflicting desires for our neural networks to remain stable in the condition to which they have converged (i.e., to retain their memories of what has been learned) while at the same time being receptive to new learning. Typically we ensure stability by reducing the learning rate during the course of a simulation but this has the obvious effect that the network cannot then respond, that is, to changing input distributions.

The ART models are based on having a mixture of top-down and bottom-up competition. The simplest model can be described as:

1. Select randomly an input from the input distribution.
2. Propagate its activation forwards.
3. Select the output neuron with greatest activation. If the activation is not high enough, create a new neuron and make its weights equal to the normalised input pattern, **x**. Go back to Step 1.

4. Check that the match between the winning neuron and the input pattern is good enough by calculating the ratio $\frac{\mathbf{w}_i . \mathbf{x}}{\|\mathbf{x}\|}$. If this does not exceed the vigilance parameter, ρ, the winning unit is discarded as not good enough. It is disabled and the competition is carried out again with the same input over all other output neurons (i.e., go back to Step 3).

5. Adjust the weights of the winning neuron using the simple competitive learning rule.

Notice how the algorithm solves the stability-plasticity problem. In order that it can continue to learn, we assume a set of unused neurons which are created as needed. On the other hand, once a neuron has learned a set of patterns (i.e., is responding maximally to those patterns) it will continue to respond to them and to patterns like them. It is possible to show that all weight changes stop after a finite number of steps.

Note also the interaction between the two criteria:

•   The winning neuron is that which is maximally firing.
•   The vigilance parameter checks whether the winning neuron is actually close enough to the input pattern.

It is the interaction between these two criteria which gives ART its power. We are actually searching through the prototype vectors to find one which is close enough to the current input to be deemed a good match. A local algorithm with top-down (checking vigilance) and bottom-up (finding winning neuron) neurons has been created.

One major difficulty with ART networks is that convergence can be extremely slow for any problem greater than a toy problem.

The Kohonen Feature Map

The interest in feature maps stems directly from their biological importance. A feature map uses the 'physical layout' of the output neurons to model some feature of the input space. In particular, if two inputs 1 and 2 are close together with respect to some distance measure in the input space, then if they cause output neurons a and b to fire respectively, a and b must be close together in some layout of the output neurons. Further we can state that the opposite should hold: if a and b are close together in the output layer, then those inputs which cause a and b to fire should be close together in the input space. When these two conditions hold, we have a feature map. Such maps are also called **topology preserving maps**.

Examples of such maps in biology include:

- The **retinotopic map** which takes input from the retina (at the eye) and maps it onto the visual cortex (back of the brain) in a two dimensional map.
- The **somatosensory map** which maps our touch centres on the skin to the somatosensory cortex.
- The **tonotopic map** which maps the responses of our ears to the auditory cortex.

Each of these maps is believed to be determined genetically but refined by usage, that is, the retinotopic map is very different if one eye is excluded from seeing during particular periods of development.

Hertz, Krogh, and Palmer (1991) distinguish between:

- Those maps which map continuous inputs from single (such as one ear) inputs or a small number of inputs to a map in which similar inputs cause firings on neighbouring outputs (left half of Figure 12).
- Those maps which take in a broad array of inputs and map onto a second array of outputs (right half of Figure 12).

There are several ways of creating feature maps. The most popular, Kohonen's (1997) algorithm is exceedingly simple. Tthe network is a simple two-layer network and competition takes place between the output neurons; however now not only are the weights into the winning neuron updated but also the weights into its neighbours. Kohonen defined a neighbourhood function of the winning neuron i^*. The neighbourhood function is a function of the distance between i and i^*. A typical function is the difference of Gaussians function; thus if unit i is at point i in the output layer then,

$$f(i,i^*) = a\exp\left(\frac{-|r_i - r_{i*}|^2}{2\sigma^2}\right) - b\exp\left(\frac{-|r_i - r_{i*}|^2}{2\sigma_1^2}\right) \tag{13}$$

The single **Gaussian** can be seen in Figure 13, while the **Mexican Hat** function is shown in Figure 14. Notice that this means that a winning neuron's chums—those neurons which are 'close' to the winning neuron in the output space—are also dragged out to the input data while those neurons further away are pushed slightly in the opposite direction.

Figure 12. Two types of feature maps: (a) a map from a small number of continuous inputs (b) a map from one layer spatially arranged to another.

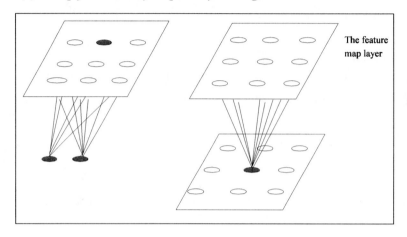

Figure 13. The Gaussian function

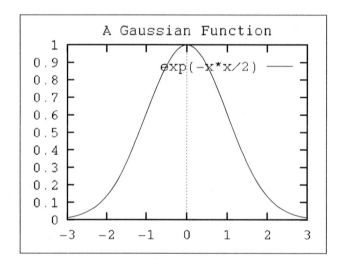

Figure 14. The difference of Gaussian function

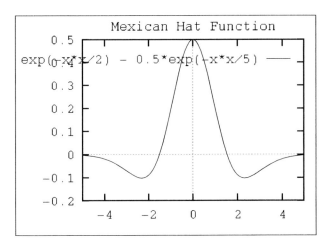

Results from an example experiment are shown in Figure 15. The experiment consists of a neural network with two inputs and 25 outputs. The two inputs at each iteration are drawn from a uniform distribution over the square from -1 to 1 in two directions. For example, typical inputs would be (0.3,0.5), (-0.4,0.9), (0.8,0.8), or (-0.1,-0.5). The algorithm is:

1. Select at random an input point (with two values).
2. There is a competition among the output neurons. That neuron whose weights are closest to the input data point wins the competition:

$$\text{winning neuron, } i^* = \text{argmin}(\|x - w_i\|) \tag{14}$$

Use the distance formula to find that distance which is smallest,

$$dist = \sqrt{(x_1 - w_{i1})^2 + (x_2 - w_{i2})^2} \tag{15}$$

3. Now update all neurons' weights using,

$$\Delta w_{ij} = \alpha(x_j - w_{ij}) * f(i, i^*) \tag{16}$$

where,

$$f(i,i^*) = a\exp\left(\frac{-|r_i - r_{i*}|^2}{2\sigma^2}\right) - b\exp\left(\frac{-|r_i - r_{i*}|^2}{2\sigma_1^2}\right) \tag{17}$$

4.   Go back to the start.

Kohonen typically keeps the learning rate constant for the first 1,000 iterations or so and then slowly decreases it to zero over the remainder of the experiment (we can be talking about 100,000 iterations for self-organising maps). Two-dimensional maps can be created by imagining the output neurons laid out on a rectangular grid (we then require a two D neighbourhood function) or sometimes a hexagonal grid.

Figure 15. A one-dimensional mapping of the two dimensional input space

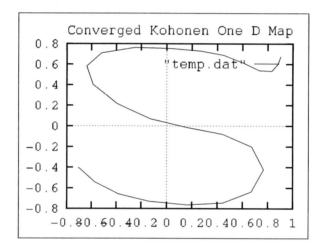

Figure 16. A 5*5 feature map which conforms well to a set of inputs drawn from a rectangular distribution but less well to a less regular distribution

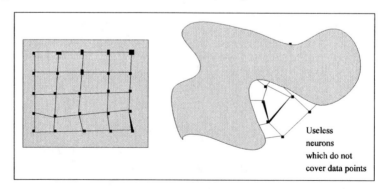

An example of such a mapping is shown in Figure 16 in which we are making a two-dimensional mapping of a two-dimensional surface. This is a little redundant and is for illustration only.

Like the ART algorithms, Kohonen's feature maps can take a long while to converge. Examples of the converged mappings which a Kohonen SOFM can find are shown in Figure 16. We can see that the neurons have spread out evenly when the input distribution is uniform over a rectangular space but with the less regular distribution in the right half of the figure there are several dead neurons which are performing no useful function that will respond to areas of the input space which are empty.

Applications

The SOFM has been used in modelling features of the human brain such as visual maps and somatosensory maps. In terms of engineered applications some of interest are:

1. Vector quantisation in which we wish to identify all vectors close to a particular prototypical vector of a particular class with the prototype. This can be useful, that is, in terms of data compression since if we transmit the code for the prototype vector (i.e., the information that it is prototype 3 rather than 2 or 4) we may be giving enough information for the vector to be reconstructed at the receiving location with very little loss of information. This can be very useful, that is, in image reconstruction where the bandwidth necessary to fully reconstruct an image may be prohibitively high.

2. Control of robot arms. Inverse kinematics problems can be extremely computationally expensive to solve. A SOFM allows an unsupervised learning of a set of standard positions of the robot end-receptors in terms of the positions of the individual angles and lengths of levers which make up a robot arm.

3. Classification of clouds from raw data.

Case Study: The Self-Organizing Map and Pong

Despite being one of the earliest video games, the game of Pong, which was described in Chapter II, is an excellent game to attempt convincing opponent AI to use a neural network. It was originally designed as a two-player game and with the help of an AI opponent it can be played as a one-player game. Pong is simple enough to demonstrate the capabilities of modern AI techniques without complicating the issue by adding ad-hoc tweaks, and the behaviour of life-like Pong players is complicated enough that creating an AI player is not a trivial problem. Nowadays, of course, there is not a market for Pong-type games. However, the principles presented in this chapter could also be applied to modern game genres such as first-person and third-person shooters. (Alternative case studies of building AI controllers using ANN are presented in Chapters IV and VIII).

AI opponents can be written with various different objectives in mind. One possible approach is to aim to produce AI players that play a game as well as possible, and are most likely to succeed in a game. Depending on the game, this can be an interesting and often difficult objective that is certainly worth pursuing (but not in the case of Pong). Another aim may be to make the gaming experience more enjoyable to the human player, and this is the approach that we will take with the AI player for Pong. This is the ultimate goal of most aspects of game design and development, and it holds more commercial value than the former objective. To achieve this objective, the AI's performance and style of play should be somewhat similar to that of a human player, providing players with believable interaction with artificial opponents or team-mates and so forth (van Waveren & Rothkrantz, 2002; Zubek & Khoo, 2002).

Two aspects of game AI that affect the enjoyment of the experience of playing the game are:

Figure 17. Screen shot of a clone of Pong

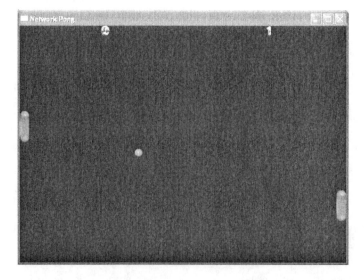

- The degree of skill of the AI player.
- The style of play of the AI player.

Let us first consider the degree of skill. An AI player that is used as an opponent against a human player should play at a level appropriate to the human player's ability. Obviously, the skill of players varies enormously, and so AI opponents should be able to provide varying difficulty levels. There is little enjoyment in playing against an opponent that is either too easy or too hard to beat; most game players like to have a challenge. In order to retain the interest of a player, AI opponents should pose a significant challenge to the human player, but it should still be beatable, even if after several attempts.

The style of play of an AI player should (in many applications) be similar to that of a human. Even if an AI player can match the performance level of a human player, if it behaves in an inhuman fashion, then the gaming experience is less convincing, less immersive, and ultimately less enjoyable. Motion of AI players should avoid being unrealistically jerky or smooth, and avoid super-human reactions to events in the game. This agrees with guidelines proposed by Spronck, Sprinkhuizen, and Postma (2002) which stated that computer controlled opponents should not cheat and should avoid ineffective behaviour.

This section presents an adaptive AI mechanism that can be used to produce computer-controlled opponents that behave in a similar fashion to human players. Data are gathered from a human playing the game and are then used to train the AI to play the game in a style similar to the human player. The AI should mimic quirks in the human's style of play, and even strengths and flaws in their play. We have implemented the AI using Kohonen's self-organizing map (SOM), which, as explained before, learns a mapping from a high dimensional data space to a low-dimensional space represented by a lattice of nodes based on the statistics of the recorded data.

The Game

Pong is such a widely recognised game that it hardly needs explaining. However, this section provides some details of our implementation, which may differ slightly from some other versions of the game.

The game is played with two player bats on the sides of the screen, each of which can move on a fixed vertical axis, using a suitable game controller. When the game begins, a ball appears near the centre of the screen, and starts moving towards the left or the right. The ball is given a random initial direction vector, $\mathbf{v}$, but it is constrained such that it is never more than $\pi/4$ radians from the horizontal direction. This direction vector is normalised to unit magnitude, and a separate scalar variable, w, represents the speed.

When the ball collides with the top or the bottom of the playing area, the vertical component of the ball's direction is negated, giving a completely elastic rebound. When the ball collides with a bat at time t, its horizontal component of direction is negated at time $t + 1$, and the resulting direction vector is rotated as in the following equation:

$$\mathbf{v}(t+1) = \mathbf{R}\mathbf{v}(t) \tag{18}$$

where:

$$\mathbf{R} = \begin{pmatrix} \cos\theta & -\sin\theta \\ \sin\theta & \cos\theta \end{pmatrix}$$

The value of θ is given by a function of the point on the bat where the ball has hit. A collision with the top of the bat gives θ a value of $-\pi/10$, and this increases linearly for other positions till a collision at the bottom of the bat gives $-\pi/10$, with the exact centre of the bat giving a value of zero. This allows the player to direct the ball's trajectory as it rebounds from the bat. The speed of the ball is also increased by a small amount each time the ball collides with a bat, and the game therefore becomes more difficult as play progresses.

Whenever a player misses the ball, the other player is awarded a point, and after a short delay, the ball is played from the centre of the screen again, in a random direction.

Several different devices could be used as a controller for the game, but we recommend a mouse, paddle, or trackball to allow the player to move their bat at different speeds, which is essential for reacting quickly, especially as the game speeds up. Digital input devices that do not allow the user this degree of control should be avoided. Analogue joystick controllers could be used, however, control of the bat is more difficult with these devices than with a mouse, and they will lead to a different style of play.

The AI Opponent

The game has several features that make it an interesting application for neural network AI. First, it is a real-time game involving human reactions. Human-like reactions are something that we aim to reproduce in the AI player. The game also allows the player to employ simple strategies and playing styles. For example, a player may try to direct the ball to move in a direction that forms an acute angle with the movement of the opponent's bat, making it more difficult for the opponent to hit the ball. Alternatively, a player may prefer the strategy of playing the ball in a more straightforward fashion to avoid getting a difficult return ball. When the AI system is trained on data captured from a human playing the game, the AI should exhibit similar playing strategies to that of the human.

Creating a realistic AI opponent for Pong is a reasonably difficult problem. It is, of course, absolutely trivial to create an unbeatable AI player that would work simply by moving the bat to a projected point where the ball is expected to intercept the bat's axis. Another even simpler option is to constantly move the bat such that its centre is equal to the vertical position of the ball. Both of these solutions would produce computer opponents that the human player can never score a point against, which is no fun for the player. This could be improved upon by adding 'artificial stupidity' to make the AI player miss occasionally. Unfortunately, this would still leave the problem that the playing style of the AI would be unlike a human player and annoying to play against. Not only would the AI sometimes miss some very easy shots, but the motion of the bat would be very obviously computer-controlled. Instead, we can achieve convincing bat motion by training an adaptive AI player on data gathered from observing humans playing the game.

Recording the Data

Game observation capture (GoCap) is the process of recording data from a live user during the execution of a game, with a view to using machine learning to train an AI player. The term 'GoCap' was introduced by Alexander (2002), and stems from the recognition that many game AI systems are written with large amounts of ad-hoc scripted code, yet they achieve a level of realism that is unconvincing and they adapt poorly to unfamiliar environments. In simple terms, Alexander describes GoCap as 'motion capture for AI.'

Using the game of Pong, the following data was collected:

- The ball's direction vector, $\mathbf{v}$.
- The ball speed, w.
- The vertical position, b, of one of the players' bats.

These values were recorded once per frame, with the game running at 60 frames per second. The speed of the ball was represented separately from the direction so that the AI system would learn to behave differently with the ball moving at different

Table 1. A sample of data recorded while playing Pong

Ball position		Ball direction				
X	y	x	y	Ball speed	Bat1	Bat 2
82.21	451.37	-0.49	-0.87	20.8	371	337
72.00	433.24	-0.49	-0.87	20.8	365	337
61.80	415.12	-0.49	-0.87	20.8	360	337
51.59	396.99	-0.49	-0.87	20.8	356	337
41.39	378.87	-0.49	-0.87	20.8	342	337
31.18	360.75	-0.49	-0.87	20.8	318	337
20.98	342.62	-0.49	-0.87	20.8	294	337
11.86	324.57	0.60	-0.80	20.9	288	337
24.41	307.85	0.60	-0.80	20.9	280	337
36.96	291.14	0.60	-0.80	20.9	263	337
49.51	274.43	0.60	-0.80	20.9	230	337
62.06	257.71	0.60	-0.80	20.9	211	337
74.60	241.00	0.60	-0.80	20.9	178	337
87.15	224.28	0.60	-0.80	20.9	156	337
99.70	207.57	0.60	-0.80	20.9	134	337
112.25	190.85	0.60	-0.80	20.9	124	337

speeds, as is the case when humans play the game. Table 1 shows a short sample of some of the collected data.

Selecting a Suitable AI Method

Given the variety of methods that we have discussed thus far, how should we decide which method to use for the AI for Pong? In this section, we will consider the merits of several methods and justify our choice of using the SOM. It should be noted that of the variety of neural network types, there are several that would perform well when applied to this problem. The decision to use one particular network is not to the exclusion of others, and we do not make the claim that the SOM will out-perform all other methods. Instead, we give suitable justification that the SOM is a reasonable choice.

The aim of this application is to learn from the complete data set, consisting of the ball's 2D position vector, its 2D direction vector, its scalar speed, and the two bat positions. After training, the data will be incomplete, missing one of the bat positions, and the objectives of the AI are to generate bat positions that are most likely to return the ball, and more importantly, to generate motion that is similar to the motion of human players. The first objective may be measured; however, we do not have a measure of the degree to which the second objective is achieved.

First, let us consider the multilayered perceptron (trained by error-backpropagation) and the radial basis function networks, which are covered in Chapters III and 6 respectively. Both of these networks have been used with success in this type of problem, where some of the dimensions of the data set are learned as target outputs. It is therefore worthwhile to apply these networks to the problem, and this we will see later in Chapter VI.

It would be possible to use one of a variety of methods (both neural and statistical) to find the principal components of the data set, then use this model to find the most likely position of a bat, given all other dimensions of a data vector. Simple linear PCA is most effective when the data set have an underlying linear structure. With the data that we are working with, they do not have this property. On the contrary, analysis shows that the data cloud has a nonlinear structure when projected onto a low-dimensional space. Another option would be to use a *piecewise linear* method, which would use a mixture of locally linear models that would be combined to give globally nonlinear models. There are several well-known methods for doing this, and the SOM can be viewed in this way, since it forms a globally nonlinear manifold of the data space.

We have not explored the use of independent component analysis because there is no theoretical reason that ICA should perform well on the problem. ICA is designed for finding a set of underlying components that have been mixed together. In this case, the bat position that we want to find out is missing from the data, and it has not been mixed with the other variables. Also, it is not an independent cause, since we can use the other variables to estimate its value.

As stated above, the SOM is known to form a globally nonlinear manifold based on the statistics of a data set. For the data that we are working with, we suggest that this degree of complexity is necessary, and a globally linear method would not sufficiently model the nonlinear structure of the data. Unlike some other methods that perform this function, the SOM has a low computational cost, particularly when optimisations are implemented. It is efficient enough that the network can be trained online with minimal processing overhead. Even in a network with a large number of nodes, the processing overhead is minimal for training and subsequent use. The computational cost does not necessarily increase when the number of nodes and weight parameters is increased. This is a major advantage of the SOM for games, since AI in games often has a very small proportion of the total available processing resource. The SOM has also been used with success in dealing with incomplete data, and our data set clearly falls in this category.

Training

A two-dimensional SOM consisting of 20×20 nodes was trained on all of the data. The learning rate, η, was set to 0.01 and this was annealed by multiplying it by 0.995 after every set of 50 iterations. The neighbourhood function in equation (20) was also annealed by multiplying the radius, r, by 0.95 after every 50 iterations, starting with an initial value of 7.

$$h_{ci} = e^{n^2/-r^2} - 0.2e^{\frac{n^2}{(\%_6)^2}},$$

(19)

(n is the distance between node c and node i.)

The training process was run for 100,000 iterations on a data set recorded from a single game of Pong played between two human players. In every iteration, a vector was selected at random from the entire data set, and the weights updated. The amount of data in the training set was typically in the region of 10,000 vectors, based on a 3 minute game played at 60 frames per second. There is no real justification for training for this number of iterations, other than experience of the SOM algorithm, and trial of different numbers of iterations. It is possible to use a convergence measure such as the 'SOM distortion measure,' and stop training only after a certain degree of convergence has been reached.

Using the SOM During Gameplay

Once a map has been sufficiently trained, the AI player works by constructing an input vector based on the ball's speed, position, and direction, feeding this into the network and then looking up the corresponding bat position from the correct component of winning node's weight vector, w_{cb}. The winner search is done by finding the node whose weight vector has the smallest Euclidean distance from the input vector; however, the component corresponding to the bat position is ignored during this search:

$$c = \arg\min_i \sum_{j \neq b} (w_{ij} x_j)$$

(20)

Compared to some other neural methods, the SOM does not have a high computational cost. On a very modest PC (e.g., with an AMD Athlon 1800 processor), a winner search can easily be run 60 times per second without imposing a severe processing bottleneck. However, this is far more often than necessary. Since the input vector in adjacent frames will always be very similar, it is perfectly acceptable to use the SOM to find a new bat position less often, for example, once every 200 milliseconds. There are further optimisations that are discussed later in this chapter which can have a very profound effect on the required processing time.

Improving the Motion

The method described so far yields reasonable results; however, there are two problems with the AI player:

- The motion of the bat appears erratic and 'jerky.'
- The bat often misses the ball by a narrow margin, even when the ball is moving slowly.

These problems can be explained by the nature of the SOM as vector quantiser (VQ), which means that it divides the data space into a set of discrete regions (called Voronoi regions), one for each reference vector. Every possible vector that in the input data space lies in one and only one of these regions, and is quantised to the weight vector of the node that wins the competition that takes place between all the nodes. As the game progresses, each input vector changes gradually, although the bat position does not change at all while the input vectors remain in the same Voronoi region. When the inputs finally cross the threshold into another Voronoi region, a different node starts winning the competitions, and the bat's position suddenly jumps to a new position, and stays there until the input pattern moves to yet another Voronoi region.

The bat position given by the AI is therefore restricted to a finite set of values, and this explains the jerky movement of the bat as it moves between these values without traversing the space in between. It also explains why the bat often misses the ball. This is illustrated by the hypothetical scenario shown in Figure 18. The

Figure 18. Missing the ball due to vector quantisation

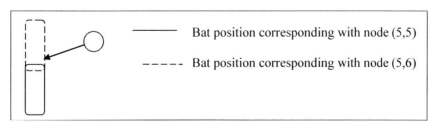

Bat position corresponding with node (5,5)

Bat position corresponding with node (5,6)

solid rectangle shows the bat position given by node (5,5), which is the winner in this case. Despite this node being the closest to the input, the input is right on the edge of the Voronoi region between node (5,5) and node (5,6). Even although the input vector is very close to the Voronoi region of node (5,6), the final bat position is not affected by it, and the bat completely misses the ball.

The problem can be solved by finding the node, d, that is the second placed winner and then interpolating between the two winners. The bat position, p, is an interpolated point between the bat position given by the winner, w_{cb} and the second placed winner, w_{db} with the point of interpolation between the two values calculated according to their Euclidean distances from the input vector (22).

$$d = \arg\min_i(\|\mathbf{x} - \mathbf{w}_i\|), d \neq c \tag{22}$$

$$p = w_{cb} + \left(1 - \frac{\|\mathbf{x} - \mathbf{w}_d\|}{\|\mathbf{x} - \mathbf{w}_c\| + \|\mathbf{x} - \mathbf{w}_d\|}\right)(w_{db} - w_{cb}) \tag{23}$$

The idea of using multiple winners in a SOM stems from the work of Stephen Luttrell (1997).

An alternative to the idea of using multiple winning nodes in a SOM is to replace the SOM with a continuous mapping model such as the generative topographic mapping (GTM) (Bishop, Svensen, & Williams, 1997) or some other continuous function, such as the parameterised SOM (Ritter, Martinez, & Schulten, 1992). However, the main disadvantage to using these methods is that they do not support the optimisations that make the SOM such an attractive choice for games development. Despite the claim that the GTM has an approximately equivalent computational cost to the SOM, this is only true when compared with the unoptimised SOM.

After using two winners, the problems identified above were helped, however, it was found to be of further benefit to smooth the movements of the AI player's bat by simulating inertia. When a human plays the game with a physical device such as a mouse or trackball, the inertia of the device constrains the way that the human can play the game, and it helps to impose a similar constraint on the computer player. This prevents the bat from moving unrealistically fast.

Optimisations

Processing efficiency is almost always a crucial consideration in games programming, and there is a major performance boost for the SOM that we can take advantage of.

Since the SOM is a topology-preserving method, its reference vectors are ordered, and therefore when the winning node is being searched out, the search space can be narrowed down to nodes that are close to the previous winner, saving a significant amount of processing time. In the examples shown, we used a two-dimensional array of 20×20 nodes, so every full winner search requires calculating 400 Euclidean distances. If we were to restrict the winner search to only those nodes in the immediate vicinity of the current winner, for example, those nodes whose Voronoi regions border with the winner's, there will be a maximum of nine Euclidean distances to be calculated on each iteration.

This is based on the assumption that successive input vectors are similar to each other, which is a suitable assumption for this application. This optimisation makes the SOM a more suitable alternative to some other clustering methods such as k-means clustering (MacQueen, 1967) which cannot be optimised in this way.

Results

In the introduction we identified the level of performance and the style of play as important factors in producing convincing game AI. First, let us consider the style of play of the AI player. The training data for our AI player were recorded from a human player, and it is possible to identify some playing quirks employed by that player, which we would expect to be apparent with the AI player. A quirk that was observed in the human player was a tendency to move the bat quickly upwards as the ball collided with the bat. Figure 19 clearly shows this quirk, which can also be seen in many other areas of the data. Immediately after the ball is hit (this occurs

Figure 19. The motion of the human player's bat as it hits the ball. The horizontal axis represents time. The origin is at the top-left and the vertical axis is positive downwards.

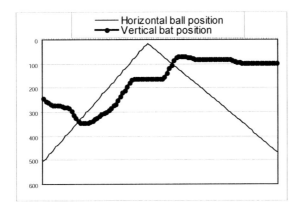

at the middle of the graph), the bat position moves up quickly. Figure 20 shows a similar quirk produced by the AI player, albeit not quite as pronounced. At the point of impact, near the middle of the graph, the bat moves quickly up. The data shown in Figure 20 are representative of typical movements made by the AI player. Note that these two graphs are taken from different games, and the other parts of the bats' motion curves should not be compared since they were captured under different conditions.

It is difficult to quantify the extent to which the AI player plays like a human. Based on the opinions of the author and three other regular games players, the AI is fun to play against, and appears human-like to a large extent. To properly investigate whether this is the case, it will be necessary to conduct a survey amongst game players to get a broader view of the extent to which this work has achieved the two objectives identified in the introduction of the chapter. Chapter XIV explores this topic further.

In terms of performance, the AI player plays reasonably well. However, it does not present a serious challenge to an experienced game player. As more work is done in this area, the level of performance should improve.

SOM: Conclusion

Our conclusion from this work is that the use of the SOM to produce an AI player from game observation data has been successful. The AI player plays the game of Pong in a style that is consistent with a human style of play, and quirks observed in the human's play are also seen in the AI player.

Figure 20. The motion of the AI player's bat as it hits the ball

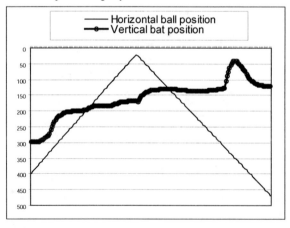

If identical situations are presented to a human player at different times in a game, they may respond a different way each time. This can be due to a lack of precision in dexterity, or it may be that the player selects one of a number of optional strategies, selecting different ones at different times. This is one area where the method presented in this chapter produces behaviour that is unlike human performance, since the outcome is always completely deterministic, based on the ball's speed, position, and direction. Having said this, it would be very difficult to notice because the game is rarely (if ever) in any particular state more than once.

An interesting area to explore is to train the network during game play, so that the computer player can learn from its opponents. A major advantage of the SOM is that it requires a small computational cost during training, and various optimisations have been used (Kohonen, 1997) to reduce this further in real-time applications.

Future research will aim to apply this method to different games and more difficult problems, including modern games such as real-time strategy (RTS) and 3D shooters.

Conclusion

Overall, in this chapter we have described how unsupervised methods may be used to effectively train ANN, and demonstrated their successful application in two different case studies. These methods may lend themselves particularly well where player data are available for use in training the ANN; to provide opponents, cooperative bots, or otherwise to populate a game world with believable characters and entities.

References

Alexander, T. (2002). GoCap: Game observation capture. In S. Rabin (Ed.), *AI game programming wisdom* (pp. 579-585). Hingham, MA: Charles River Media.

Bishop, C., Svensen, M., & Williams, C. (1997). GTM: The generative topographic mapping. *Neural Computation 10*(1), 215-234.

Grossberg, S. (1991). Adaptive pattern classification and universal recoding, II: Feeback, expectation, olfaction and illusions. In Carpenter & Grossberg (Eds.), *Pattern recognition in self-organising neural networks*. Cambridge, MA: MIT Press.

Hebb, D. O. (1949). *The organization of behaviour*. Wiley.

Hertz, J., Krogh, A., & Palmer, R. G. (1991) *Introduction to the theory of neural computation*. Addison Wesley.

Hyvarinen, A., Karhunen, J., & Oja, E. (2001). *Independent component analysis*. Wiley

Kohonen, T. (1996). *The speedy SOM* (Tech. Rep. No. A33). Espoo, Finland: Helsinki University of Technology, Laboratory of Computer and Information Science.

Kohonen, T. (1997). *Self-organizing maps* (2nd ed.). New York: Springer-Verlag.

Luttrell, S.P. (1997). Self-organisation of multiple winner-take-all neural networks. *Connection Science 9(1)*, 11-30

MacQueen, J. (1967). *Some methods for classification and analysis of multivariate observations*. Paper presented at the Fifth Berkeley Symposium on Mathematics, Statistics and Probability (Vol. 1, pp. 281-297). Berkeley: University of California Press

Oja, E. (1982). A simplified neuron model as a principal component analyzer. *Journal of mathematical biology, 15*, 267-273.

Oja, E. (1989). Neural networks, principal components and subspaces. *International Journal of Neural Systems, 1*, 61-68.

Oja, E., Ogawa, H., & Wangviwattana, J. (1992). Principal component analysis by homogeneous neural networks (Parts I and II). *IEICE trans. on Information and system*, (75), 366-375.

Ritter, H., Martinez, T., & Schulten, K. (1992). *Neural computation and self-organizing maps*. Reading, MA: Addison-Wesley

Sanger, T. D. (1989). An optimality principle for unsupervised learning. *Advances in Neural Information Processing Systems, 1*, 11-19.

Shannon, C. E. (1948). A mathematical theory of communication. *Bell System Technical Journal, 27*, 379-423.

Spronck, P., Sprinkhuizen, I., & Postma, E. (2002) Improved opponent intelligence through offline learning. *International Journal of Intelligent Games & Simulation, 2*(1), 20-27.

van Waveren, J. M. P., & Rothkrantz, L. J. M. (2002). Artificial player for quake III arena. *International Journal of Intelligent Games & Simulation, 1*(1), 25-32.

Zubek, R., & Khoo, A. (2002). Making the human care: On building engaging bots. In *Proceedings of AAAI Spring Symposium on Artificial Intelligence and Interactive Entertainment*, Menlo Park, California (AAAI Tech. Rep. SS-02-01). AAAI Press.

Chapter VI

Fast Learning in Neural Networks

Introduction

We noted in the previous chapters that, while the multilayer perceptron is capable of approximating any continuous function, it can suffer from excessively long training times. In this chapter we will investigate methods of shortening training times for artificial neural networks using **supervised learning**. Haykin's (1999) work is a particularly good reference for **radial basis function** (RBF) networks. In this chapter we outline the theory and implementation of a RBF network before demonstrating how such a network may be used to solve one of the previously visited problems, and compare our solutions.

Radial Basis Functions

Note. Activation is fed forward from the input layer to the hidden layer where a (basis) function of the Euclidean distance between the inputs and the centres of the

Figure 1. A typical radial basis function network

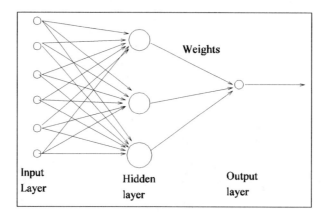

basis functions is calculated. The weighted sum of the basis function outputs is fed forward to the output neuron.

A typical radial basis function (RBF) network is shown in Figure 1. The input layer is simply a receptor for the input data. The crucial feature of the RBF network is the function calculation which is performed in the hidden layer. This function performs a *nonlinear* transformation from the input space to the hidden-layer space. The hidden neurons' functions form a basis for the input vectors and the output neurons merely calculate a linear (weighted) combination of the hidden neurons' outputs.

An often-used set of basis functions is the set of Gaussian functions whose mean and standard deviation may be determined in some way by the input data (see below). Therefore, if $\mathbf{f}(x)$ is the vector of hidden neurons' outputs when the input pattern $\mathbf{x}$ is presented and if there are M hidden neurons, then,

$$\mathbf{f}(x) = (f_1(x), f_2(x), ..., f_M(x))^T$$
$$\text{where } f_i(x) = \exp(-1_i \|x - c_i\|^2)$$

where the centres i of the Gaussians will be determined by the input data. Note that the terms i represent the Euclidean distance between the inputs and the centre. For the moment we will only consider basis functions with i. The output of the network is calculated by,

$$y = \mathbf{x}.\mathbf{f}(x) = w^T f(x)$$

where $\mathbf{w}$ is the weight vector from the hidden neurons to the output neuron.

Figure 2. A 'tiling' of a part of the plane

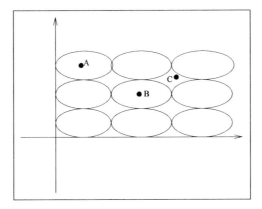

To get some idea of the effect of basis functions, consider Figure 2. In this figure we have used an elliptical tiling of a portion of the plane; this could be thought of as a Gaussian tiling as defined above but with a different standard deviation in the vertical direction from that in the horizontal direction. We may then view the lines drawn as the 1 (or 2 or 3, etc.) standard deviation contour. Then each basis function is centred as shown but each has a nonzero effect elsewhere. Thus we may think of *A* as the point (1,0,0,0,0,0,0,0,0) and *B* as (0,0,0,0,1,0,0,0,0).

Since the basis functions actually have nonzero values everywhere this is an approximation since *A* will have some effect particularly on the second, fourth, and fifth basis functions (the next three closest) but these values will be relatively small compared to 1, the value of the first basis function.

However the value of the basis functions marked 2,3,5 and 6 at the point *C* will be non-negligible. Thus the coordinates of *C* in this basis might be thought of as (0,0.2,0.5,0,0.3,0.4,0,0,0), that is, it is nonzero over 4 dimensions.

Notice also from this simple example that we have increased the dimensionality of each point by using this basis.

We will use the XOR function to demonstrate that expressing the input patterns in the hidden layer's basis permits patterns which were not linearly separable in the original (input) space to become linearly separable in the hidden neurons' space (Haykin, 1999, p. 241).

XOR Again

We will use the XOR pattern which is shown diagrammatically in Figure 3. We noted earlier that this set of patterns is not linearly separable (in the input (X,Y)-

space). Let us consider the effect of mapping the inputs to a hidden layer with two neurons with,

$f_1(x) = \exp(-\|x - c_1\|^2)$, where $c_1 = (1,1)$
$f_2(x) = \exp(-\|x - c_2\|^2)$, where $c_2 = (0,0)$

Then the two hidden neurons' outputs on presentation of the four input patterns is shown in Table 1.

Now if we plot the hidden neuron's outputs in the 12 basis, we see (Figure 3) that the outputs are linearly separable.

Table 1. The activation functions of the hidden neurons for the 4 possible inputs for the XOR problem

Input pattern	1	2
(0,0)	0.135	1
(0,1)	0.368	0.368
(1,0)	0.368	0.368
(1,1)	1	0.135

Figure 3. The hidden neurons' activations are plotted on a graph whose axes are the neuron's functions. One (of many possible) discriminating lines is drawn.

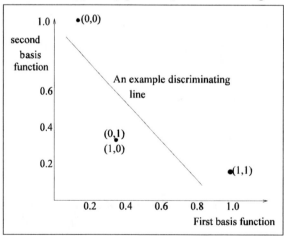

Learning Weights

However we still have to find the actual parameters which determine the slope of the discrimination line. These are the weights between the basis functions (in the hidden layer) and the output layer.

We may train the network now using the simple LMS algorithm (see Chapter III) in the usual way. If the sum of the errors over all N patterns is,

$$E = \frac{1}{2}\sum_{i=1}^{N}(t^i - o^i)^2 = \frac{1}{2}\sum_{i=1}^{N}\left(t^i - \sum_j w_j \varphi_j(\mathbf{x}^i)\right)^2 = \frac{1}{2}\sum_{i=1}^{N} e_i^2$$

where, as before, represents the target output for the input pattern, then we can represent the instantaneous error (the error on presentation of a single pattern) by,

$$E^i = \frac{1}{2}\left(t^i - \sum_j w_j \varphi_j(\mathbf{x}^i)\right)^2 = \frac{1}{2}e_i^2,$$

and so we can create an online learning algorithm using,

$$\frac{\partial E^i}{\partial w_k} = -\left(t^i - \sum_j w_j \varphi_j(\mathbf{x}^i)\right)\varphi_k(\mathbf{x}^i) = -e^2 . \varphi_k(\mathbf{x}^i).$$

Therefore we will change the weights after presentation of the ith input pattern x^{th} by,

$$\Delta w_k = \frac{\partial E^i}{\partial w_k} = e^i . \varphi_k(\mathbf{x}^i).$$

Approximation Problems

We may view the problem of finding the weights which minimise the error at the outputs as an approximation problem. Then the learning process described above is equivalent to finding that line in the hidden layer's space which is optimal for approximating an unknown function. Note that this straight line (or in general hyperplane) in the hidden layer space is equivalent to a curve or hypersurface in the original space. Now, as before, our aim is not solely to make the best fit to the data points on which we are training the network, but our overall aim is to have the network perform as well as possible on data which it has not seen during learning.

Previously we described this as generalisation. In the context of the RBF network, we may here view it as interpolation: we are fitting the RBF network to the actual values which it sees during training but we are doing so with a smooth enough set of basis functions that we can interpolate between the training points and give correct (or almost correct) responses for points not in the training set.

If the number of points in the training set is less than the number of hidden neurons, this problem is underdetermined and there is the possibility that the hidden neurons will map the training data precisely and be less useful as an approximation function of the underlying distribution. Ideally the examples from which we wish to generalise must show some redundancy, however if this is not possible we can add some constraints to the RBF network to attempt to ensure that any approximation it might perform is valid. A typical constraint is that the second derivative of the basis functions with respect to the input distribution is sufficiently small. If this is small, the weighted sum of the functions does not change too rapidly when the inputs change and so the output values (the y's) should be reasonable approximations of the true values of the unknown function at intermediate input values (the x's) between the training values.

RBF and MLP as Approximators

We examine the approximation properties of both a multilayered perceptron and a radial basis function on a problem which we met in Chapter III: a noisy version of a simple trigonometric function. Consider the set of points shown in Figure 4 which are drawn from $\sin(2\pi x)$ + noise.

Figure 4. 15 data points drawn from a noisy version of sin(2πx)

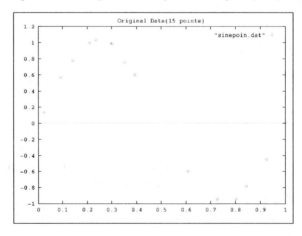

Figure 5. Approximation of the above data using radial basis function networks with 1, 3, and 5 basis functions

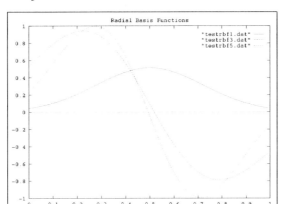

The convergence of radial basis function networks is shown in Figure 5. In all cases the centres of the basis functions were set evenly across the interval [0,1]. It is clear that the network with 1 basis function is not powerful enough to give a good approximation to the data. That with 3 basis functions makes a much better job while that with 5 is better yet. Note that in the last cases the approximation near the end points (0 and 1) is much worse than that in the centre of the mapping. This illustrates the fact that RBFs are better at interpolation than extrapolation; where there is a region of the input space with little data, an RBF cannot be expected to approximate well.

Figure 6. The data points which were corrupted by noise, the underlying signal, and the network approximation by a radial basis function net with 15 basis functions

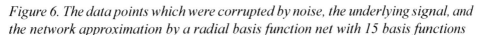
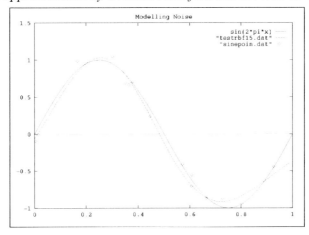

Figure 7. A comparison of the network convergence using multilayered perceptrons on the same data.

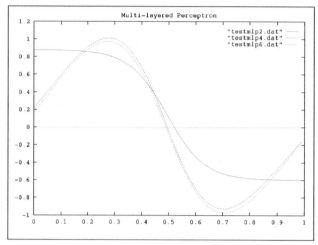

The above results might suggest that we should simply create a large RBF network with a great many basis functions, however if we create too many basis functions the network will begin to model the noise rather than try to extract the underlying signal from the data. An example is shown in Figure 6.

In order to compare the convergence of the RBF network with an MLP we repeat the experiment performed in Chapter III with the same data but with a multilayered perceptron with linear output units and a *tanh*() nonlinearity in the hidden units. The results are shown in Figure 7.

Notice that in this case we were *required* to have biases on both the hidden neurons and the output neurons and so the nets in the figure had 1, 3, and 5 hidden neurons *plus* a bias neuron in each case. This is necessary because:

- In an RBF network, activation contours (where the hidden neurons fire equally) are circular (or ellipsoid if the function has a different response in each direction).

- In an MLP network, activation contours are planar. The hidden neurons have equal responses to a plane of input activations which must go through the origin if there is no bias.

However the number of basis neurons is not the only parameter in the RBF. We can also change its properties when we move the centres or change the width of the basis functions. We illustrate this last in Figure 8 in which we illustrate this fact on the same type of data as before but use a value of $\lambda = 1$ and $\lambda = 100$ for the parameter λ when calculating the output of the basis neurons.

$$y = \sum \exp(-\lambda \|\mathbf{x}_i - \mathbf{c}_i\|^2)$$

Comparison with MLPS

Both RBFs and MLPs can be shown to be universal approximators, that is, each can arbitrarily closely model continuous functions. There are however several important differences:

1. The neurons of an MLP generally all calculate the same function of the neurons' activations, for example, all neurons calculate the logistic function of their weighted inputs. In an RBF, the hidden neurons perform a nonlinear mapping whereas the output layer is always linear.
2. The nonlinearity in MLPs is generally monotonic; in RBFs we use a radially decreasing function.
3. The argument of the MLP neuron's function is the vector product $\mathbf{w}.\mathbf{x}$ of the input and the weights; in an RBF network, the argument is the distance between the input and the centre of the radial basis function, $\|\mathbf{x} - \mathbf{w}\|$.

Figure 8. Using a basis function with a wide neighbourhood is equivalent to smoothing the output. A narrower neighbourhood function will more closely model the noise.

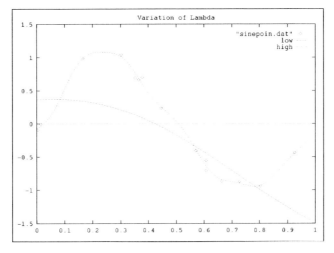

4.   MLPs perform a global calculation whereas RBFs find a sum of local outputs. Therefore MLPs are better at finding answers in regions of the input space where there is little data in the training set. If accurate results are required over the whole training space, we may require many RBFs, that is, many hidden neurons in an RBF network. However because of the local nature of the model, RBFs are less sensitive to the order in which data is presented to them.

5.   MLPs must pass the error back in order to change weights progressively. RBFs do not do this and so are much quicker to train.

Finding the Centres of the RBFS

If we have little data, we may have no option but to position the centres of our radial basis functions at the data points. However, as noted earlier, such problems may be ill-posed and lead to poor generalisation. If we have more training data, several solutions are possible:

1.   Choose the centres of the basis functions randomly from the available training data.

2.   Choose to allocate each point to a particular radial basis function (i.e., such that the greatest component of the hidden layer's activation comes from a particular neuron) according to the *k-nearest neighbours rule*. In this rule, a vote is taken among the k-nearest neighbours as to which neuron's centre they are closest and the new input is allocated accordingly. The centre of the neuron is moved so that it remains the average of the inputs allocated to it.

3.   We can use a generalisation of the LMS rule:

$$\Delta c_i = -\frac{\partial E}{\partial c_i}$$

This unfortunately is not guaranteed to converge (unlike the equivalent weight change rule) since the cost function E is not convex with respect to the centres and so a local minimum is possible.

Error Descent

The backpropagation method as described so far is innately slow. The reason for this is shown diagrammatically in Figure 9.

Figure 9. The path taken by the route of fastest descent is not the path directly to the centre (minimum) of the error surface

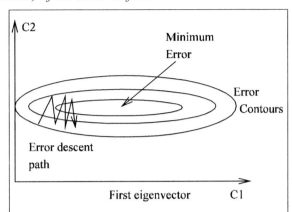

In this Figure, we show (in two dimensions) the contours of constant error. Since the error is not the same in each direction we get ellipses rather than circles. If we are following the path of **steepest descent**, which is perpendicular to the contours of constant error, we get a zig-zag path as shown. The axes of the ellipse can be shown to be parallel to the eigenvectors of the Hessian matrix. The greater the difference between the largest and the smallest eigenvalues, the more elliptical the error surface is and the more zig-zag the path that the fastest descent algorithm takes.

There are now a variety of methods which attempt to take additional information into account when the weights are changed. Such methods are described in many of the very good textbooks on this subject and are described further in Appendix *E*. We note however that such methods do speed up learning but can often be computationally intensive.

Pong: A Comparative Study, MLP vs. RBF

We trained our networks on a data set created by two human players playing a game of Pong (the same data set used in the previous chapter). During the game, the ball made approximately 80 double traverses of the pitch. This gave us 16,733 samples but we cleaned the data by ignoring those samples when the ball was outwith the pitch, that is, in the few samples when one player had missed the ball. This left us with 15,442 samples. The input data was the ball's *x*-coordinate, *y*-coordinate, *x*-velocity, *y*-velocity, and a parameter which determined the overall speed of the ball. The target data was the player's bat position which had to be learned from the input data.

We will call the left player Stephen and the right player Danny. We trained separate artificial neural networks on these data sets, that is, one network is trained on the input data + Stephen's bat position while the other is trained on the input data + Danny's bat position so that there is no interference in the network from the other function which must be learned.

We wish to compare two types of supervised learning networks, the multilayered perceptron (MLP) and the radial basis function network (RBF) on a level playing field. We attempt to level the field by giving each network approximately 100 parameters which will be learned during training.

Semi-Final 1: Radial Basis Networks

We first compare two radial basis networks. Ten-fold cross validation suggested that the radial basis network should be trained for 500,000 iterations with inverse width parameter =0.0001. We used 100 basis functions since that gives us 100 parameters (weights) which can be adjusted; comparative experiments showed little improvement when we increase the number of basis functions and a small decrease in performance as we decrease the number of basis functions. The learning rate was annealed from 0.1 to 0 during the simulation. When the trained networks played each other $\text{rbf}_{\text{Danny}}$ beat $\text{rbf}_{\text{Stephen}}$ by 14 games to 2 on new games (i.e., not data in the training set) over 10,000 time instances. If the number of basis functions is halved to 50, $\text{rbf}_{\text{Stephen}}$ beats $\text{rbf}_{\text{Danny}}$ by 33 games to 26.

An important point to note is that we select the centres randomly from the data points at the start of the game and do not adjust their positions during the game. The *same* centres are used for both RBF networks.

Semi-Final 2: Multilayered Perceptrons

We repeat the experimental situation with multilayered perceptrons. We note that if we have n inputs, h hidden neurons, and 1 output, the number of adjustable parameters for the MLP is $(n+1)h+h+1$[1]: we use 20 hidden neurons so that we have 141 parameters to adjust.

Again, cross validation showed that 20 hidden neurons and a slope parameter of 0.000000001 were appropriate. We also allowed 500,000 iterations but used a lower initial learning rate (=0.001) since the higher learning rate produced overfitting with this number of iterations. With the same test set as before (i.e., the ball appeared at the same position for the first shot of any rally), we find that $mlp_{Stephen}$ beat mlp_{Danny} by 37 to 19.

The Final

In the final, we play $mlp_{Stephen}$ against rbf_{Danny} and find that the latter wins by a convincing 10 games to 1. Even if we reduce the number of basis functions to 50, rbf_{Danny} beats $mlp_{Stephen}$ by 18 games to 14.

We also might consider, for example, improving the RBF's performance by selecting the centres only from points close to the position from which the ball must be played. Thus we might select each RBF's centres only from points within 100 units (the pitch is 600 long) from the appropriate side.

This does improve performance even more but between shots the RBF networks output nothing, meaning the bat returns to 0 (the bottom of the pitch) after each shot and only comes up the pitch as the ball reenters the 100 wide strip near where the ball must be played. This is hardly a human-like performance and so will not be considered any further.

CAVEAT

The above might seem to suggest that we might always favour the radial basis network over the multilayered perceptron. However, there are advantages and disadvantages to be aware of in both networks. In particular, the MLP performs a global mapping while the RBF is best considered a sum of local mappings. This means that the MLP is better placed to extrapolate (into new regions of data space) than the RBF and also that the RBF can be too data-specific. Ideally we wish our machines to be robust and able to perform under new conditions not specifically met during training.

For example, the human players modelled above tried to hit the ball with the edges of their bats, something which the artificial neural networks also learned. If we reduce the size of the bat from 64 pixels to 34 pixels, $mlp_{Stephen}$ beats rbf_{Danny} (with 100 basis functions) by 23 games to 16 and by 46 to 17 when the RBF uses only 50 basis functions. The RBF has learned to hit the ball with the edge of the bat; presumably the MLP's edge hitting behaviour has been moderated by its neurons learning the global mapping.

Conclusion

In a number of texts on game AI, when ANN are discussed the MLP is the only example ANN presented, yet as we have seen in this and the previous chapter, there have are many alternative forms of ANN. While the MLP performs well in many cases, there are many cases where it is out-performed by some of the other forms of ANN. To make the best use of ANN in game AI, a developer should be aware of a range of the varieties available and their relative strengths and weaknesses.

Reference

Haykin, S. (1999). *Artificial neural networks: A comprehensive foundation* (2nd ed.). Prentice Hall.

Endnote

[1]   The extra 1 appears because of the bias term.

Chapter VII

Genetic Algorithms

Introduction

The methods in this chapter were developed in response to the need for general purpose methods for solving complex optimisation problems. A classical problem addressed is the **travelling salesman problem** in which a salesman must visit each of n cities once and only once in an optimum order, that which minimises his travelling. While not typical of a problem encountered in a computer game context, the problem of optimising responses or strategies clearly is applicable. There are two traditional methods for tackling optimisation problems:

- **Enumeration:** Basically we test the whole search space with respect to some optimisation function to find the best point with respect to this function. This can be a long process for substantial problems.

- **Calculus-based methods:** We may divide these into:
  - *Direct methods,* which use the gradient at each point in the space to guide in which direction to search next. This is comparable to the error descent

methods we used earlier and is effective in well-behaved problems (problems for which there are no local minima and which have continuous cost functions).

° *Indirect methods* which attempt to solve the nonlinear set of differential equations to get those points where the gradient is zero that is, stationary points of the evaluation function. Such solutions are often difficult or even impossible to find.

Because of these drawbacks, alternative methods which may be characterised as involving guided random searches have arisen. Such methods are based on enumerative techniques but allow some knowledge of the domain to permeate the search process. We will look at one of these types of methods which is based on processes which seem to involve the solution of difficult problems in the real world.

Genetic Algorithms

The attraction of simulating **evolution** as a problem solver is similar in many respects to the attraction of simulating neurons: evolution seems to offer a robust method of information processing. We will begin by briefly examining natural evolution and then consider the aspects of such evolution which are deemed to be important when we simulate it.

Natural Evolution

Evolution is a process of change for living beings. But whereas learning is a process which happens to an individual in the space of a lifetime, evolution is a process which changes species over a much longer timescale. Notice that the individual is unaware of evolution; evolution is happening on a different timescale to the individual's time-scale. In addition, evolution has no memory itself. It does not matter what happened last generation or the generation before, the only material with which evolution has to play is the current version of life.

It is important to be clear about the fact that evolution acts upon **chromosomes** rather than on living beings. We can view chromosomes as a code which determines life. Therefore we require a process which will decode the chromosomes. The individual parts of a chromosome are **genes**. It is the positioning of certain genes in specific positions in the chromosome which determine the features of the resulting life. In natural evolution, there is an alphabet of only four values; GAs typically use a binary 1/0 alphabet.

Natural selection is a process by which those chromosomes which encode successful life forms get more opportunity to reproduce than others. The method which is most commonly used is **survival of the fittest**. In this method, those individuals who are most fit for their current environment get more chances to reproduce and thereby transmit their chromosomes to the next generation.

In going from one generation to the next there is a process of reproduction in which there is some explicit probability of the genetic material which exists in this generation being passed on to the next generation. All high level organisms on earth use sexual reproduction which requires parents of two sexes. Some very simple organisms use asexual reproduction in which the genetic material from the single parent is passed onto its children.

The Simple Genetic Algorithm

Genetic algorithms were invented single-handedly by Holland (Holland, 1975) in the 1970s. His algorithm is usually known now as the simple genetic algorithm (GA) since many of those now using GAs have added bells and whistles. Holland's major breakthrough was to code a particular optimisation problem in a binary string, a string of 0s and 1s. We can by analogy with the natural world call the individual bit positions **alleles**. He then created a random population of these strings and evaluated each string in terms of its fitness with respect to solving the problem. Strings which had a greater fitness were given greater chance of reproducing and so there was a greater chance that their chromosomes (strings) would appear in the next generation. Eventually Holland showed that the whole population of strings converged to satisfactory solutions to the problem. Since it is so important, we reproduce the algorithm in how-to-do-it form.

1.   Initialise a population of chromosomes randomly.
2.   Evaluate the fitness of each chromosome (string) in the population.
3.   Create new chromosomes by mating. Mutate some bits randomly.
4.   Delete the less fit members of the current population.
5.   Evaluate the new (child) chromosomes and insert them into the population
6.   Repeat Steps 3-5 until convergence of the population.

Notice that the population's overall fitness increases as a result of the increase in the number of fit individuals in the population. Notice, however, that there may be just as fit (or even fitter) individuals in the population at time $t-1$ as there are at time t. In evolution, we only make statements about populations rather than individuals.

There are several aspects of the problem which merit closer scrutiny. We will do so in the context of a particular optimisation problem. The description given below owes much to Davis (1991).

The Knapsack Problem

The knapsack problem is one of those deceptively simple problems for which no algorithm is known for the solution of the general problem (other than exhaustive enumeration of the potential solutions). Consider a knapsack which can hold at most W kg. We wish to load the knapsack with as many objects as we can in order to maximise their value subject to this weight constraint. (We may in addition have a constraint on the total number of objects which the knapsack can hold). Then, letting v_i be the value and w_i the weight of the ith object, we wish to maximise $\Sigma_i v_i$, subject to the constraint $\Sigma_i w_i < W$.

In the simple knapsack problem, we are only allowed one of each type of object and so we can model this as a binary string which has value 1 in the bit if object i is selected for the knapsack and 0 otherwise. An example seven-object knapsack problem is shown in Table 1.

The knapsack problem is characterised by having optima which are often far apart in Hamming distance and so is a difficult problem for calculus-based methods. Notice how simple the coding is in this case. There is no necessity to use a binary alphabet though most GAs use only 0s and 1s.

Table 1. The weights and values of seven objects and the optimal objects held when the total weight is limited to 50

Object Number	Object Value	Object Weight	Optimal String (W=50)
1	70	31	1
2	20	10	0
3	39	20	0
4	37	19	1
5	7	4	0
6	5	3	0
7	10	6	0
Total:	188	93	2

Evolution of Fitness

The evaluation of fitness in this problem is extremely simple: if the weight constraint has been violated we give the chromosome a large negative value; otherwise the fitness value of the chromosome is the value of the objects which it has loaded into the string. Practitioners of GAs generally talk about hill-climbing (as opposed to error descent). The basic idea is that the population of chromosomes here are climbing up a hill corresponding to a surface measuring their fitness. Some problems are simple, particularly those consisting of a single hill; in this case, a calculus-based method would be capable of finding the summit of the hill. Of more interest, though, are problems in which there are a number of nonrelated peaks. Many knapsack problems are of this form. For example, the string 1001000 shown above has fitness (value) of 107 whereas the next best string 1100011 has fitness of 105. Notice that the Hamming distance between these strings is 4 or over half the maximum distance across the space. In a high-dimensional problem this can have serious consequences.

There are a number of refinements to this naive method of evaluating fitness which may be found useful in specific problems:

- **Windowing:** Find the minimum fitness in a population and then assign as fitness the amount by which a chromosome's fitness exceeds this value. Sometimes a minimum value is set so that every chromosome has some nonzero fitness value.
- **Linear normalisation:** Order the chromosomes by decreasing fitness values; assign a maximum and minimum fitness for the population and then assign intermediate values between these two according to the position of the chromosome in the assigned order.

The second technique is especially useful if there is a possibility of a **super-individual** in the population. A super-individual is so called because its evaluated fitness greatly exceeds that of its contemporaries. This can be a major problem if, by chance, a super-individual appears in the population early on. It will have no real competitors and will soon dominate the population; clones of the super-individual will far outweigh any other chromosome. However, the super-individual may only be relatively super and it may represent the coding of a local maximum of the problem.

Reproduction

Typically we imagine reproduction to be carried out in two stages: the parent chromosomes are copied into the child chromosome bits and then some functions which alter the child chromosomes are applied to each child. The three original operations are crossover, mutation, and reversal. The last of these has fallen from favour but is included here for completeness. Crossover is the major power behind genetic algorithms and usually is assigned high probability; mutation is less important and is given a lower probability. Finally the parameters are often varied during the simulation: mutation becomes more important as the simulation progresses and the population becomes less varied. Reproduction with more than two parents has not been found to be an improvement.

Crossover

Crossover is the driving force of a genetic algorithm. It mimics sexual reproduction which is used by almost all of the earth's complex species. The basic GA uses a random number generator to select a point in each parent at which the crossover of genetic material takes place. For example, if we have two parents, PARENT A 01010101 and PARENT B 11110000, then if the point between bit 2 and bit 3 is the crossover point we will get two new chromosomes CHILD A **11**010101 and CHILD B 01**110000** where the bold font is used for the bits which have come from parent B. Notice that bit 4 has not changed in either child since it was the same in both parents. The crossover described here is also known as one-point crossover; it is entirely possible to allow crossover at two or more locations.

Mutation

Unfortunately if we only allow crossover in our population, there may be regions of the search space which are never explored; even if every part of the search space is potentially in our original population, it may be that the direction of increasing fitness initially may remove potentially valuable bits from our chromosomes. Thus we have a mutation operator which assigns at reproduction time a small though nonzero probability of change in any single bit position. This keeps diversity in our population ensuring that convergence to a suboptimal minimum is not complete.

Note that we can define mutation as the probability of changing a bit's value or the probability of randomly selecting a bit's value; with a binary alphabet, the latter description leads to a probability of change equal to half that of the former.

Inversion

Inversion was an operator which was used with the original GA because of its biological plausibility. The inversion operator inverts all the bits in a bit-string between a start and an end point. For example, with an original of 0110101010, inverting between bits 3 and 6 gives new chromosome 0101011010.

There is conjecture that inversion may be found to be useful with longer chromosomes.

Selection

There are a variety of strategies for selecting which members of the population should reproduce. The original GA used **roulette-wheel selection** (see Figure 1).

Each individual is given a chance to reproduce which is proportional to its fitness. A fit individual should be given more chances to reproduce than an individual who is unfit. This is a mirror of real evolutionary situations in that, in order to reproduce, an individual must survive. Therefore a fitter individual which survives longer will have more chance to reproduce. We calculate the fitness of the whole population and then set the probability of an individual being selected for reproduction to be equal to the fraction of its fitness over the whole population's fitness. Therefore if we randomly generate a number between, for example, and and determine in which slice the random number falls, we will give each individual the appropriate chance. Now we simply select two individuals at random from the population and mate them, repeating this operation as often as is necessary until we have a replacement population.

Other possible strategies include **elitism** in which we ensure that we do not lose the best individuals from each generation by copying immediately the best of each generation into the next generation.

Figure 1. We envisage a roulette wheel in which the ball has equal chance of stopping anywhere on the circumference. Each individual is given a slice of the wheel in proportion to its fitness.

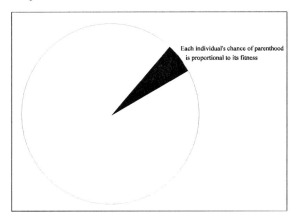

Each individual's chance of parenthood is proportional to its fitness

Another possible strategy is **steady-state reproduction** in which we only allow a few individuals at a time to reproduce. We may refine this by using steady-state with no duplicates in which we do not allow children which are duplicates of strings which already exist in the population. (By insisting that there are no duplicates at all in the population, we are ensuring genetic diversity). This has the great advantage of ensuring no premature convergence of the algorithm. It has however been found that steady-state reproduction methods do not work well when the evaluation function is noisy. In this case, a bad chromosome can get a spuriously good evaluation which will allow it to propagate its equally bad offspring throughout the gene-pool; if the evaluation function is deterministic, however, this problem does not arise.

Comparison of Operators

It is generally held that while crossover is essential to GAs, mutation alone is not sufficient to account for the algorithm's effectiveness. Note that crossover produces children which can be very different from their parents while mutation alone produces children which are only changed in one bit (or at most a few bits) from their parents. One argument for the relative importance of crossover goes like this: consider a population which uses mutation alone to change. Then if the population as a whole has a certain set chromosome values in certain positions and if it requires two changes to its chromosomes to give an individual an edge in the reproduction game, then it may take a very long while to get an individual with both of these changes at once. If P(good mutation) $=0.001$ for each position, then P(both mutations at once) $= 0.000001$. However, if we allow crossover in our reproduction cycle we need only have P(both mutations at once) $\propto P$(good mutation), a considerable improvement.

The Schema Theorem (The Fundamental Theorem of Gas)

Holland has developed a theorem which describes the effectiveness of the GA known as the Schema Theorem. This roughly states that the probability of useful strings being generated and kept in the population's chromosomes depends on the length of the strings (since longer strings are more likely to be disrupted themselves) and on the distance across the string from the first to last position in the string. It must be emphasised that the Schema Theorem is not universally accepted.

We first note that we may describe a particular template or **schema** using the alphabet which we are using for the chromosome with the addition of a '*' for do not care. Thus if we are particularly interested in strings with a 1 in position 3, a 0 in position 4, and a 1 in position 8, we describe the schema, H, of this state as **10***1** for the 10 bit string. The **schema order**, $O(H)$, is defined as the number of fixcd positions (1s and 0s in the binary alphabet); thus in the above example, the schema order is 3.

The **schema defining length** $\delta(H)$ is the distance from the first to the last fixed position in the schema. Thus in the schema above, $\delta(H) = 5$.

Holland's argument runs as follows: each individual chromosome is a representative of a great number of schema. For example, the string 10101 represents the schema $= 1****$ and $2 =*01**$ and so forth. Thus the GA may be thought of as a parallel search mechanism which is evaluating a great number of schema simultaneously. Now suppose at a particular time, t, there exists m examples of a particular schema, H, within the population. Let the average fitness of the schema be f and the average fitness of the population be F; then at time $t +1$ we would expect to have 1 examples of schema H where $m_1 = \dfrac{m * f}{F}$. That is, a schema's incidence grows as its relative fitness with respect to the population as a whole grows. So schema with above average fitness will come to dominate the population.

This much seems qualitatively obvious. Now we try to quantify the effect of the two operators, crossover and mutation. Consider a string 010001010. Then it is representative of (among others) the schema $*1**0****$ and $*1*****1*$. If the probability of crossover occurring at any point is c then the probability that the first schema will be untouched by crossover in this generation is while the probability that crossover will not disrupt the second schema is . Clearly longer strings are more likely to be disrupted. Therefore we can see that the defining length of a schema is essential to its chances of survival into the next generation; short schema have greater chances than long schema.

Alternatively we may say that the survival probability of a schema with respect to simple crossover is given by $P_s = 1 - P_c \dfrac{\delta(h)}{(l-1)}$ where l is the length of the chromosome. Now if reproduction and crossover occur independently, then we have,

$$m' = m.\frac{f}{F}\left(1 - P_c \frac{\delta(H)}{l-1}\right).$$

Now we must consider the effects of mutation. Let the probability of mutation at any gene position be m. Then since there are $O(H)$ positions of importance for each schema (those which are specified by 0s and 1s) we have the probability of a particular schema surviving mutation $= (1 - P_m)^{O(H)}N$. Now since m, high order powers of m can be ignored and so we get the survival probability as approximately $(1 - O(H).P_m$.

Therefore our completed expected number of instances of the schema H in the new generation is given by,

$$m' = m.\frac{f}{F}\left(1 - P_c \frac{\delta(H)}{l-1} - O(H).P_m\right) \tag{1}$$

This is known as the fundamental theorem of genetic algorithms or the schema theorem.

A First Example

Consider the fitness function shown in Figure 2. It represents a fitness function defined by fitness, $0 £ x £ 1$. This is a trivial problem to solve using calculus-based methods since we have an explicit derivative at each point and can use,

$$\Delta x = \eta \frac{dF}{dx} = \eta - 2(x - 0.5) \tag{2}$$

So we start off with a random value of x in the interval $[0,1]$ and if x is less than 0.5, Δx is positive and so x will increase towards 0.5 while if x is more than 0.5, Δx is negative and so x will decrease towards 0.5.

However we will use this easy problem to illustrate the GA solution. We first have to decide the correct coding. Let us use a binary coding and wish to have the answer correct to six decimal places. The range of possible answers is from 0 to 1 and so we wish to slice this range up into enough bit positions to get the desired accuracy. We are looking for that value m which is such that $2^{m-1} < 10^6 < 2^m$, that is, that value of m which is just big enough to give the required degree of accuracy. Therefore m

Figure 2. A simple hill-climbing algorithm will find this maximum

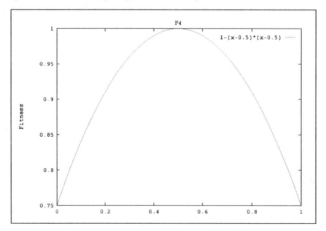

must be 20 and so our chromosome will be 20 bits long. When we decode a chromosome we will use $x = \Sigma_j 2^{-j-1} bit_j$.

If our range of possible solutions had been $[a,b]$, we would have required the value of m such that $2^{m-1} < (b - a)*10^6 < 2^m$, and decoded chromosomes using $x = a + \Sigma_j 2^{-j-1} bit_j * (b - a)$.

Now we generate a number of solutions randomly.

Consider a population of 3 comprising :

$v_1 = 10101010101010101010$

$v_2 = 11001101010100101100$

$v_3 = 00101001011011100101$

Then v_1 is equivalent to the point ≈ 0.66667 which has fitness $F = 1-(x - 0.5)^2 = 1-(0.66667 - 0.5)^2 = 0.972222$. Similarly v_2 is equivalent to the point ≈ 0.80204 which has fitness $F = 1-(x - 0.5)^2 = 1-(0.80204 - 0.5)^2 = 0.908$. Similarly v_3 is equivalent to the point ≈ 0.16183 which has fitness $F = 1-(x - 0.5)^2 = 1-(0.16183 - 0.5)^2 = 0.8856$.

A roulette wheel selection procedure simply adds the three fitnesses together and allocates the probability of each gene being selected for parenting of the next generation as $p_I = \dfrac{F(I)}{\Sigma_j F(j)}$. So $p_1 = \dfrac{0.972222}{2.7658}, p_2 = \dfrac{0.908}{2.7658}, p_3 = \dfrac{0.8856}{2.7658}$. Clearly the definition of fitness has a lot to do with the probability that genes are selected in the next generation.

Premature Convergence

There is a trade-off between fast convergence of a GA and searching the whole search space: the danger is that fast convergence will lead to a convergence point which is only locally optimal. On the other hand, we live in a real world where we do not have infinite time or an infinitely large population. Premature convergence is often associated with a super-individual in the population. An individual whose fitness is so much greater than the fitness of those around that the individual will breed so quickly that the population will become dominated by the individual. Sometimes GAs insist that each new generation totally replaces the old. At other times, it may make more sense to retain the best individual between generations. This is known as elitism.

Case Study: GA and Backpropagation ANN for Motocross Controllers

At this point it is worth presenting an example application of the methods described in this and previous chapters in the context of a modern video game application. The task we will look at is developing an AI controller for a computer player in a motocross racing game. This example along with the game itself has been developed by one of our colleagues, Benoit Chaperot.

In the game, a physically modelled motorbike must be ridden round a track which features a number of turns, bumps, and jumps. The physics modelling is detailed sufficiently to include the effects of riders shifting their seated position as they navigate the track (Chaperot & Fyfe, 2005a). The level of detail in the physical modelling makes control challenging for human players, more so than in typical arcade style games.

In his work, Benoit compares the effects of training a MLP ANN against date recorded from a human expert riding the bike round a track against those achieved by using the GA to evolve weights for the MLP (Chaperot & Fyfe, 2005b).

Choose the Inputs and Outputs

Being set in a continuous model, it is important to limit and select the number of inputs that the ANN will use. The outputs are limited to acceleration and braking and turning (left or right) values, being equivalent to the controls available to human players. Each pair of values is represented as a single floating point value in the range [-1...1].

A number of way-points mark the direction and centre position of the track at one meter intervals along its length. The ANN then uses the position and orientation of the bike relative to the nearest way point for one set of inputs, along with the bike velocity. Additional inputs indicate the track centre at a small number of sampled positions in front of the bike and a large number of ground height samples. Both sets of samples are provided relative to current bike position. The track centre samples are required to enable the ANN to control turning and the height samples hopefully allow the ANN to learn how to handle jumps, bumps, and pits.

The ANN itself is a simple multilayered perceptron network (See Chapter III).

Training the ANN

Data was recorded of a human expert playing the game, similar in principle to the work described in the previous chapters where ANN were trained to play Pong.

Twenty minutes of play time resulted in a training set consisting of 120,000 data samples. For 10 million iterations, randomly selected samples from the set were trained against. Experiments were repeated to allow suitable values to be found for learning rate and for the number of training iterations used. Training used the standard back-propagation algorithm (Chapter III).

Evolving the ANN

An alternative approach to training ANN is to evolve the weights using the GA (in this case real valued rather than binary valued chromosomes were used, making this work more like the evolution strategies described earlier). A population of random network weights is created and evaluated for fitness. Weight chromosomes are then selected using roulette wheel selection where the chance of selection is proportional to the fitness of the chromosome, and pairs of chromosomes used to create pairs of offspring using crossover and mutation. Elitism is also applied to pass the two fittest members of any one generation directly into the next.

To evaluate fitness, a fitness function was created which scored each chromosome with points and penalties for passing way points, missing way points, crashing, final distance, and test time. The values for these bonuses were set manually after a small amount of experimentation. A population of 80 ANN chromosomes was evolved for 100 generations. More extensive experimental details are made available by Chaperot and Fyfe (2005b). We also look at evolving ANN in more detail in a later chapter.

Results

An expert human player was able to complete the test track (which was not used for training) with times ranging from 2 minutes 10 seconds to 3 minutes. Training and evolving the ANN as described above created AI riders which were able to complete the test track with time of between 2 minutes 25 seconds and 3 minutes 15 seconds for the trained ANN and between 2 minutes 50 seconds and 3 minutes 30 seconds for the evolved ANN. These times are considered quite respectable given the complex nature of the task and the large number of inputs required for decision making.

In an effort to improve results a specialised training regime was attempted. Tricky parts of the course where crashes are more likely to occur were identified. For training the ANN with backpropagation, these tricky cases were then presented more often by making the chance with which a training sample is selected proportional to the error that was produced the last time the sample was presented to the ANN.

Interestingly, this actually had a negative effect, increasing average lap times from 2 minutes and 40 seconds to 3 minutes. In fact, the exact opposite of the original supposition turned out to be true with an inverted training regime improving the best lap times to 2 minutes and 20 seconds. This brought the trained ANN's performance very close to that achieved by the human expert, and improved its ability to recover from accidents.

Further Reading

There have been a wide range of academic efforts aimed at developing biologically-inspired controllers for robots (real or simulated). Much of this work has influenced current game AI, but not all is so well known. Not directly based on biological controllers, Rodney Brooks' (1991) subsumption architecture is a significant inspiration behind a lot of modern agent-based AI architectures. At around the same time, Karl Sims (1994) was exploring the use of artificial evolution for computer graphics, and went on to evolve simple creatures whose bodies adapted over many generations. Since then, work on evolving robotic controllers and morphologies has become a particularly active and productive field, with a number of research groups worldwide focussing on this particular area (e.g., Harvey, Husbands, Cliff, Thompson, & Jakobi, 1997) with many of the findings with potential relevance to the commercial games industry.

Some of these ideas have already made their way into commercial games, but generally with limited success. As previously mentioned, 'Creatures' is likely the best example of the application of GA and ANN to computer entertainment. Each creature is controlled by an ANN 'brain,' with inputs from the environment and their own artificial biochemistry, and mating of creatures produces eggs from which new creatures are born, with initial weights and values determined through recombination and mutation of the parent chromosomes (Grand, 1998). In comparison, the critically acclaimed 'Black and White' used a very simple—single neuron!—neural controller for its creatures.

'Colin McRae Rally 2' is a commercial game where AI drivers were created using ANN trained on human player data in a manner similar to the case study presented above, albeit with cars instead of physically modelled motorbikes (Buckland, 2002, p. 426).

Rather than using GA to evolve the weights of a network, there has also been significant work done on using the GA to evolve the topology of a network to evolve the number of neurons and the network of connections between them. One of the first approaches used as a start point chromosomes where for each possible network connection (one for every possible pairing of neurons, plus one for a connection feeding activation from a neuron back into itself) a single bit of the chromosome determined if a connection existed (Miller, 1989). Later approaches looked at evolving the topology more generally, such as by using chromosomes which encode rules for 'growing' a network, rather than directly encoding the network itself (e.g., Kitano, 1990). A particularly interesting approach is that used by the NEAT algorithm (Stanley & Miikkulainen, 2002) which uses additional information on the changes to network structure to help prevent crossover from combining unrelated changes such that progress is disrupted. A more detailed description of NEAT than presented here, along with sample code for implementing it, was written by Buckland (2002). A real-time extension of NEAT, rtNEAT, featuring simultaneous and asynchronous evaluation and evolution, is presented with an experiment where it was used to evolve controllers for combat units in a simple RTS game (NERO) by Stanley, Bryant, and Miikkulainen (2005). In this last chapter, a game training environment was established where students could edit the training environment in order to present increasingly complex combat situations to the rtNEAT agents. Initial training might focus on simply targeting and attacking opponents with later training on combat with movement and obstacles, and all training occurring in real-time during play.

Summary

In this chapter we introduced the standard genetic algorithm and its operators. A variety of selection methods were described and the formal schema theorem presented. Some simple problems solvable with the GA were presented as examples along with a more detailed case study showing a possible application of the GA (with ANN) in the context of modern video games.

Over recent years, awareness of the GA has grown significantly amongst commercial game developers, although some issues relating to their development are still less well known. The next chapter will focus on some of the potential pitfalls which are currently less well appreciated both by a large portion of the academic community and by game developers who are starting to use evolutionary techniques more and more. Tthe subsequent chapter presents a range of extensions and variations to the GA.

References

Brooks, R. A. (1991). Intelligence without representation. *Artificial Intelligence Journal, 47*, 139-159.

Buckland, M. (2002). *AI techniques for game programming*. Ohio: Premier Press.

Chaperot, B., & Fyfe, C. (2005a, November). Issues in the physics of a motocross simulation. In Q. Mehdi & N. Gough (Eds.), *Game-On 2005*. Leicester.

Chaperot, B., & Fyfe, C. (2005b, November 8-9). Motocross and artificial neural networks. In M. Merabti, N. Lee, M. H. Overmars, & A. El Rhalibi (Eds.), *Game design and technology workshop. Liverpool.*

Davis, L. (1991). *Handbook of genetic algorithms*. Van Nostrand Reinhold.

Grand, S., & Cliff, D. (1998). Creatures: Artificial life autonomous software agents for home entertainment. *Autonomous Agents and Multi-Agent Systems, 1*(1), 39-57.

Harvey, I., Husbands, P., Cliff, D., Thompson, A., & Jakobi, N. (1997). Evolutionary robotics: The Sussex approach. *Robotics and Autonomous Systems, 20*(2), 205-224

Holland, J. H. (1975). *Adaptation in natural and artificial systems*. Ann Arbor, MI: University of Michegan Press.

Kitano, H. (1990). Designing neural networks using genetic algorithms with graph generation system. *Complex Systems, 4*, 461-476.

Miller, G. F., Todd, P. M., & Hegde, S. U. (1989). Designing neural networks using genetic algorithms. In D. Schaffer (Ed.), *Proceedings of the Third International Conference on Genetic Algorithms*. Morgan Kauffman.

Sims, K. (1994). Evolving 3D morphology and behavior by competitio. In R. Brooks & P. Maes (Eds), *Proceedings of artificial life IV* (pp. 28-39). MIT Press.

Stanley, K. O., Bryant, B. D., & Miikkulainen, R. (2005, April). Evolving neural network agents in the NERO video game. In G. Kendall & S. Lucas (Eds.), *IEEE 2005 Symposium on Computational Intelligence and Games (CIG'05)* (pp. 182-189). Essex: Colchester.

Stanley, K. O., & Miikkulainen, R. (2002). Evolving neural networks through augmenting topologies. *Evolutionary Computation, 10*(2).

Chapter VIII

Beyond the GA:
Extensions and Alternatives

Introduction

The last two chapters introduced the standard genetic algorithm (GA), presented an example case study, and explored some of the potential pitfalls in using evolutionary methods. This chapter focuses on a number of extensions and variations of the standard GA. While there is not room to cover them all, many extensions to GAs have been proposed usually in response to situations in which the simple GA does not perform particularly well. Two such situations are:

1.   Deceptive problems
2.   Changing environments

In this chapter we will first describe these particular problems before presenting some GA variants which may be able to deal more successfully with them.

Deceptive Problems

Much recent research has been in the area of **deceptive problems**. The simplest deceptive problem is as follows.

Consider a population in which the string '11' is most fit and the following conditions characterise the fitness landscape:

$f(11) > f(00)$

$f(11) > f(01)$

$f(11) > f(10)$

$f(*0) > f(*1)$ or $f(0*) > f(1*)$

Then the order 1 schemata do not contain the optimal string 11 as an instance and lead the GA away from 11. Now in this simple example, the structure of the problem itself occasioned the deception; however, the nonlinearity in crossover and mutation, the finiteness of population sizes, and poor problem representation have all been shown to contribute to deception in a problem. These are hard problems for the simple GA to solve and so attempts have been made to modify the simple GA.

A particular type of deceptive problem is known as a *trap* **function** which is based on the *unitation* or number of 1s in the representation of the problem. Let the unitation of a string of length 1 be *u*. Then define the fitness of a chromosome with *u* unitation as,

Figure 1. A fitness function which is deceptive. The basin of attraction of the maximum at a is much larger (dependent on z and l) than that of the maximum at b.

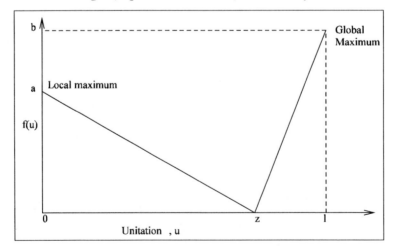

$$f(u)= \begin{cases} \dfrac{a}{z}(z-u), & if \quad u \le z \\ \dfrac{b}{1-z}(u-z), & otherwise \end{cases}$$

where the parameters, a, b, and z determine the shape of the function. An example is shown in Figure 1. Clearly by altering the parameter z, the function can be made more or less deceptive as the basin of attraction of the maximum at a increases or decreases.

The Structured GA

A number of extensions to the basic GA have been proposed; they are often based on the fact that real biological material has great redundancy within it. It has been estimated that only a small fraction of genetic material is really used in creating a new individual (a figure of 80% of genetic material being junk has been quoted). Further biologists have long realised that as cells differentiate they switch some genes on and others off making it possible for a single fertilised egg to self-organise to create a new bird, bee, or baboon. Yet the differences in DNA are remarkably small, for example, a chimpanzee shares 99% of our genetic material; or put another way, a change of only 1% in our genes would make us chimpanzees. Consider how little differences then must there be between the genetic material of different humans.

One example of such an extension is the **structured genetic algorithm (SGA)** (Dasgupta, 1993) in which we imagine a two-layered genetic algorithm such as shown in Figure 2.

Figure 2. The structured genetic algorithm

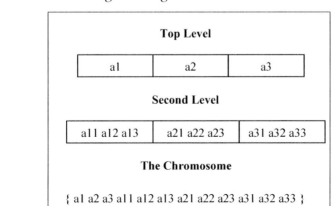

Here we have a two layered genetic structure. Genes at either level can be either active or passive; high level genes either activate or deactivate the sets of lower level genes, that is, only if gene $a1$ is active will genes $a1$, $a2$, and $a3$ determine a phenotype. Therefore a single change in a gene at a high level represents multiple changes at the second level in terms of genes which are active. Genes which are not active (passive genes) do not, however, disappear since they remain in the chromosome structure and are carried invisibly to subsequent generations with the individual's string of genes. Therefore a single change at the top level of the network can create a huge difference in the realised phenotype whereas with the simple GA we would require a number of changes in the chromosome to create the same effect. As the number of changes required increases, the probability of such a set of changes becomes vanishingly small.

Figure 3. The best in each generation using the SGA and the average fitness during that generation when the constraints were changed every 50 generations

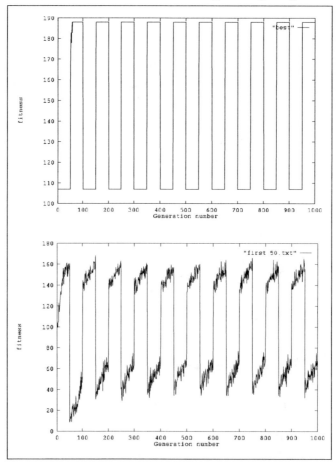

Such extensions have been found to be most helpful in problems in which the simple genetic algorithm does not perform well.

For example, the structured genetic algorithm has been shown to perform well in dynamic situations, that is, when the environment is changing within the course of an experiment. For example, in the knapsack problem described above, let us allow the simulation to converge (so that the population has converged on some solution of the problem [maximisation of value] under the constraint that the weight in the knapsack does not exceed 50Kg). Now change the constraint so that individuals must now optimise their value under the constraint that the weights do not exceed 75Kg. The simple GA will not perform well in this change of environment since the individuals of the population have been optimised for a different environment.

The structured GA, on the other hand, retains enough genetic diversity within its string to quickly converge to optimal values. Further if we set up an experiment so that the environment changes systematically and regularly, the structured GA will quickly adapt to these conditions since even the phenotypes which are most fit with respect to the 50Kg constraints may retain (as passive genes) genetic material which would make their offspring fit with respect to the 75Kg constraints (and recall that these genes can be switched on with a single change at the top level). An example of the convergence of such a GA is shown in Figure 3, in which the constraints were changed every 50 generations.

While we have considered only 2 level chromosomes here, clearly a multi-layered approach would be possible.

Tabu Search

In this section and the next we consider algorithms related to GAs but different in some way from a GA. Tabu search is not a genetic algorithm yet shares some similarities with genetic algorithms particularly in the encoding of the problem. Consider again the knapsack problem. A tabu system will encode the problem in exactly the same way as the genetic algorithm. However the tabu search uses only a single chromosome randomly initialised.

First Algorithm

Since we have only a single chromosome there can be no crossover; therefore mutation plays the role of sole provider of genetic change. The algorithm can be described as:

1.   Randomly select a single point on the chromosome and mutate the gene at that point. Using our binary alphabet we will be changing a 0 to a 1 or vice-versa.

2.   Test the fitness of the new gene. If it is more fit than its predecessor (parent seems the wrong term) the change is accepted. If it is more fit, the change is rejected.

3.   In either case, we return to Stage 2.

The search is continued until no change in the fitness of the gene is recorded after a given number of generations or until the fitness is deemed to be good enough. (We cannot get caught in a loop since we are always lowering fitness at each stage; if we opt to accept all changes that do not leave the phenotype less fit, we must test explicitly for loops.)

Notice the second crucial difference between this search method and GAs is a directed search in that we only accept changes to the gene which make the phenotype more fit. This is both a strength and a weakness in that, on the one hand, the convergence of this algorithm is typically much faster than a GA, but on the other hand we may not find a global minimum since the whole search space may not be reachable from our initial position. Since it is very easy for a tabu search to get stuck in a local optimum, the tabu search is usually repeated from many different starting points and the best final answer taken.

A Second Tabu Search

We have not yet explained the term 'tabu.' In this type of search we typically retain a short term memory of previous changes and ensure that a change cannot be performed if it reverses one which has recently been done. Such a change is tabu. We do not have to be black and white about tabus; we can classify the quantity of tabuness of a move numerically. Consider the problem of using seven modules of insulating material to create the best insulator over all. The quality of the final insulator is dependent on the order in which the layers are laid down. An initial gene might be 2-5-7-3-4-6-1. Let us consider the operator 'pairwise exchange.' So to swap modules 5 and 4 would result in 2-4-7-3-5-6-1. We do not then allow the reswap of modules 5 and 4 for, say, 3 iterations. Using this method, we can allow some swaps which will decrease the overall fitness of the string *if there is no alternative.* One option is to evaluate all possible swaps and opt for the best nontabu swap. Sometimes the tabu rule is overruled if the new solution is better than any solution which has been found previously (the aspiration criterion). Occasionally we use longer term statistics to guide the search as well as the short term memory.

Population-Based Incremental Learning

The tabu search described above is a hill-climbing algorithm: the chromosome at time $t + 1$ is always better than the algorithm at time t. However the algorithm has lost the property to search the whole search space since there is no crossover operations which will allow the chromosome to jump to a different region of the space. We would like to retain the GAs stochastic elements which enable all points of the space to be reachable from each starting point but improve the convergence properties of the GA.

One possibility is the **population-based incremental learning (PBIL)** algorithm (Baluja, 1994). This abstracts out the operations of crossover and mutation and yet retains the stochastic search elements of the GA by:

- Creating a vector whose length is the same as the required chromosome and whose elements are the probabilities of a 1 in the corresponding bit position of the chromosome.

- Generate a number of samples from the vector where the probability of a 1 in each bit position of each vector is determined by the current probability vector.

- Find the most fit chromosome from this population.

- Amend the probability vector's elements so that the probability of a 1 is increased in positions in which the most fit chromosomes have a 1.

The process is initialised with a probability vector each of whose elements is 0.5 and terminated when each element of the vector approaches 1 or 0. The update of the probability vector's elements is done using a supervised learning method,

$$\Delta p_i = \eta(E_{bestj}(chromosome_{ji}) - p_i)$$

where $E_{bestj}(chromosome_{ji})$ is the mean value of the ith chromosome bit taken over the most fit chromosomes and p_i is the probability of a 1 in position i in the current generation.

Therefore to transmit information from generation to generation we have a single vector—the probability vector—from which we can generate instances (chromosomes) from the appropriate distribution. Notice that,

$$\Delta p_i \to 0 \leftarrow \to p_i \to E_{bestj}(chromosome_{ji})$$

This would suggest that the number of vectors chosen to represent each generation might be a factor which will play off the speed of hill climbing with the need to search the whole search space.

Evolution Strategies

Evolution strategies (ES) or evolutionary algorithms were developed independently from GAs but have a similar basis in biological evolution. ES are programs designed to optimise a particular function (whereas GAs were developed as general search techniques which are used in function optimisation). Therefore ES use a floating point number representation. Consider again the optimisation of 0£×£1. Then it is more natural to represent x with a floating point number rather than a discretised version.

Representation and Mutation

ES represents a potential solution of a problem by a pair of real-valued vectors (x,σ). The first vector x represents a point in the search space. In the example, x would in fact be a scalar. The second vector (σ) is a vector of standard deviations which measures the spread of a distribution. If σ is large, we have a large spread in our distribution; if σ is small, the distribution is very compact. The σ parameter is used in mutating the current vector x to its new value:

$$x(t+1) = x(t) + N(0,\sigma)$$

$N(0,\sigma)$ represents a normal (Gaussian) distribution with zero mean and standard deviations (σ). If the new vector is more fit than its parent (and satisfies any constraints within the problem) it replaces its parent. If not, it is rejected. In our simple example, let us have $x(t) = 0.3$ and $\sigma = 0.2$. Then we generate a random number from the Gaussian distribution $N(0,0.2) = 0.15$ say and add this to $x(t)$ to get $x(t+1)$ = 0.45. Since the fitness of $x(t+1)$ is greater than $x(t)$, it is accepted and $x(t)$ is removed from the population.

A refinement is to have a population of N individuals and generate M children. We can then keep the best of the $(M+N)$ individuals in the new population, this is known as $(M+N) - ES$, or delete the N parents and keep only the best N of the M children, this is known as $(M,N) - ES$.

It can be shown under certain not-too-severe conditions that the simple ES described above will converge to the optimal function value with probability 1.

The parameter σ is usually adapted dynamically during the run of the program dependent on the fraction of mutations which prove to be successful. If you are having a lot of successful mutations, this suggests that your current solution is far from an optimum and we can increase the amount of mutation. If on the other hand you are having very few successful mutations, you should decrease the magnitude of the mutations in order to search the local space more intensely.

When we use a multimembered ES, we can introduce crossover, for example,

$$(x_1, \sigma_1) = (x_{11}, x_{12}, x_{13}, ..., x_{1n}, \sigma_{11}, \sigma_{12}, ..., \sigma_{1n})$$
$$(x_2, \sigma_2) = (x_{21}, x_{22}, x_{23}, ..., x_{2n}, \sigma_{21}, \sigma_{22}, ..., \sigma_{2n})$$

Then we can either select child vectors based on discrete crossover or can use an averaging operator, for example,

$$(x_3, \sigma_3) = (x_{21}, x_{12}, x_{23}, ..., x_{2n}, \sigma_{11}, \sigma_{22}, ..., \sigma_{2n})$$

$$(\mathbf{x}_2, \sigma_2) = \left(\frac{x_{21} + x_{11}}{2}, \frac{x_{12} + x_{22}}{2}, ..., \frac{x_{1n} + x_{2n}}{2}, \frac{\sigma_{11} + \sigma_{21}}{2}, ..., \frac{\sigma_{1n} + \sigma_{2n}}{2} \right)$$

Comparison with Genetic Algorithms

There are a number of differences between GA and ES, not just in the implementation details but also in the concepts that guided their development. For example, GAs were developed as general purpose adaptive search techniques, while ESs were developed as real valued optimisers. An obvious difference is the ES use of floating point representations where the standard GA uses a discrete representation. Further points of comparison are:

- In GAs each individual has a particular probability of being selected for parenthood whereas in ESs each individual will be a parent of a child in the next generation, that is, it is deterministic.

- Similarly in GAs a fit individual has a chance of being selected a great many times for parenthood. In ESs each individual is selected exactly once.

- In ESs we have recombination-selection-fitness evaluation. In GAs we have fitness evaluation-selection-recombination.

- In GAs the reproduction parameters remain constant whereas in ESs the parameters are varied continually.

- In GAs, constraint violations are usually dealt with by adding a penalty to the fitness function; in ESs, violators are removed from the population.

Having made these points, there is a convergence between these two sets of algorithms and the underlying methods certainly come under the general heading of algorithms based on evolution.

We consider the use of GAs in a 'game' which is a standard from classical game theory: the prisoners' dilemma.

The Iterated Prisoners' Dilemma (IPD)

The **prisoner's dilemma** is a simple game played by two players. Each is asked independently to help the authorities 'grass' the other. If both refuse to comply, both

Figure 4. The prisoners' dilemma: The four outcomes of a single game

		What you do	
		COOPERATE	DEFECT
COOPERATE		Fairly good REWARD 3pts	Very bad SUCKER'S PAYOFF 0pts
What I do			
DEFECT		Very good TEMPATION 5pts	Fairly bad PUNISHMENT 1pt

Table 1. The prisoners' dilemma. The important feature is that the maximal gain for the population of prisoners is if both cooperate.

Player 1	Player 2	1	2
Defect	Defect	1	1
Defect	Cooperate	5	0
Cooperate	Defect	0	5
Cooperate	Cooperate	3	3

will be jailed for one year. If one complies and the other does not, the complier gets freedom and the noncomplier gets 10 years imprisonment. If both comply, each gets three years imprisonment. We can put this in score-terms as shown in Table 1.

The important feature of the scoring is that the benefits of both cooperating outweigh the benefits of only one cooperating *for the population*.

We wish to have a GA learn the optimal strategy for the population. Notice that the iteration is an important point in the game. If there is to be only one game, then deception is better than cooperation.

Representation

We consider only deterministic strategies. Assume each move made by an individual takes account of the previous three moves. Since there are four possible outcomes for each move we have 4*4*4 = 64 different histories for the last three moves. Therefore we require 64 bits each of which will represent a strategy for one of the histories. We also have to specify what strategy to use initially, that is, whether to cooperate or defect on the first move and use 6 bits to represent its premises about the three hypothetical moves which preceded the game.

Axelrod (1990) used a tournament to optimise the fitness of the population. Each player's fitness was determined by its score when it played against other members of the population. The player's fitness is its average score. In selecting players to breed, a player with an average score is allowed one mating, one with a score one standard deviation above the average is given two, and one with a score one standard deviation below the average does not breed. Successful players are paired off randomly and crossover and mutation are performed. Axelrod used a GA to breed a population of nice guys who did much better on average than the bad guys.

Results

Axelrod found that the population converged to a population which cooperated rather than defected on average, that is, after (CC)(CC)(CC) C(ooperate). But the population was not wholly gullible since this would allow a rogue D(efector) to gain ground. Thus after a defection, the individual should also defect. Thus after (CC)(CC)(CD) D(efect). But it was also the case that the best individuals were forgiving, that is, after (CD)(DC)C(ooperate). These are usually summarised as 'do unto others...'

N-Persons Iterated Prisoners' Dilemma (NIPD)

We investigate the relevance of the above result in the context of cooperation among N prisoners when $N > 2$. This game has been analysed, for example, in the context of oligopolies, when there are a few major players in a market who are able to co-operate with one another (and in effect form cartels).

The payoff matrix can be represented as in Table 2, which shows the gain for a single prisoner in a population of N-players. It is important to note that the return is dependent on the actions of the other $N-1$ players in the population. The term $C_i(D_i)$ refers to the payoff to the current strategy if it cooperates (defects) when there are *i other* cooperators in the population. This payoff determines the fitness function in our simulations.

The payoff matrix of the NIPD must satisfy,

- It pays to defect: $D_i > C_i$ for all i in $0,\ldots,N-1$.

- Payoffs increase when the number of cooperators in the population increases: $D_{i+1} > D_i$ and $C_{i+1} > C_i$ for all i in $0,\ldots,N-1$

- The population as a whole gains more, the more cooperators there are in the population: $C_{i+1} > (C_i + D_{i+1})/2$ for all i in $0,\ldots,N-2$. Notice that this last

Table 2. The payoff matrix for a single prisoner in a population of N players. There may be 0,1,...,N-1 cooperators in the remainder of the population.

Number of Cooperators	0	1	2	...	N-1
Cooperate	C_0	C_1	C_2	...	C_{N-1}
Defect	D_0	D_1	D_2	...	D_{N-1}

Table 3. Chromosome length for a memory of four rounds

Round	R1	R2	R2	R3	R3	R3	R3	
History	-	D	C	DD	CD	DC	CC	
Length	1	N+1	N+1	$(N+1)^2$	$(N+1)^2$	$(N+1)^2$	$(N+1)^2$	
	R4	R4	R4	R4	R4	R4	R4	R4
	DDD	CDD	DCD	CCD	DDC	CDC	DCC	CCC
	$(N+1)^3$	$(N+1)^3$	$(N+1)^3$	$(N+1)^3$	$(N+1)^3$	$(N+1)^3$	$(N+1)^3$	$(N+1)^3$

gives a transitive relationship so that the global maximum is a population of cooperators.

Colman (1982) has indicated that the NIPD is qualitatively different from the 2-prisoner's dilemma (2IPD) and that certain strategies that work well for individuals in the 2-prisoners' dilemma fail in larger groups.

We have shown that the chromosome in Table 3 can be used to evolve solutions to the NIPD. The first bit determines if the strategy will cooperate ('1') or defect ('0') on the first round. In Round 2, the decision is taken dependent on whether the strategy cooperated or defected in Round 1 (second and third blocks respectively). And then in each block, the bit that determines whether to cooperate or to defect in this round is identified dependent on the number of cooperators in Round 1. This may vary from 0 to N, so $N+1$ bits are necessary. In Round 3 the decision depends on the strategy"s previous decisions: DD, CD, DC, or CC. Within each block there are $(N + 1)*(N + 1)$ histories determined by the number of cooperators in each of the first two rounds, that is, 00, 10, 20, 30, 01, 11, 21, and so on.

In this section, we consider the N-player prisoners' dilemma game where $N > 2$. Previous experiments (Wang, 2002) have shown that the $N = 7$ is a critical value; if $N > 7$, cooperation is very difficult to achieve.

When GAs are used, many simulations (Wang, 2002) show local fitness optima in which players mutually defect at the first few rounds then mutually cooperate after that. These situations appear no matter which selection operators are used. It is an open question as to whether the problem is innate in genetic procedures.

Population-Based Learning

The object of the PBIL (Baluja, 1994) is to create a probability vector which, when sampled, reveals high quality solution vectors with high probability with respect to the available knowledge of the search space.

The vector of probabilities is updated at each generation. The change in the probability vector is towards the better individuals of the population and away from the worst individuals. Each bit or component of the probability vector is analysed independently. This method does not pretend to represent all the population by means of a vector, but it rather introduces a search based on the better individuals.

The two parameters in the PBIL method that must be defined for each problem are the population size (number of samples generated) and the learning rate (LR).

We may show that the PBIL can be used to evolve cooperation but that we often get only partial cooperation, for example, the whole population may defect at Round 2 but regain cooperation at subsequent rounds. A typical result is shown in Figure 7.

The numbers of competition outcomes stay relatively steady throughout hundreds of generations, especially the number of 0-cooperators and 7-cooperators. That means the players either all mutually defect or they all mutually cooperate. We note that they also try other competition outcomes in some rounds. We check the probability vector at the end of simulation from the trial shown in Figure 5 and find that the first left bit is 0 and that only some bits at the right part of the probability vector are not 1 or 0. That means this population almost converges and the difference between strategies that individuals have is very small. However, the created individuals under this probability vector defect at the first round before finding a route to cooperation. Because of the lack of the exploration capability in the converged population, the population can not move out but sinks into this local fitness optimum and remains there throughout the generations. Since there are so many local fitness optima that the simulation could sink into in this set of simulations, we consider the original PBIL with the learning rate = 0.1 is not a suitable search method to simulate the 7-player IPD game.

Also, there is a hitchhiker problem which happens in PBIL. The bits on the chromosomes of the winners which might not be used during the competition can be changed during the simulation. The reason for these individuals' success is not affected by what values they have on these bits which have never been used. The upgrade process does not consider the factors for success in the winners and changes all the probabilities on the vector. It updates every position of the probability vector using the information from the winners even though some bits of the winners have not been used during previous competitions and might also lead to worse results if they were used. This hitchhiker problem decreases the performance and quality of the search. The cooperative PBIL algorithm is designed to meet this problem.

Figure 5. Convergence of the PBIL algorithm on the 7_IPD

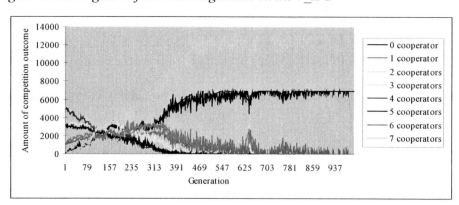

The Cooperative PBIL Algorithm

Ben-Jacob (1998a, 1998b) challenges the new Darwinian view of the chromosome as static code which may be decoded to create phenotypes. Ben-Jacob notes the experimental evidence that mutations in bacteria exist prior to there being a need for or benefit from such mutations, however, while this might suggest that random mutations do exist in populations, it does not preclude nonrandom mutations. Ben-Jacob (1998b) then notes experimental evidence that bacteria may demonstrate genomic changes other than during replication. There is further evidence that a specific mutation will occur in high frequencies only when needed to remove the selective pressure and further that such mutations will not trigger any other mutations. It is the view of Ben-Jacob (1998a, 1998b) that major evolutionary changes occur in response to a population meeting paradoxical environmental conditions. Ben-Jacob contrasts paradoxes with problem solving: the normal processes of evolution may be sufficient when a population meets a problem in this environment but a paradox calls for a more directed evolution in which change is directed by the population as a whole onto individuals within the population. Let us consider that paradoxes in the NIPD are created when a prisoner wishes to respond nicely to other cooperators but retaliate against the defectors. However with only one action, each prisoner can only respond in the same way to all.

Thus we design an improved PBIL, the **cooperative PBIL** algorithm, which will use the environmental input to direct the evolutionary process but which will not cause unnecessary side effects in genes which need not be changed in response to environmental paradoxes. This improved algorithm is described below.

1.   Find the highest fitness chromosomes as the winner just as in the PBIL algorithm.

2.   Select representative chromosomes among the population randomly. This step and Step 3 were repeated 20 times in the simulations below.

3.   The winners compete against these representative chromosomes and the bits of the chromosomes used through these competitions are recorded.

4.   Use the recorded bits in the chromosomes of the winners to upgrade the values of the same positions of the probability vector.

5.   Recreate the new population randomly under the probabilities of the probability vector.

This procedure guarantees that only the bits which contribute to the success of the winners will be upgraded and the other unused bits will not influence the probability vectors. If the bit has not been used throughout the generations, the probability of this bit still remains around 0.5 and allows continuing exploration of these bits by

Figure 6. Convergence of the cooperative PBIL algorithm

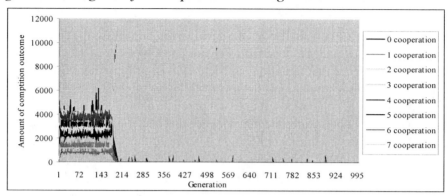

the population if needed. The creation of the unused strategies encoded on these bits when the learning rate is 0.2 creates variation in the population which is not affected by the previous competitions which did not involve them.

The crucial difference between the cooperative PBIL algorithm and the ordinary PBIL algorithm is that there is no genetic drift in this algorithm; only those bits which are actually used in determining fitness are used in modifications to the chromosome.

If we increase the learning rate, exploitation works more strongly and exploration becomes weaker. The population converges quickly and the search may improve in quality. However, if learning experience and selection moves the chromosome in a wrong search direction, the search may fall into a local fitness optimum due to weak exploration. We may expect that there are many trials in which the simulation falls into a local fitness optimum, and so we should find a suitable learning rate to keep the balance between exploration and exploitation to keep the performance high and the quality of search satisfactory. From the simulation of the last section, we know that, with $\eta = 0.1$, the search works well in finding mutual cooperation.

We investigate how a higher learning rate affects the appearance of mutual cooperation and which rate is the best for the simulated NIPD game.

Firstly, we use a learning rate of 0.2 to investigate the 7-IPD via the cooperative PBIL and find that in 10 of 25 trials, we can achieve total mutual cooperation. The number of successful trials to achieve mutual cooperation is slightly lower than when we use a learning rate of 0.1. We also note the strong effect of exploitation in that many trials achieve a local fitness optimum and maintain this population of very stable strategies. Six of these 10 simulations achieve the global fitness. There are four trials which achieve mutual cooperation in a local fitness optimum in which the players mutually defect at the first round or at the first two rounds. Comparing the simulations which achieve the global fitness optimum when we use 0.2 as the learning rate with that when 0.1 is used, we find that this stronger exploitation, due to the higher learning rate, does not improve the performance of the search.

Figure 7. The cooperative PBIL, η=0.2

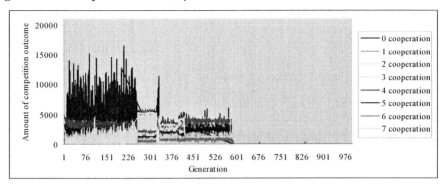

There are also some trials which still need several hundred generations to evolve mutual cooperation (See Figure 6). A qualitatively similar behaviour is seen in Figure 7 from a different simulation with the same parameter set; there is a period of turmoil, sometimes with quieter periods embedded followed by the emergence of cooperation.

From the simulation using the PBIL with different learning rates, we can draw a graph to show the influence of the learning rate on the emergence of cooperation (See Figure 8). We see that too high or too low a learning rate applied to the cooperative PBIL makes the performance worse. Too high a learning rate leads to a lack of exploration and too low a learning rate means little information is passed to the next generation. Both extremes lead to a bad performance, that is, mutual cooperation is not achieved. However, from the experimental results, we can not say which interval of values of learning rates is optimal for a search with the PBILs. Two similar learning rates can give different results. Therefore, we do not suggest which learning rate is optimal for the investigation of the evolutionary game. However, almost half the trials achieve mutual cooperation when a learning rate of 0.5 is used for the investigation with the Cooperative PBIL. We may say that this performance is acceptable and comparable for the investigation of the 7-IPD with other evolutionary methods.

Even though the Cooperative PBIL is an improved PBIL method, the optimal learning rates for the cooperative PBIL and the standard PBIL are different. The investigation of the NIPD shows that a good learning rate for a simulation with thecCooperative PBIL does not work well with the standard PBIL. Performance is best with the cooperative PBIL when the learning rate is 0.5. However, with the standard PBIL, the best learning rate is 0.05.

Figure 8. The number of cooperators varies with the learning rate

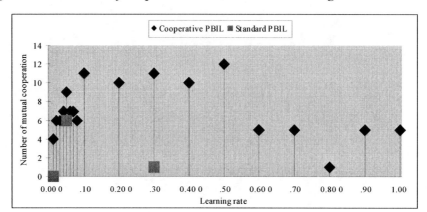

References

Axelroord, R. (1990). *The evolution of cooperation*. Penguin Books.

Baluja, S. (1994). Population-based incremental learning: A method for integrating genetic search based function optimization and competitive learning (Tech. Rep. CMU-CS-94-163). Carnegie Mellon University.

Ben-Jacob, E. (1998a). Bacterial wisdom. *Physica A*, *249*, 553-557.

Ben-Jacob, E. (1998b). Bacterial wisdom, Godel's theorem and creative genomic webs. *Physica A*, *248*, 57-76.

Champandard, A. J. (2004). *AI game development*. New Riders Publishing.

Colman, A. M. (1982). *Game theory and experimental games*. Oxford, England: Pergamon Press.

Dasgupta, D. (1993). Optimisation in time-varying environments using structured genetic algorithms (Tech. Rep. IKBS-17-93). U.K.: The University of Strathclyde.

Davis, L. (1991). *Handbook of genetic algorithms*. Van Nostrand Reinhold.

Fyfe, C. (1999). Structured population-based incremental learning. *Soft Computing*, *2*(4), 191-198.

Holland, J. (1975). *Adaptation in natural artificial systems*. Ann Arbor: University of Michigan Press.

Rapoport, A. (2001). *N-Person game theory, concepts and applications*. University of Michigan Press.

Wang, T.-D. (2002). *The evolution of cooperation in artificial communities*. Unpublished doctoral thesis, University of Paisley.

Chapter IX

Evolving Solutions for Multiobjective Problems and Hierarchical AI

Introduction

Multiobjective problems (MOP) are a class of problems for which different, competing objectives are to be satisfied and for which there is generally no single best solution, but rather for which a set of solutions may exist which are all equally as good. In commercial real-time strategy (RTS) games, designers put a lot of effort into trying to create games where a variety of strategies and tactics can be employed and where (ideally) no single simple optimal strategy exists. Indeed, a great deal of effort may be spent in 'balancing' the game to ensure that the main strategies and units all have effective counters (Rollings & Morris, 1999). It may be the case, then, that RTS games may be considered as MOP. If not in terms of the overall goal of winning the game, which is clearly a single overriding objective, then in terms of the many different objectives that must be met in order to achieve victory. There may be a number of strong, potentially *winning* strategies, each of which is formed from the combination of a large number of tactical and strategic decisions and where improvement in one area will lead to increasing a weakness elsewhere.

Due to the obviously combative nature of RTS, it has also been seen as an ideal area for attempting to evolve strategies using competitive coevolution. The nature of the problem—which combines individual unit control, localised tactical behaviour, and global strategies—also promotes the development of hierarchical AI systems. The use of coevolution and hierarchical AI both have potential hidden problems, which experimenters and game developers should be aware of should they plan to use this approach. We begin this chapter looking at MOP before considering the specific issues relating to the use of coevolving hierarchical AI methods.

Multiobjective Problems

MOP are a distinct class of problem from those presented in Chapter VII where a single solution is better than all other possible solutions. The different objectives in a MOP might entail some degree of conflict such as an airplane attempting to maximise both the number of passengers and the distance that can be travelled on a load of fuel. A more detailed example will highlight the problem.

The Multiobjective Knapsack Problem

In the last chapter, the knapsack problem was presented. There also exists a multiobjective version of this problem where the second objective is to minimise the weight of the knapsack (Steuer, 1986). Obviously the most valuable load would simply include one of every item, while the lightest would not include any. Thus the two objectives clearly conflict. Rather than a single solution, we need to find a set of solutions where improvements for one objective cannot be achieved without impairing performance in the second. This set of solutions is known as the pareto-optimal set, or simply the pareto-set.

For the MOP knapsack problem, fitness can be evaluated on the basis of whether a solution is dominated or not (Zitzler, 1999). A solution is dominated if there exists another solution of the same (or lesser weight) and is of greater value, or if there exists another solution of the same value but of lesser weight. The set of *nondominated* solutions forms the pareto-set.

This is clearly related to the situation desired in RTS games, where designers try to design games which support a number of nondominated strategies.

Coevolution in Hierarchical AI for Strategy Games

Real-time strategy games present an interesting problem domain for artificial intelligence research. We review current approaches to developing AI systems for such games, noting the frequent decomposition into hierarchies similar to those found in real-world armies. We also note the rarity of any form of learning in this domain and find limitations in the work that does use learning. Such work tends to enable learning at only one level of the AI hierarchy. We argue, using examples from real-world wars and from research on coevolution in evolutionary computation, that learning in AI hierarchies should occur concurrently at the different strategic and tactical levels present. We then present a framework for conducting research on coevolving the AI.

Introduction

In recent years advances in computing power have enabled the development of simulations and models in which (very) large numbers of individual agents are explicitly modelled, allowing individual based models to be used alongside more traditional mathematical modelling techniques in a variety of scientific disciplines (see, for example, the range of papers by Adami, Belew, Kitano, and Taylor [1998]). Other uses have been found in the entertainment industries for computer generated mobs, masses, and armies in films (recently used to great effect in the Lord of the Rings film trilogy), and to create interactive mobs, masses, and armies in computer and video games (such as the hugely successful Total War series of games).

However, where traditional approaches to agent based modelling usually require that agent activity, communication and coordination is done within an autonomous framework, for example (Rebollo, Botti, & Onaindia, 2003), commercial games generally have no such requirements. The goal of such AI is to entertain, and it is of no concern if principles of autonomy or embodiment are broken, as noted by Buro (2004).

However, ignoring the demand for the AI to be entertaining, there are some interesting research problems in developing AI for RTS games, including planning in an uncertain world with incomplete information learning, opponent modelling, and spatial and temporal reasoning (Buro, 2004).

In a similar vein, Corruble, Madeira, and Ramalho (2002) discuss the different AI problems that exist in computer-based war-games, and generally consider the difficulty inherent in designing AI systems for such games. Particular problems, they argue, are caused by the large search spaces—environments consisting of many thousands of possible positions for each of hundreds, possibly thousands, of units—and the parallel nature of the problem. Unlike traditional games, any number of moves may be made simultaneously.

In this chapter we review some of the current approaches to building AI systems for RTS games, and propose a framework for developing learning AI for RTS games in which adaptation occurs at different tactical and strategic levels, which coevolve over time.

Hierarchical AI in RTS Games

Hierarchical approaches to developing AI systems are not new. For example, Brooks' (1991) famous subsumption architecture uses a hierarchy of behaviours within a single agent. The application of hierarchies for military organisation is considerably older. Throughout human history armies have long been organised along very strictly defined hierarchical principles, the ancient Roman armies providing but one good example.

Hierarchies are also very natural control structures for use in RTS games, allowing the development of separate AI systems for controlling high level strategic behaviours of the army as a whole and for low level tactical behaviours which can be given to individual units (Kent, 2004). Hierarchal AI can also be used more generally in other games in which very large organisations are modelled (Wallace, 2004), and in games which might only model small groups of units but in which there is some form of group command (van der Sterren, 2002).

In an RTS AI hierarchy, the uppermost level will be some form of command agent with overall strategic control. The lowest level will be a—potentially very simple—agent AI responsible for the control of an individual soldier (tank, horse, etc.), and there may be any number of intermediary layers of AI representing command over groups of individual soldiers (such as squads) and progressively larger groupings of combat units.

Within this problem domain we will not currently concern ourselves with problems such as path planning or terrain evaluation, which remain problems of interest. Instead we will concentrate on the problems raised by, and on the benefits of, attempting to build adaptive learning AI systems which may exist at multiple levels of the command hierarchy, and which coevolve over time.

Current Hierarchical AI in Video Games

A number of hierarchical AI architectures for use in video games have already been proposed and documented.

For control of small squads, van der Sterren (2002) considers a decentralised approach whereby squad agents communicate and form emergent strategies, such as for fire-and-move behaviours, illustrating how team tactics can emerge from interactions between a number of agents. The advantages and disadvantages of the decentralised approach are illustrated using an example of having the squad wait in ambush. The key limitation appears to be that there is no single AI responsible for the strategic deployment of the squad; a solution to this is presented in the following chapter (van der Sterren, 2002) which modifies the architecture from a self-organising one into a simple hierarchical one. This presents two distinct command styles: authoritarian, where the member agents always perform the actions they are commanded to do; and coach, where a higher level squad AI (not an explicit agent commanding the squad, but some strategic controller AI) sends requests to the agents, which then evaluate them in light of their current circumstances before deciding which action to perform. It is suggested that a third style, which combines elements of the first two might be the most successful.

This idea of using command hierarchies for controlling units of agents is also used by Reynolds (2002), again for the control of small squads of agents. For controlling larger numbers of agents, Kent (2004) provides an architecture for a nonadaptive hierarchical strategic/tactical AI to control armies in a RTS game. The principal behind the architecture is to mirror the hierarchical structure of real armies in the simulated one.

At the top level is a human or AI game player, which makes the highest level decisions; below this are AIs for individual armies, divisions, brigades, companies, platoons, and squads as required by the sizes of the forces involved and the complexity of the game. Finally, at the bottom level of the hierarchy are AIs to control individual soldiers.

Ramsey (2004) presents a similar approach, less specifically focussed on military organisation, which he calls the 'multi-tiered AI framework' (MTAIF). This contains four levels of intelligence: strategic, operational, tactical, and individual unit. Within this more generalised framework, the AI approach is similar to that advocated by Kent, but the tasks to be carried out by the different units can vary more, including resource gathering and city and empire building. This chapter, like that of Kent (2004), devotes much discussion to solving the problems of message passing and coordination with large hierarchies.

One notable aspect of these AI architectures is the absence of any form of learning. One of the rare occurrences of learning in war games is in an online report

(Sweetser, Watson, & Wiles, 2003) which presents work on developing command agents for strategy simulations using cognitive work analysis and machine learning approaches, but here the learning is only to aid the decisions of the overall commander, not for the subordinate units.

A hierarchical learning example is presented by Madeira, Corruble, Ramalho, and Ratitch (2004), who focus on the problem of partially automating the design of AI for strategy games, proposing a system in which the AI learns how to play the game during development, rather than having the AI manually programmed. While their work uses reinforcement learning in a strategy game environment, they note that in principal a wider range of machine learning techniques may be used. It is noted that strategy games currently primarily use rule-based systems. Advantages and disadvantages of such an approach are discussed before reinforcement learning and machine learning are introduced as alternatives.

Again, the problem is decomposed using the natural hierarchical decomposition of the command-structure, allowing decision making to be carried out on several different levels. They repeat the observation that this allows higher levels to focus on more abstract strategic reasoning, leaving fine-grained tactical reasoning to units involved in combat.

They train a reinforcement learning AI player against a rule-based AI player, allowing learning to take place over thousands of games.

Madeira et al. (2004) note that enabling learning at different levels simultaneously can be problematic, with a reference to the difficulty of concurrent layered learning (Whiteson & Stone, 2003), and instead train a single level of their AI hierarchy at a time. Accordingly, they initialise their learning AI with rule-based system controllers for each level of the AI hierarchy and train the top level only. Once training of the top-level is complete, its AI is fixed and training of the AI for the next level down is started, and so on down to the soldier level. While this work is still in progress, with learning yet to be extended to levels below the top level player, we can note that by limiting learning to a single layer at a time (Madeira et al., 2004) and limiting the search space available to their learning AI, this, and the potential benefits of enabling simultaneous adaptation at multiple levels, is what we consider next.

Adaptation at Multiple Levels in Battle Strategies

It is actually quite easy to find real-world examples that highlight the limitations of the approach proposed by Madeira et al. (2004). Whenever new technology is introduced into the battlefield, or new formations and methods of organising units at a low level are developed, high level strategies must adapt to make good use of the new opportunities. New formations may be ineffective without a new strategy for using them, and new strategies might simply not be available without the new formations or technologies they depend on, as the following two examples demonstrate.

World War I featured the first large scale use of machine guns—yet tactics for infantry assault remained unchanged. These typically entailed sending large lines of men marching steadily towards enemy positions, an ideal target for opposing machine gunners. It was only towards the end of the war that General Oskar von Hutier of Germany introduced new tactics for his attacking units and a strategy ('Infiltration') for using them: having loose formations of lightly encumbered soldiers (Storm Troopers) rapidly advance over and beyond the enemy lines, bypassing then attacking strong-points from the rear. This finally allowed infantry to effectively attack enemy lines despite the presence of the deadly machine guns, enabling the Central Powers to briefly make significant advances against the Allies (Makepeace & Padfield, 2004).

In the middle ages, spearmen were often used defensively against cavalry. The schiltrom was a particularly effective defensive formation presenting bristling spear points in every direction, a deadly barrier for oncoming cavalry. At Bannockburn, Robert the Bruce trained his spearmen to charge as a phalanx, and to change formation between schiltrom and phalanx at command (Bingham, 1998, p. 222), and the strategic use of these new tactics aided his decisive victory at that battle.

This clearly implies that we should make use of a coevolutionary approach. However, the advantages of using a coevolutionary method are not necessarily clear cut and there are some potential disadvantages that we need to be aware of.

Problems with Coevolution

It has been known for some time that coevolution can lead to the development of suboptimal solutions (Cliff & Miller, 1995), and that these conflict with the advantages of coevolutionary processes. Watson and Pollack (2001) provide several concrete examples of coevolution leading to suboptimal solutions. One particular cause of this is that in typical coevolution scenarios where the coevolving populations and individuals are competing for resources and the fitness of agents is relative. Rather than having an external objective measure of fitness (as typically used in evolutionary computation), fitness is found by determining which of a number of competitors is best.

One consequence of this is that the best solution may drift into worse solutions, as long as it remains the best of the solutions available, and if a chance mutation does improve the best strategy, it may not be selected for as it will not actually improve its fitness. One solution to this problem is to keep examples of previous best solutions in the population (Cliff, 1995).

Intransitive Superiority

Another problem investigated by Watson and Pollack (2001) is that caused by intransitive superiority. Intransitive superiority exists in any situation where for three (or more) strategies or players no single strategy or player is the best; instead, and rather like scissors-paper-stone, some form of circular superiority relationship exists between them. For example, Strategy A beats B, and B beats C, but C beats A. In such a situation it is may be troublesome even to find the most fit individuals in populations of coevolving strategies.

Of particular note, Watson and Pollack (2001) show that coevolution with intransitive superiority can not only allow best solutions to drift to poorer ones, but can in some cases drive the evolution towards poorer general performance. This is of particular concern to the domain of RTS games, where intransitive superiority is often deliberately designed into the game (Rollings & Morris, 1999).

A variety of algorithms and techniques are able to overcome problems caused by intransitive superiority, and the possibility of cycling that can exist even where superiority is transitive (de Jong, 2004b). Solutions generally involve the addition of some form of memory or archive to the underlying evolutionary computational technique used.

In the next chapter we will look at artificial immune systems (AIS) (Dasgupta, 2000), a biologically inspired approach in which memory of previous good solutions is a core feature.

Coevolution in AI Hierarchies

It should be noted that all of the problems described assume that the coevolution occurs between competing players or populations. In our case we are actually interested in a quite different situation where the coevolving strategies are not opponents, but partners operating at different levels. This is somewhat similar to the problem of concurrent layered learning in individual agents explored by Whiteson and Stone (2003). While the difficulties of such an approach were cited by Madeira et al. (2004) as a reason not to coevolve the different levels in an AI hierarchy (in the third section), the point made by Whiteson and Stone (2003) is that concurrent layered learning is beneficial in certain situations and can outperform traditional, one layer at a time, layered learning (as we argued it may be earlier).

In our case we can potentially avoid some of the problems of coevolving opponent AI by pitting our evolving hierarchical AI against fixed, nonevolving opponents. In doing so we may lose some of the advantages of coevolving against another hierarchical AI, such as having an opponent that presents a 'hittable' target, or allowing for more open-ended evolution instead of having evolution merely drift once the fixed AI has been beaten (Watson & Pollack, 2001).

But issues remain. Let A be the set of possible high level strategies and B the set of low level tactics. Further, let $a1$ and $a2$ be two high level strategies and $b1$ and $b2$ be two low level strategies. We can easily imagine a situation where, against a fixed opponent, the fitness, f, of these strategies is such that $f(a2,b2) > f(a1,b1)$. Now what if, as suggested in the forth section, the fitness advantages of $a2$ and $b2$ only exists when these strategies are used together. In other terms, there exists a linkage between the variables (de Jong, 2004b). Then we may also have $f(a1,b1) > f(a1,b2)$ and $f(a1,b1) > f(a2,b1)$. The fitness landscape presented by coevolving hierarchical AI is likely to be high-dimensional and feature many suboptimal maxima and may feature hard-to-find global maxima, presenting a significant challenge.

de Jong (2004a) notes that if the order of linkage—the maximum number of linked variables—is small and some exploitable structure exists, a hierarchical genetic algorithm is most likely able to find the globally optimal solution, given that such a solution exists.

Conclusion

RTS games provide a rich environment for artificial evolution and other AI approaches to problem solving. Good players, human or AI, need to reason at multiple levels of detail, from overall grand strategies down to highly localised decisions. RTS games also possess very natural and intuitive levels of detail, allowing the problem to be quite neatly decomposed into a number of smaller problems, although these are not independent of one another.

While current approaches to building AI systems for RTS games already use a hierarchical decomposition, these generally do not include learning or adaptation. Those systems that exist that do enable learning, and those that have been proposed enable learning in single layers only in order to simplify the search involved. One proposal to extend this to enable learning at successively lower levels after each higher level of learning is complete in turn.

We note that such a solution may fail to exhaustively search the space of possible solutions, as some good solutions may depend on combinations of adaptations at multiple levels. Accordingly, we propose to develop a system in which the different levels of the hierarchical AI coevolve. We have noted a number of issues regarding this and further proposed a basic framework for future progress on this.

References

Adami, C., Belew, R. K., Kitano, H., & Taylor, C. E. (1998). *Artificial life VI.* UCLA: MIT Press.

Bingham, C. (1998). *Robert the Bruce.* London: Constable and Company.

Brooks, R. A. (1991). Intelligence without representation. *Artificial Intelligence, 47,* 139–159.

Buro, M. (2004, July). Call for AI research in RTS games. In D. Fu & J. Orkin (Eds.), *AAAI workshop on challenges in game AI* (pp. 139-141). San Jose.

Cliff, D., & Miller, G. F. (1995). *Tracking the red queen: Measurements of adaptive progress in co-evolutionary simulations.* Paper presented at the Third European conference on Artificial Life (pp. 200-218). Springer-Verlag.

Corruble, V., Madeira, C., & Ramalho, G. (2002). Steps towards building a good AI for complex wargame-type simulation games. Game-On 2002. In Q. Mehdi, N. Gough, & M. Cavazza (Eds.), *The third international conference on intelligent games and simulation* (pp. 155-159). London.

Dasgupta, D. (2000). *Artificial immune systems and their applications.* Springer-Verlag.

de Jong, E. D. (2004a, September). *Hierarchical genetic algorithms.* Paper presented at the 8th International Conference on Parallel Problem Solving from Nature (pp. 232-241), Birmingham, U.K.

de Jong, E. D. (2004b, September). *Intransitivity in coevolution.* Paper presented at the 8th International Conference on Parallel Problem Solving from Nature (pp. 843-851), Birmingham, U.K.

Kent, T. (2004). Multi-tiered AI layers and terrain analysis for RTS games. In S. Rabin (Ed.), *AI game programming wisdom 2.* Hingham, MA: Charles River Media, Inc.

Madeira, C., Corruble, V., Ramalho, G. & Ratitch, B. (2004, July). Bootstrapping the learning process for the semi-automated design of a challenging game AI. In D. Fu & J. Orkin (Eds.), *AAAI workshop on challenges in game AI* (pp. 72-76). San Jose.

Makepeace, D., & Padfield, A. (2004). *Trench hell and the role of the 'Stosstruppen.'* Retreived October 5, 2006, from http://www.wargamesjournal.com/

Ramsey, M. (2004). Designing a multi-tiered AI framework. In S. Rabin (Ed.), *AI game programming wisdom 2.* Hingham, MA: Charles River Media, Inc.

Rebollo, M., Botti, V., & Onaindia, E. (2003, June). Formal modeling of dynamic environments for real-time agents. In V. Marík, J. Müller, & M. Pchouek (Eds.), *CEEMAS 2003* (Lecture Notes in AI, 2691) (pp. 474-484). Prague: Springer

Reynolds, J. (2002). Tactical team AI using a command hierarchy. In Rabin S. (Ed.), *AI game programming wisdom*. Hingham, MA: Charles River Media, Inc.

Rollings, A., & Morris, D. (1999). *Game architecture and design*. Scottsdale, AZ: Coriolis.

Steuer, E. (1986) *Multiple criteria optimization: Theory, computation, and application*. New York: Wiley.

Sweetser, P., Watson, M., & Wiles, J. (2003). Intelligent command agents for command and control simulations using cognitive work Analysis and machine learning. *The University of Queensland, Brisbane, Australia*. Retrieved June 14, 2007, from http://www.itee.uq.edu.au/~penny/

van der Sterren, W. (2002a). Squad tactics: Planned maneuvers. In S. Rabin (Ed,), *AI game programming wisdom 2*. Hingham, MA: Charles River Media, Inc.

van der Sterren, W. (2002b). Squad tactics: Team AI and emergent maneuvers. In S. Rabin (Ed.), *AI game programming wisdom 2*. Hingham, MA: Charles River Media, Inc.

Wallace, N. (2004). Hierarchical planning in dynamic worlds. In S. Rabin (Ed.), *AI game programming wisdom 2*. Hingham, MA: Charles River Media, Inc.

Watson, R. A., & Pollack, J. B. (2001). Coevolutionary dynamics in a minimal substrate. L. Spector & et al. (Eds.), *Genetic and evolutionary computation conference (GECCO 2001)*. Morgan Kaufmann.

Whiteson, S., & Stone, P. (2003). *Concurrent layered learning*. Paper presented at the Second International Joint Conference on Autonomous Agents and Multi-Agent Systems (pp. 193-200), Melbourne. ACM Press.

Zitzler, E., & Thiele, L. (1999). Multiobjective evolutionary algorithms: A comparative case study and the strength pareto approach. *IEEE Transactions on Evolutionary Computation, 3*(4), 257-271.

Chapter X

Artificial Immune Systems

Introduction

We now consider the problem of introducing more intelligence into the artificial intelligence's responses in real-time strategy games (RTS). We discuss how the paradigm of **artificial immune systems** (AIS) gives us an effective model to improve the AI's responses and demonstrate with simple games how the AIS work. We further discuss how the AIS paradigm enables us to extend current games in ways which make the game more sophisticated for both human and AI.

In this chapter, we show how strategies may be dynamically created and utilised by an artificial intelligence in a real-time strategy (RTS) game. We develop as simple as possible RTS games in order to display the power of the method we use.

As discussed in the last chapter, units are powerful against one unit and weak against another. In a typical game world, scissors dominates paper which dominates stone which dominates scissors. For example, in Rise of Nations from Microsoft, cavalry are powerful against light infantry who are good against bowmen who are powerful against heavy infantry who in turn can overcome cavalry. Therefore knowing what strategy your opponent is going to use gives the human player a very great advantage.

In these games, the computer player's strategy is often extremely predictable. Typically, it will select what seems initially to be an optimal balance of each type of fighter but if that is known, it can be defended against. Thus the game reduces to the human player(s) simply identifying how the artificial intelligence (AI) will play and devising a strategy which will overcome the AI's strategy. The AI generally has no flexibility in its responses to the human strategies and so the game quickly becomes boring. At core is the fact that, for the AI, the strategies of the human player form an important part of an evolving environment. In giving it an *a priori* optimal strategy, the games developers may be giving it the best single static strategy but this will always be beaten by strategies which are learned during the course of the game and dynamically changed in response to the changing strategies met during the course of the game. We propose a system which allows the AI to respond dynamically to the strategies used by its human opponent; in effect, we wish to give the AI enough adaptability so that it may respond as a second human player would to the strategies of its human opponent.

The prototypical situation which we have in mind is that which exists when the AI and the human are both building civilisations with limited resources. Often during such games, the civilisations interact with one another in a hostile manner: the AI will typically launch attacks against the human player's civilisation and the human strategy becomes one of defending a civilisation whilst building up enough resources in order to be able to launch an overwhelming attack. While success in this type of game is initially satisfying, the fact that the same strategy can be used each time diminishes the enjoyment of the game. By giving the AI the ability to adapt, we hope that the human will gain more lasting enjoyment from the game.

Thus we propose to use artificial immune system (Dasgupta, 2000) methods; the immune system response attributes of specificity, diversity, memory, and self/non-self recognition are just what is needed in this situation. The next section discusses the immune system before we go on to describe the artificial immune system and how it may be used to optimise the AI's responses to human opponents. Finally we consider how the use of the immune system paradigm may allow us to develop more sophisticated games which are more like real life engagements.

The Immune System

We discuss only those aspects of artificial immune systems which are relevant to this chapter. For a fuller discussion, see for example works by Dasgupta (2000) and De Castro and von Zeuben (1999, 2000).

The immune system is a complex system that enables a mechanism by which certain dangers to the organism can be identified. These dangers can be roughly classified as those which arise from dysfunction within the organism's own cells and those which are due to the action of exogenous pathogens. We will concentrate on the latter since we will consider the case in which the actions of a human player are treated by the AI as pathogens to which it must respond by creating actions which optimally confront those of the human player.

The root of the system we will be emulating is a set of cells known as the B-lymphocytes which are created in the bone marrow. They are responsible for producing specific antibodies in response to the identification of specific antigens; each antibody will respond optimally to a specific antigen rather like a key which fits into a keyhole. The key part of the antigen is known as the epitope and the keyhole part of the antibody is known as the paratope.

The immune system itself is partly innate—we are born with an active immune system—and partly adaptive where the body learns to respond appropriately to the attacks which the organism meets in life. There are limited resources available for the production of antibodies so that in responding to a particular antigen by creating specific antibodies, the system inevitably has fewer resources available to respond to other antigens.

The adaptive immune system is believed to be continually creating antibodies in a somewhat random fashion. It is rather as though it is exploring the space of antigens always on the lookout for new dangers to the organism. This could be used in creating probing attacks on human positions and in readying the AI for optimal response to new threats; we anticipate that a more intelligent response from the AI will lead to an arms race. The human opponent will have to be continually changing strategies in order to overcome the AI which in turn will be responding by developing new strategies.

One further feature of the immune system which is of interest in the current context is its memory: the adaptive immune system remembers which attacks the organism had to withstand and retains a response mechanism which is optimal for attacks of the same or a similar type in future. We will use this feature so that the AI learns typical tactics from the player(s) it meets most often so that it learns how to respond optimally to those humans it meets.

A final feature of the immune system in which we will be interested is based on Jerne's (1974) **immune network theory**. This proposes that the various parts of the immune system itself recognise other parts of the same system and indeed affect the production or suppression of other parts of the system. A positive reaction between components can lead to cell proliferation and activation while a negative response can lead to cell tolerance and suppression.

Artificial Immune Systems

Perhaps the definitive difference between traditional artificial intelligence and the studies which comprise contemporary artificial intelligence (which we take to encompass evolutionary algorithms, artificial neural networks, artificial life, and artificial immune systems) is the emphasis on the program writer not solving the problem but merely creating conditions whereby a program, if exposed to sufficient training examples, will learn to extract sufficient information from a problem in order to solve it itself. The artificial immune system does just that.

We consider initially a situation in which there is a limited alphabet of attack-defence pieces such as cavalry, infantry, and bowmen. Let this be the set $\{s_1, s_2, ..., s_k\}$ and let the optimal response to s_i be r_i. Then if the human strategy is to defend (or attack) with k_i of unit s_i, the AI must learn to respond with l_i of unit r_i. Let $L=\{l_1, l_2, ..., l_k\}$. Then initially L will be random or, at best, the optimal a priori strategy. However during play, the values in L will change to mirror the strategies used by its human opponent. Now we have a moving target for the human player. It is playing against an opponent which is not preprogrammed to make specific moves but is treating the game as a dynamic challenge and responding to the situation, as does the human.

Thus the AI's response, L, to its human opponent will approximate L^*, the current optimal strategy, and because of the nature of the artificial immune system, it will retain a memory of L in its memory of how to respond to a future attack by the human opponent.

However, when the human changes strategies, the AI will respond to that because of the adaptive nature of the artificial immune system.

An Illustrative Example

To illustrate these ideas, we construct a simple game which abstracts the basic ideas. The game has three types of resources labelled A, B, and C. Using '>' for dominates, we have $A < B$, $B < C$, and $C < A$. The game is almost deterministic; if a unit of type A meets an opponent of type B, the type B unit wins. The only stochastic element occurs when the opponents are of the same type in which case we randomly select the winner. For the first experiment (and it should be noted reversing the current position in games), we let the human have a fixed strategy and allow the AI to respond to this. The human's strategy is to have 12 units of resource A, 8 of resource B, and 5 of resource C. The AI initially has 25 units randomly selected from A, B, and C. At each round, we select one unit from the human's side and one from the AI's side and play them off against each other.

- If the human's unit wins, we delete the AI unit and randomly select a new unit from our alphabet {A, B, C}.

- If the AI wins, we randomly delete one of the other units in the AI's resources and replace it with a new unit of the type which has just won. This is the AIS response. We have defeated this antigen but there may be more of the same around and so we therefore create similar antibodies.

Note that these rules can be made much more sophisticated while remaining within the artificial immune system paradigm. The results of one simulation of 1,000 rounds are shown in Figure 1. The average number of units of each type is shown in Table 1. We see that the values approximate the optimal values of 5, 12, and 8 showing that even this very simple system can learn to optimise its response. Notice that the number of units of each type continually changes throughout the simulation. This is due to the random nature of selecting opponents from a small population (25 units

Figure 1. The proportion of each type of unit in the AI's resources during 1,000 rounds of the simple game

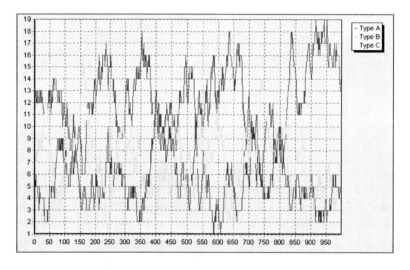

Table 1. The average number of units of each type during the simulation shown in Figure 1

Type	A	B	C
Average	5.400	12.446	7.154

for each side in this experiment); if we use a larger population these effects are less evident. Simulations over a greater number of rounds show short periods of time when populations move to extreme values but inevitably they return to respond to the main threats fairly quickly. Over 10 runs of 10,000 rounds each, the AI won an average of 5458.5 times with a standard deviation of 42.

Now we return a little intelligence to our human player. At round 1,000, the player realises the AI is countering the moves and changes strategies. The player switches the proportion of *A* and *C* units so that there is now 5 units of type *A* and 12 of type *C*. The AI's response is shown in Figure 2. Note the fast nature of the change. Within 20 rounds or so, the AI has responded to the new environment created by the human's changing strategy.

However the above simulation does not utilise the memory aspect of the AIS. We thus equip the AI with a number of generals each of which remembers how to respond to particular types of attacks; each general is, in AIS terms, a *B* cell with a memory of which particular antibody to produce to combat a specific antigen. This is most easily done by having a variable measuring the amount of local winning done by the current general. When this falls to too low a level, a new (randomised) general is created or one of the existing ones is let loose on the human. If a human wins $(s_i > l_i)$, let $\delta = 0$; if the AI wins $(l_i > s_i)$, let $\delta = 1$. Then a simple rule for updating the local memory, *m* is,

$$m = 0.99m + 0.01(2\delta - 1)$$

Figure 2. The human changes the strategy at round 1,000 and the AI's response is clearly seen

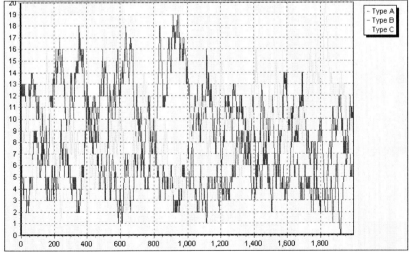

Figure 3. Two generals used by the AI to counter the human's changing strategies. Each general uses different concentrations of the three types of resource and so can be used for different types of attacks.

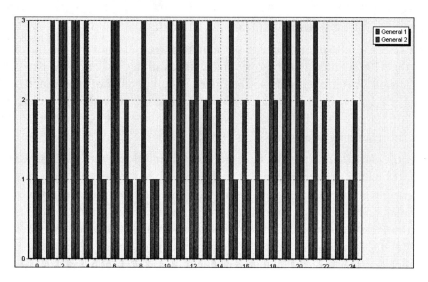

When *m* falls below some reference level (in the simulation from which Figure 3 is taken this was 0.05), a new general is tried. Figure 3 shows the result of a simulation from a game in which the AI had potentially up to 30 generals; it actually only used four in this game though only two are shown for clarity. We see that the generals tend to have different concentrations of the three types of resource: a bar of height 1 indicates resource type *A*, height 2 indicates resource type *B*, and height 3 indicates a resource type *C*. Identifying the general with the colour of the bar in this diagram, we see that the red general had 4 *A*s, 12 *B*s ,and 9 *C*s while the blue general had 11 *A*s, 3 *B*s, and 11 *C*s; each is optimal for responding to quite different strategies from human opponents.

The number of generals used in a game can be controlled by altering the parameters used for updating m and by the reference level.

Hypermutations

We stated that one of the important features of the immune system is that it retains a memory of previously encountered antigens which primes it to fight new attacks from the same antigens in future. However this priming is even more important because the cloning of new antibodies comes with a feature known as **hypermutation**: the cloning is not perfect in that each new clone of a previously useful antibody has a high probability of being a slightly mutated version of the antibody. The 'hyper' is because this probability is much greater than is seen with standard genetic variation in evolution. Thus in effect the priming is arming the system with responses both to the specific antigen and to any close relatives of that antigen. Considering the space of potential antibodies, the hypermutation process acts like a shotgun firing antibodies into the system around this space in positions close to the previously useful antibody. Of course, if used long term against a single form of opponent, this will have the effect of fine tuning the system's response to that opponent. However, we can use this system to create more sophisticated games.

We have previously considered a system in which resource A < resource B and so forth. This views each resource as a one dimensional resource. In real life, we may have more than a single aspect to consider. To train an infantryman, we may consider expending so much time on his physical fitness, so much on his marksmanship, so much on his intelligence, and so forth. Thus we have a resource which varies along several, perhaps many, dimensions. Now we may consider a game in which each player is able to expend so many resources on individual units and within each unit may redistribute the resources in a way which seems optimal. However the AI can now respond in that it may have a unit which responds very well to a general infantryman but, through the process of hypermutation, it will identify which type of unit will optimally respond to the human player's typical specific type of units.

To illustrate this feature, we create a game in which each player has three-dimensional resources, such as speed, strength, and intelligence. Since there is a limited quantity of resources available, we normalise the variables so that the vector of resources for each player sums to 1. This may be written as:

$$\mathbf{a} = \{a_1, a_2, a_3\}, \mathbf{b} = \{b_1, b_2, b_3\} \text{ where } 0 \leq a_i, b_i \leq 1 \text{ and } \Sigma a_i = \Sigma b_i = 1, i = 1, 2, 3.$$

Now let the rules of the game be that when two units meet, the unit with greater value in two of the three elements is the winner. Note that because of the constraints, no unit can be greater in all three elements. Let us begin with a population of N antibodies selected randomly and let the optimal antibody be the one which has values in two of its elements greater than the human-selected unit but which has most value in the third element. For Figure 4, the human initially chose $\mathbf{a} = \{0.4, 0.4, 0.2\}$; the figure shows the convergence of the $\mathbf{b}$ vector when we used a population of 10 antibodies and replaced the current population of antibodies with noisy versions of the best antibody from the previous generation. We see very fast convergence to an approximation of the optimal value.

This enables us to change the nature of the games themselves so that they are more challenging for both the human player and the AI opponent.

Figure 4. Very fast convergence from the hypermutations leads to optimal values

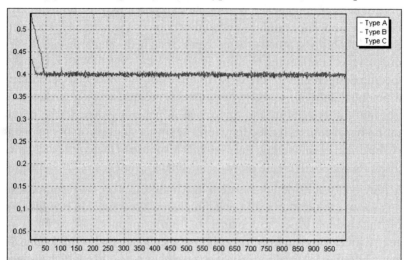

The Immune Network

We stated earlier that Jerne had developed a theory that there were interactions between the various parts of an immune system: the production of one antibody can suppress or activate the production of a second type of antibody. To illustrate this feature we require to devise a slightly more complex game in which a resource of type *A* can dominate both a type *B* resource and a type *C* resource but which will be dominated by a joint attack from a $(B + C)$ combination. Therefore we have $A > B$, $A > C$, $B > C$ but $(B + C) > A$. We require to introduce a cost constraint rather than a constraint on number of pieces and so we have costs $C_A = 4$, $C_B = 3$, and $C_C = 2$ so that it costs more to create a $(B + C)$ combination than it does an *A*. Now we set up a game between a human army consisting of a number of *A*s, *B*s, and *C*s (the number is determined by the human but must meet a certain cost constraint) and an AI army which must also meet the constraint. When a unit from either group meets a weaker one it will prevail except when the unit is a type *A* in which case the weaker opponent (a *B* or *C*) will have the option of enlisting the support of a colleague (of type *C* or *B*, respectively) *if such a colleague exists*. Thus we must use meetings of armies this time rather than individuals since we must model the situation in which there are finite resources. If, during the game, a $(B + C)$ combination wins, new copies of *B* and *C* are both put in the population. This only very slightly more complex game can provide a range of behaviours dependent on the strategy used by the human.

For example in Figure 5, the human strategy was to use 12 of type *A*, 8 of type *B*, and 5 of type *C*. The AI's response was to devote most resources to type *B* since $B > C$

Figure 5. The population very quickly converges on a relatively stable population for the immune network game

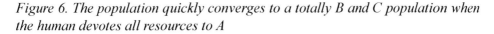

and $(B + C) > A$, next most resources to C since it can be used in conjunction with a B to defeat an A and a very much lesser amount to A production.

It should be emphasised that the AI's initial army is totally random in all simulations and thus we see that the convergence to the values shown is very fast. We show 1,000 iterations of the game each time to illustrate that the solutions found are very stable.

On the other hand, Figure 6 shows the AI response to a human strategy of devoting all its resources to type A: the AI creates an army compose only of Bs and Cs in equal quantities. Every contest is the AI's $(B + C)$ against an A from the human army.

Figure 6. The population quickly converges to a totally B and C population when the human devotes all resources to A

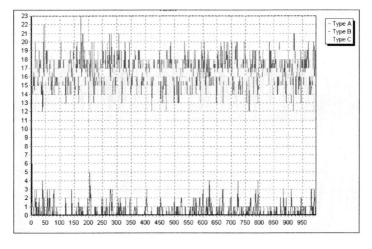

Figure 7. Response of the AI to a human strategy of using only Bs and Cs

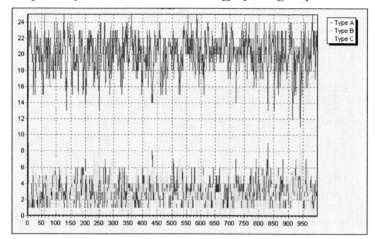

On the other hand, if the human should use this strategy (i.e., uses only types *B* and *C*), the AI puts all of its resources into type *B* alone (Figure 7) since when a *B* meets another *B* the winner is selected randomly while when a *B* meets a *C*, the *B* wins. Naturally if the human opts to use only *B*s, the AI puts all its resources into creating *A*s which will defeat a lone *B* every time.

The take-home message from even this simple game is that there is no guaranteed winning strategy. The use of the artificial immune system's priming mechanism allows the AI to develop counter strategies to any strategy which is developed by the human. It is, in a very real and practical manner, responding to the human moves. Note also that the speed of the response makes it a potentially valuable method even on today's hardware.

Agent Wars

The above simulations are rather limited in that we allow the AI to adapt its strategies quickly but do not permit the human to do so. Let us now extend the above simulation in order to have two AIs which are playing each other. Let one AI have 10 strategies initialised randomly while the other is initialised with noisy versions of a particular strategy {0.4, 0.4, 0.2}. In order to create some inequality between the two AIs, we give one 5 times the exploratory capacity of the other, that is, when we clone the winner, we make the magnitude of the mutations 5 times greater for one AI than the other. Results are shown in Figure 8. We see that the two AIs perform a dance in which the actions of one are completely mirrored in the actions of

Figure 8. Top: the strategies of the AI with the high mutation rate. Bottom: the strategies of the AI with the low mutation rate.

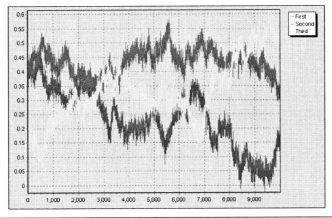

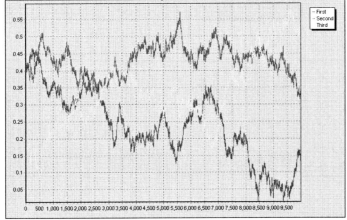

the other. The top diagram is from the AI with the high mutation rate; the bottom diagram is from the AI with the low mutation rate.

This type of dance can be shown to continue for 100,000s of iterations. However, if we explicitly ensure that, if one or other side has won no competition, it takes random values as its new starting point, we get a much more interesting situation shown in Figure 9.

We see that sudden transitions in one AI's strategies are followed by very fast transitions in the other AI's strategies. This is very close to human behaviour. If you are being beaten 10-0 in a game, you are clearly not in the sort of position in which fine tuning your strategies is going to be effective; only a major change in strategy-set is going to be effective.

The last diagram in Figure 9 shows the number of times out of 10 that each AI won.

When one AI reaches 10, its opponent who won 0 of the last round is completely randomised. Rather counter intuitively, if we decrease the rate of mutation, we increase the number of times this randomisation kicks in. This is due to the fact that a low mutation rate leads to more exploitation and less exploration and so the AI which finds a good niche first, is able to wipe out its opponent very quickly.

The punctuated equilibrium of such simulations is clearly shown in Figure 10 in which we give one AI a much higher mutation rate than the other.

Cooperating Strategies

Now we wish to investigate whether our AIs can **cooperate** with each other. To do this, we create a typical game situation: we have three AIs each with slightly different interests. We create a payoff function discussed by Fudenberg and Tirole (1991, p. 15). Let us have thee AIs labelled 1, 2, and 3 and let the possible strategies be labelled *A*, *B*, and *C*. The game consists of each of the AIs choosing a strategy

Figure 9. By randomising the AIs strategies when it has won no competitions, we get much more interesting behaviours. The last diagram shows the number of times out of 10 that each AI won.

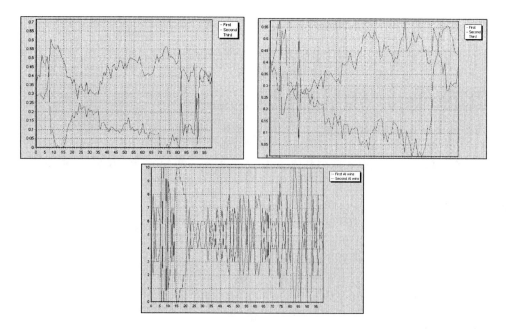

Figure 10. A type of punctuated equilibrium is found when we use randomisation. For this simulation we used two different mutation rates.

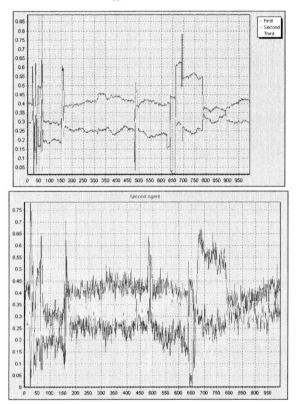

and the strategy with the highest number of votes wins. If no strategy has a higher number of votes than any other, A wins by default. The payoff functions are:

$$\mu_1(A) = \mu_2(B) = \mu_3(C) = 2$$
$$\mu_1(B) = \mu_2(C) = \mu_3(A) = 1$$
$$\mu_1(C) = \mu_2(A) = \mu_3(B) = 0$$

where we are using $\mu_i(X)$ as the payoff for AI$_i$ on strategy X. At each stage, we give the AIs no global information, we merely select from each population of strategies separately a strategy which gives that particular AI the best payoff at that stage in the simulation. If there is more than one strategy, a strategy is selected randomly from the optimal ones.

The results of one typical simulation are shown in Figure 11. The figure shows one of the strategies during each round which was optimal for each agent.- AI_1 in red, AI_2 in green, and AI_3 in yellow. Level 0 indicates strategy A, level 1 indicates strategy *B*, and level 2 indicates strategy *C*. The AIs initially all compete, and then there is a short spell from round 200 to round 450 when each AI prefers its own optimal strategy to get a payoff of 2 each time. During this time, the diversity is being driven from the population till there comes a time when AI_2 can no longer find another *B* in the population to gain a payoff of 2. At this time its only chance of escaping the payoff of 0 is to switch to cooperate with AI_3 (i.e., vote for strategy *C*) to get a payoff of 1. This it does for the remainder of the simulation. At the end the population is totally converged to AI_2 and AI_3 voting for *C* while AI_1 continues to vote for *A* (there is no incentive for it to change).

Thus we have in effect a consortium involving AI_2 and AI_3 playing together against AI_1. AI_3 might be thought of as the stronger partner in this consortium since it is gaining the greatest payoff each time but there is no incentive for AI_2 to change. If AI_1 were really intelligent, it would change to strategy *B* since then AI_2 would change its strategy to 2 and both AI_1 and AI_2 would gain. This might be done with randomisation.

Incomplete Information

Perhaps one of the most interesting aspects of modern computer games is the 'fog of war' in which players are playing a game with **incomplete information**. We now investigate responses to incomplete information.

Figure 11. Level 0 indicates strategy A, level 1 indicates strategy B, and level 2 indicates strategy C.

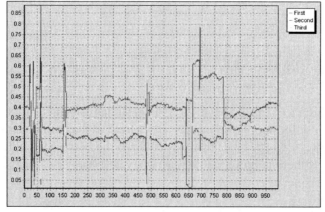

We create a Russian roulette game in which the AI player's strategies are created by an artificial immune system. The AI takes turns with its human opponent to pull the trigger of the gun (six chambers, only one bullet) when the gun is pressed to the player's temple. Each player may opt out of the game but in doing so loses face which is however preferable to losing life if the player pulls the trigger and the bullet happens to be in that chamber. Thus we have three possible outcomes for the AI, which in order of preference are:

1.   The AI wins either because the human has been killed or opted out; the AI does not care which of these it is since it wins in either case.
2.   The AI opts out of the game.
3.   The AI is killed.

We initially set up a situation in which the AI has 10 random strategies and play the game 100 times. Each strategy will have two integer values: a 1 equivalent to pulling the trigger at this round, and a 0 equal to opting out of the game at the current round. Each round of the game in which the AI pulls the trigger and is not killed, the AI gains one point. If the current strategy opts out of the game at any round, it gains 0.5. If it pulls the trigger and dies, it gains 0. The best strategy each round is cloned up to the death round. Figure 12 shows the results of six simulations. The first 100 columns show the total number of trigger pulls in each of the three rounds over the 10 strategies in the population when the bullet is in the first chamber. If the AI pulls the trigger the first time, it will die. Therefore the most successful strategy is to quit the game immediately. That this happens is shown by the quick drop of the red line to zero. Since the other two strategies occur after the AI has dropped out of the race they remain at their original levels for the whole game. The second round shows the strategies of the AI when the bullet is in the second chamber (which will be used by the human). Now it pays the AI to pull the trigger on the first round and so the red line climbs to 10: the whole population of strategies opts to pull the trigger the first time. Again the second and third round strategies are unaffected since they come after the game has finished. The third hundred shows what happens during the third game when the bullet is in chamber 3. Now the AI pulls the trigger the first time but opts out of the game on the second round (the green line drops to 0 showing that the whole population has opted out of the game at that round.). Continuing in this way we see that for each game of 100 rounds the AI has found the optimal strategy for playing the game each time. Note that at no time are we giving the AI information as to where the bullet is. Clearly the AI is responding to the position of the bullet appropriately.

Figure 12. Each group of 100 shows the response of the AI to a game of 100 rounds when the bullet is in the first chamber (1-100), when the bullet is in the second chamber (101-200), and so forth.

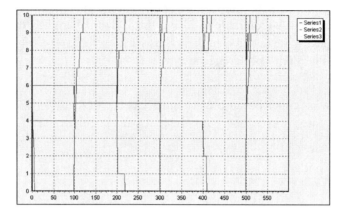

Changing the Game

The game described above is somewhat unrealistic since God has decided where the bullet is and determined that the bullet is in the same position each time the game is played. Let us now alter that. For each iteration of the game, we use a different randomly chosen chamber for the bullet. The results for a simulation with 100 strategies over 1,000 iterations are shown in Figure 13.

Figure 13. The red line is the number of strategies out of 100 which pull the trigger in the first round. The green is the number of strategies who pull the trigger in the second round. The blue is the number of strategies who pull the figure in the third round.

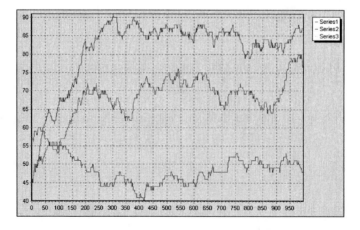

For the first round of each game, the probability of being killed if you pull the trigger is 1/6. Therefore the probability of not being killed is 5/6 (~0.83). We see that the red line which is the number of strategies out of 100 which pull the trigger first time is around this value. Similarly, if we get to round 2, there are four chambers left only one of which contains the bullet and therefore the probability of not being killed by pulling the trigger is 3/4. The green line is around this value. Finally if we get to the third round, the probability of being killed by pulling the trigger is 1/2 and the blue line is around this value.

Duelling

The classic one-on-one shoot'em up game may be characterised as a duel between two opponents who are trying to kill each other as they move towards each other. Let us again abstract out the important features of this game. Let the opponents be initially at a distance $D = 1$ from each other. Let each of two AIs have a set of binary strategy vectors each of length 10. Then if $AI_1[i] = 1$, AI_1 will fire when it is at the ith position. If $AI_1[i] = 0$, AI_1 will wait. Similarly with AI_2. Now we must give each a probability vector for hitting the other and this probability vector is dependent on the distance apart the two AIs are. Let $p_1(d)$ be the probability that AI_1 hits AI_2 when they are a distance d apart and $p_2(d)$ be the corresponding probability for AI_2 to hit AI_1. Let $p_1(d) = 1 - d$ and $p_2(d) = 1 - d^2$. Then, since $d < 1$, AI_2 is a better shot than AI_1.

In our artificial immune system simulation, we give each AI 100 strategies and run the simulation for 1,000 iterations. Each time we randomly select a pair of strategies, one from AI_1 and one from AI_2, to duel with each other. We clone the winning AI strategy up to the point that the shot is fired. Results are shown in Figure 14.

From the top figure, we see that the preferred AI_1 strategy is to wait for five time intervals and shoot on the sixth. AI_2's strategy is slightly more complex. About 75% of the games, AI_2 also waits five times and shoots on the sixth. But on the other 25% of the games AI_2 waits six time intervals and shoots on the seventh.

These figures accord well with the theoretic value given by Binmore (1992, page 132).

Discussion

The immune system discussed by Jerne considered sets of lymphocytes which are all identical, particularly with respect to their capability for generating antibodies

Figure 14. Top: AI$_1$'s strategy. Five waits (0s) followed by one shot(1s). Some times corresponding to those distances smaller than the distance the shot is fired are unchanged; one is changed by chance. Bottom: the corresponding strategy for AI$_2$.

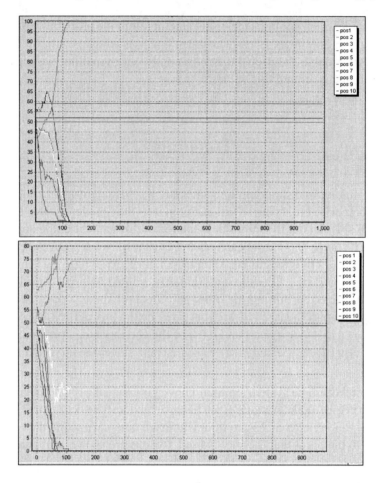

of a particular type. Let the number of antibodies of type i be s_i. Then the rate of change of the s_i is characterised by:

$$\frac{ds_i}{dt} = s_i \sum_{j=1}^{N_1} f(e_j) - s_i \sum_{j=1}^{N_2} g(i_j) + k_1 - k_2 s_i \qquad (1)$$

where k_1 is the rate at which new instances of type i enter the population and k_2 is rate at which these lymphocytes are removed from the population. $f()$ models the excitatory effect of another N_1 lymphocytes in the network while $g()$ models the inhibitory effect from another N_2 lymphocytes.

The **Lotka-Volterra equations** were derived to explain the relationship between the numbers of predator-prey systems. Let there be x prey and y predators in a population. The basic assumption of the system is that the rate of growth of x in the absence of predators is constant that is, $\dfrac{x}{x} = a$ but that it decreases linearly in the presence of a population y of predators. This leads to $x = x(a - by)$.

Similarly one can argue that, if there were no prey, the predators would have to die but, the more prey there are, the more predators there can be. This gives us $y = y(-c + dx)$ so that a, b, c, and $d > 0$. This set of equations has been extensively analysed (e.g., Hofbauer & Sigmund, 1998).

The Lotka-Volterra equations can be generalised for n populations as:

$$s_i = s_i \left(r_i + \sum_{j=1}^{n} a_{ij} s_j \right) \tag{2}$$

where s_i is the size of the ith population. The r_i is the intrinsic growth or decay of the ith population and a_{ij} is the (linear) effect which population j has on population i.

There are only two differences between the two models:

1. The first model (1) presupposes a decay rate whereas the second (2) allows a growth rate.

2. The rate k_1 at which new instances of type i enter the population is independent of the current value of s_i.

Thus only a very small adjustment to Jerne's model allows us to state that the second model is a linear version of:

$$\frac{ds_i}{dt} = s_i \left\{ \sum_{j=1}^{N_1} f(e_j) - \sum_{j=1}^{N_2} g(i_j) + k_1 - k_2 \right\} \tag{3}$$

Now Jerne's main point was that there is dynamics at work in the immune system so that it is continually changing even in the absence of any attack by any antigen. Thus there are no specific interactions in his equations between the immune system and antibodies. However we can simply treat antigens as new populations thus including them in the N_1 or N_2 populations, depending on their effect on the current lymphocyte.

Interestingly, Hofbauer and Sigmund (1998) have also considered systems of equations from dynamical games theory known as replicator dynamics. Consider the situation in which we have n strategies in a population all competing with each other and let us allow the process of evolution to work on the population. If the fitness of strategy i is f_i, then using the terminology above, the rate of increase of the ith strategy $\frac{\dot{s_i}}{s_i}$ depends on how fit the ith strategy is compares to the general population at that time. That is, $\frac{\dot{s_i}}{s_i} = f_i - \overline{f}$ where $\overline{f}$ is the average fitness of the population.

Hofbauer and Sigmund show that if $f()$ is a linear function of $\mathbf{s}$, the population at that time, then the orbits of the replicator dynamics are equal to the orbits of the generalised Lotka-Volterra system.

Comparison with Gas

There is clearly a family resemblance between AIS and the genetic algorithms (Gas) described in Chapter VII. We investigate this in the context of path planning in a very simplified environment.

Path Planning

Path planning is a common problem in the field of game AI because we desire our characters to be able to navigate around game worlds. Navigation is most often performed in computer games with symbolic AI algorithms such as A*. Such algorithms are now standard fare and somewhat distant from leading edge research in artificial intelligence. We investigate in this chapter some of the more recent algorithms applied to this task.

In this example, we assume a graph based navigation system and investigate the problem of static obstacle avoidance using the computational intelligence techniques: genetic algorithms (GAs), artificial immune systems (AIS), and ant colony optimisation (ACO). These techniques have individually been applied to path planning in the past but the time is now apposite for a comparative study of their performances. We accept that there is little incentive to use techniques such as these for path planning in commercial software when $A*$ (and its many variants) work extremely well at solving such problems, and with superior performance than that likely to be offered by evolutionary approaches. Nevertheless, the path planning examples presented here does provide useful demonstrations of the modern techniques.

Formulating the Environment

For this experiment, we will set up the terrain/search space as follows: We set up an m by n grid with each possible location labelled as:

$$n-1 \quad 2n-1 \quad 3n-1 \qquad . \qquad . \qquad . \qquad m*n-1$$

$$n-2 \quad 2n-2 \quad 3n-2 \quad . \qquad . \qquad . \qquad .$$

$$.$$

$$.$$

$$. \qquad\qquad\qquad .$$

$$.$$

$$0 \qquad n \qquad 2n \qquad . \qquad . \qquad . \qquad (m-1)n$$

We use a grid where $m = n = 10$, and place obstacles on the terrain at the following locations: $30 - 36$, 39, $70 - 71$, and $74 - 79$ so that the terrain is as shown in Figure 15. Note that the game is played on a cylinder where we have wraparound so that for example, location 29 is adjacent to location 30.

We wish to find a path from the 'START' side of the grid to the 'FINISH' side. We restrict the movement of the path to forward ($\rightarrow$), left ($\uparrow$), and right ($\downarrow$). However,

Figure 15. The artificial terrain: A path must be found from the start side to the finish side avoiding the two walls

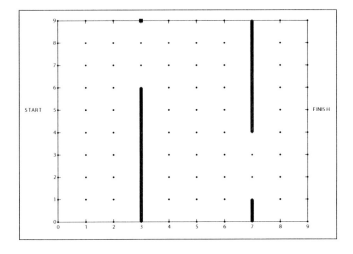

we allow the path to wrap around the grid; that is, moving left from location $n - 1$ will lead to location n, and moving right from location n will lead to location $n - 1$. The paths may not traverse the obstacles.

Each chromosome in the population represents a path that starts from the START side of the grid and complies with the constraints defined above, and consists of an array of grid points which constitute the path. Figure 16 illustrates the two paths:

a) | 0 | 1 | 2 | 12 | 22 |

b) | 5 | 6 | 16 | 26 | 27 | 37 | 47 | 57 | 56 | 55 | 65 | 64 | 63 | 73 | 83 | 93 |

If the two chromosomes are not the same length then we crop the longer chromosome to the length of the shorter one. A crossover point is then randomly selected, and from this point for each chromosome we change the genetic material so that it

Figure 16. Two examples of chromosomes representing possible paths through the terrain. (a) Shows a path which goes from START and stops at an obstacle whilst (b) represents a path between START and FINISH.

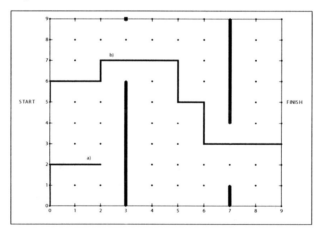

Figure 17. The modified crossover operator ensures no invalid paths are followed

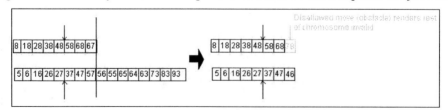

follows the same path shape as the other. If at any point, the path moves to a location that is disallowed, we discard the rest of the chromosome.

Simulations

We report on two sets of simulations:

4.   Finding any possible path from START to FINISH.
5.   Finding the shortest path.

Finding any Possible Path (GA and AIS)

We ran each simulation for 10,000 generations/iterations, using a fitness function of,

$$f(d) = \frac{1}{d+1} \qquad (4)$$

where d is the distance of the end point of the path from the FINISH side. The parameters used were,

GA parameters: Population size: 100, Crossover rate: 0.01, Mutation rate: 0.01
AIS parameters: Population size: 100, Mutation rate: 0.1, ß: 0.01

Table 2 shows average values and standard deviation of the time taken to find a path to the finish. Both algorithms find a possible path; the artificial immune system is somewhat faster.

It was found that the both the GA and AIS converge to a solution that finds a path to the FINISH side. Figure 18 shows the typical evolution of the mean and best fitness

Table 2. Mean and standard deviation of time taken to find path to finish

Mean generation which first found path to finish	Σ
37.0	47.8
19.2	8.2

with each generation/iteration, and shows that both path planning algorithms quickly converge to valid possible paths across the terrain (i.e., have fitness of 1).

The crossover and mutation operators act as a way of exploring the search space for the GA. The exploration is done by the mutation operator in the AIS. The Roulette wheel selection enables exploitation of good solutions for the GA while the clone operator performs the same function in the AIS.

Figure 18. The evolution of mean and best fitness of the population for the AIS (top) and GA (bottom) path planning algorithms with each iteration and generation respectively. Those solutions with fitness 1 represent possible valid paths that connect the START to the FINISH side of the terrain.

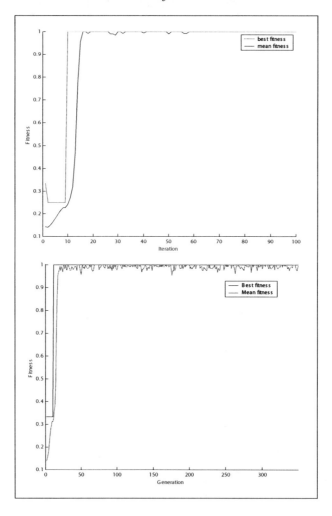

The AIS outperformed the GA. However it may be possible that the GA solutions are in some way better than those found by the AIS. We thus, in the next section, penalise poor quality solutions, that is, longer meandering solutions.

Finding the Shortest Possible Path (GA and AIS)

To find the shortest possible path from the START side of the terrain to the FINISH side, we modified the fitness function used in the previous section to include a penalty for longer paths:

$$f(d,l) = \frac{1}{d+1} - \alpha l \tag{5}$$

where d is the distance of the end point of the path from the FINISH side, and l is the length of the path.

GA parameters: Population size: 100, Crossover rate: 0.01, Mutation rate 0.01

AIS parameters: Population size: 100, Mutation rate 0.1, ß: 0.01

Figure 19. Fitness function used to find the shortest possible path across the terrain

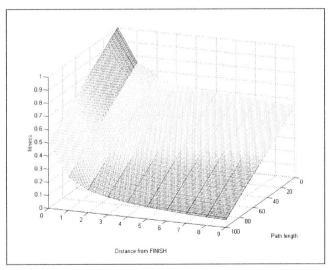

We ran each simulation for 100 iterations, using $\alpha = 0.01$ giving a fitness function of:

$$f(d,l) = 0.5\left(1 + \frac{1}{d+1} - 0.01l\right)$$

which has been scaled to give fitness values between 0 and 1, as shown in Figure 19.

Figure 20 shows the best paths found by the GA at generations 500, 3000, and 8000.

Table 3. Both algorithms find similar lengths of paths with the AIS again somewhat better.

Path algorithm	Average length of best shortest path
GA	23.5
AIS	21.8

Figure 20. The best path found by the GA at generations 500 (top left), 3000 (top right), and 8000 (bottom).

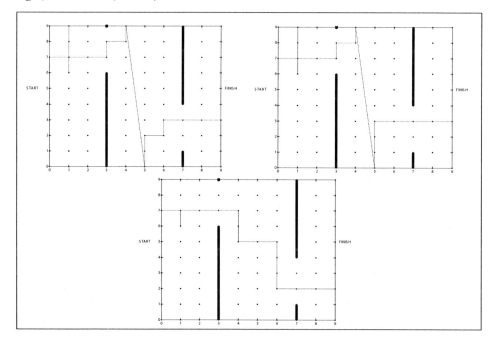

Figure 21. The best paths found by the AIS at iterations 10 (top left), 200 (top right), 600 (bottom left), and 800 (bottom right) respectively.

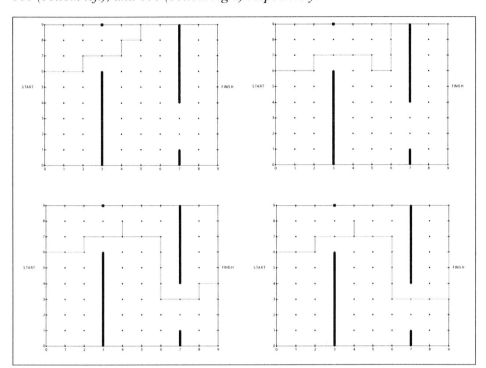

Note that while we have shown the path as crossing the terrain from location 49 to location 50 in the top two diagrams, the actual route uses the wrap around effect due the map lying on a cylinder.

Figure 21 shows the best paths found by the AIS at iterations 10, 200, 600, and 800. Note that both the final best GA path and the final best AIS path both contain an irrelevant lateral movement. Such movements contribute nothing to the fitness of the chromosome or antibody (indeed are penalised under the new fitness function) but are difficult to mutate out of the path with the current definition of the operators.

Both algorithms do not find the optimal shortest path for the terrain. We also find that due to the way that the mutation operator is defined in both cases, that the algorithms cannot correct suboptimal (i.e., not the shortest) sections of path near to the START side of the terrain.

Conclusion

We have in this chapter shown, in the context of a very simplified abstract real-time strategy game, how the concepts from the realm of artificial immune systems can be used to give the AI more intelligence in dealing with a human who is creating novel strategies in the game in real time. In all simulations discussed in this chapter, we have initiated the AI's strategy randomly yet shown that the AI's response to the human's strategy is approximately optimal and very fast. The fact that in each simulation we see that the AI's response gets to approximately the correct level but changes rather a lot around this level is, perhaps, no bad thing; after all, when two humans play, their play will not be exactly the same each and every day. Some randomness in the AI's response is liable to make its strategies appear more human-like.

The proposed method creates AIs which are optimal for the particular environment in which they have learned; in other words, each AI's strategy is determined by the strategies which have been used against it by the human player. Thus AIs which have been playing against different humans will be different: each human player has a individualised opponent. This opens up the possibilities of:

- Having AIs play against each other. A tournament of AI players with learning turned off would determine the most successful overall strategies.
- Having AIs learn from each other. Each AI has learned slightly different strategies and by learning from other AIs would create opponents for the human which are much more difficult than the human's own AI alone.

References

Binmore, K. (1992). *Fun and games*. DC: Heath and Co.

Dasgupta, D. (2000). *Artificial immune systems and their applications*. Springer-Verlag.

De Castro, L. N., & von Zuben, F. J. (1999). Artificial immune systems: Part 1—Basic theory and applications (Tech. Rep. TR DCA 01/99). Retrieved December 2006, from ftp://ftp.dca.fee.unicamp.br/pub/docs/vonzuben/Inunes

De Castro, L. N., & von Zuben, F. J. (2000). Artificial immune systems: Part 2—A survey of applications (Tech. Rep. TR DCA 02/00). Retrieved December 2006, from ftp://ftp.dca.fee.unicamp.br/pub/docs/vonzuben/Inunes

Fudenberg, D., & Tirole, J. (1991). *Game theory*. Boston: MIT Press.

Hofbauer, J., & Sigmund, K. (1998). *Evolutionary games and population dynamics*. Cambridge University Press.

Jerne, N. K. (1974). Towards a network theory of the immune system. *Annals of Immunology*, *125C*, 373-389.

Chapter XI

Ant Colony Optimisation

Introduction

Ants are truly amazing creatures. Most species of ant are virtually blind; some of which have no vision at all, yet despite this, they are able to explore and find their way around their environment, discovering and 'remembering' routes between their nest and food sources. Ants exhibit complex social behaviours, with different roles assigned to different ants, and they are able to perform organised operations, even, for example, relocating their entire nest. Even a casual observer of an ant colony can see the efficiency and organisation with which they perform tasks such as foraging food. They are able to find and follow shortest paths between locations, negotiating obstacles between them, and this problem is an active area of interest in computer science, particularly in computer game AI.

What makes all of this possible is the acute sense of smell that ants have, and the secretion of *pheromones*, odorous chemicals that are deposited by the ants, and are subsequently smelt by other ants. For example, if an ant discovers a rich food source, it will return to the nest, secreting some *'trail pheromone'* (a particular type of pheromone chemical) on the way. Other ants will detect the pheromone trail and follow it, and they too will be likely to find the food source and will return to the nest depositing more trail pheromone on the way, making the trail even more likely to be discovered by other ants. The more ants that discover the food by the pheromone trail, the more likely it is that other ants will also discover it. It is as a result of this positive reinforcement that many ant species are observed to move in narrow trails that follow shortest paths.

These behaviours have inspired artificial intelligence algorithms that have produced impressive results in various combinatorial optimisation problems. Artificial ant colonies can be simulated in a computer, and can be used to find shortest paths in a similar way to biological ants. This idea was originally proposed by Moyson and Manderick (1988) and their ideas have been developed by several researchers, but most notably Dorigo and Stutzle (2004). Various artificial ant colony algorithms have been developed and successfully applied to problems such as the travelling salesman problem (TSP), network routing, and resource scheduling. Much of this research is recent, within the past seven years or so, and it is a vibrant and growing area of academic activity. This chapter provides an overview of the topic of ant colony optimisation (ACO) and shows how it can be applied to path finding and other general problems relevant to computer games.

Foraging Behaviour of Ants

Before we look at artificial ACO algorithms, we will provide a brief account of the behaviour of real ants observed under laboratory conditions. This account is not intended to be an in-depth study of ant behaviours, since our objective is not to accurately describe ant behaviours, but to provide a background to implementing intelligent algorithms inspired by ant species. As stated before, ants exhibit many different complex social behaviours; this section will focus on one of these behaviours: *foraging*.

During foraging, ants will leave their nest and search for food. We shall assume for now that no prior pheromone trails exist, and that the ants have no prior knowledge of the location of the food. With no scents to guide their paths, the ants will explore the area in random directions. A small number of ants may discover food sources by chance. They will take some of the food and carry it back to the nest, leaving a pheromone trail behind. As explained before, the trails will be positively reinforced by more ants, and the trails will be established with strong pheromone scents, guiding ants to the food. With some ant species, it has been observed that when an ant finds a food source, the amount of pheromone that it deposits depends (amongst other things) on:

- The richness of the food source.
- The length of the route that led the ant from its nest to the food source.

If an ant finds food, but it followed a very long route to find it, it will leave a weaker trail of pheromone than if it had found a short route to it. Moreover, if the ant found food, but did not perceive it to be a rich and plentiful source, the trail would also be weak. This means that a strong scent is more likely to lead to a plentiful food source that is nearby; weak scents may follow a long route, or may lead to a poor food source.

Finding the Shortest Path

Consider the situation where there is one ant nest and one food source, but two equal-length paths to the food, both of which have no pheromone trails at the start of the experiment. This situation has been investigated experimentally by various researchers (e.g., Goss, Aron, Deneubourg, & Pasteels, 1989) and it has been found that initially, the ants will follow both paths *almost* equally. However, given enough time, the ants will tend to favour one of the two paths. This observance has been explained by random favouring of one of the two paths. Due to random fluctuations in the ants' decision-making behaviour, one of the paths may be selected by slightly more ants that the other path, and this leads to slightly more pheromone being deposited on that path, which in turn results in more ants using it. This feedback continues and one path is therefore favoured over the other one.

Investigations have been conducted by observing the behaviour of ants using two paths of different lengths, with varying ratios of the short path to the longer path, l_s/l_l (Deneubourg, Aron, Goss, & Pasteels, 1990; Goss et al., 1989). The results were that initially both paths are used by the ants, but as time progresses, more ants use the shorter of the two paths. This behaviour can be explained in two ways. First, suppose that an equal number of ants choose each of the paths, and for each path, we count the number of ants that travelled from the nest to the food and back again within a given period of time. We would expect more of these journeys to be completed for the shorter of the two paths, and there will therefore be more pheromone deposited on the shorter path, establishing the shorter path as the favoured one. This holds true, even if the ants deposit pheromone at the same rate, regardless of the path that they followed.

The other explanation takes the concentration of pheromone deposition into account.

At the start of the experiment, the ants cannot detect any strong pheromone trail, and so they select one of the two paths without particular preference. At the end of the trail they will find food, although those that chose the longer path will have walked longer to find it and on their return journey they deposit a weaker concentration of pheromone than the ants that chose the shorter path. After a sufficient period of time it is the shorter of the two paths that has the strong pheromone trail.

Simulating Artificial Ant Colonies with the S-ACO Algorithm

The previous section showed that by having a simple decision-making process in each ant, collectively the ants are able to solve problems that appear to be intelligent. This can be simulated in software to find shortest paths. The objective of this chapter is to introduce the reader to the topic of ACO in the context of computer game AI. For a fuller coverage of the topic, and a more rigorous theoretical analysis, see work by Dorigo and Stützle (2004). The algorithm that is described is known as simple ant colony optimisation, or S-ACO for short.

Goal Seeking

To begin with, we will consider artificial ants moving on a graph data structure. The simplest problem to start with is the double bridge problem shown in Figure 1(a).

This graph shows three nodes: node 1 represents the nest, and node 3 represents the food source. The three arcs are deemed to be of equal length. Two paths from the nest to the food are in this graph, and one is twice the length of the other. (For now, all arcs of the graph are deemed to be of equal length, although we will later consider using weighted graphs that have arcs of varying length or cost.) Each arc connecting two nodes, i and j has an amount of pheromone on it, τ_{ij}, which is initialised to a small positive amount, α, the same across all arcs. (The value of α is not critical, although in our experiments we have used a value of 0.1) When an ant, k, is at a node, i, the probability of selecting the arc leading to node j is expressed as the amount of pheromone on the arc ij as a proportion of the sum of the amounts of pheromone on *all* arcs in the *neighbourhood* of the ant. This neighbourhood is the set of nodes that an ant, k, may choose as the next node to travel to, and is represented by N_i^k. This may be the same thing as the set of nodes, S_i, directly connected to node i but it can be beneficial to restrict the choice to a set $N_i^k \subseteq S_i$. For example, it is advisable to omit from N_i^k the node that was last visited to prevent ants from turning back or even repeatedly oscillating over the same arc or group

Figure 1. (a) A graph showing two possible paths from the nest to a food source. One route is twice the length of the other. (b) A graph showing four possible routes to a food source.

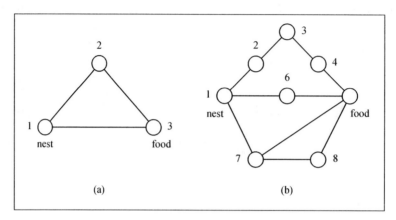

of arcs. (This could easily happen if one arc had a much higher concentration of pheromone than the others close to it.) The probability calculation is summarised in the equation below:

$$p_{ij}^k = \frac{\tau_{ij}}{\sum_{l \in N_i^k} \tau_{il}}, \text{ if } j \in N_i^k \tag{1}$$

If nodes i and j are not connected by any arc, then $p_{ij}^k = 0$. The denominator in the above equation should always be nonzero, and it is for this reason that nodes should be initialised to have a positive amount of pheromone, rather than zero.

Suppose that an ant follows a path and finds a food source. The ant must then return to the nest, depositing pheromones on the way. Each ant must therefore have states associated with it. For the time being, we will consider two states: 'find food' and 'return to nest.' When in the 'find food' state, the ant should start from the nest and at every branch a route should be selected at random. The selection of a branch, while random, should be according to the probabilities defined by equation (1). In the 'return to nest' state, the ant should simply retrace its steps back to the nest using the reverse route that it took to find the food.

Deposit of Trail Pheromone

As an ant moves back towards the nest in the 'return to nest' state, it should deposit some trail pheromone. The amount of pheromone deposited by ant k is denoted $\Delta\tau^k$, and the pheromone on an arc at time t is updated as follows:

$$\tau_{ij}(t+1) = \tau_{ij}(t) + \Delta\tau^k \qquad\qquad (2)$$

The value of $\Delta\tau^k$ is open to different implementation strategies. For example, it is possible for the algorithm to learn shortest paths by using a constant value of $\Delta\tau^k$ for all ants at all times since ants that choose shorter paths will deposit pheromone earlier and more frequently than ants that choose longer paths (as explained earlier). However, it is advisable to determine $\Delta\tau^k$ by a monotonically decreasing function of the path length from the nest to the food. This increases the favour shown to shorter paths, and causes the algorithm to converge more quickly. Good results have been achieved by using the reciprocal of the length L^k of the path found by ant k, as in the following equation:

$$\Delta\tau^k = \eta\frac{1}{L^k} \qquad\qquad (3)$$

The parameter η is normally a constant; all pheromone deposits are a proportion of this value.

Evaluating the Shortest Path Found

Suppose that the algorithm described so far is run for a required number of iterations, and we need to find the path that the algorithm has identified as being the shortest. This can be found by starting at the nest, and at each branch, following the arc that has the most pheromone on it. This is described by the recursive procedure shown in Figure 2 below.

Figure 2. Pseudo-code for a procedure to identify the shortest path according to the current state of the graph

```
procedure shortestPath(in: previousNode, in: currentNode, in/out: path)
        add currentNode to end of path
        if current node is food
                return
        else
                greatestPheromoneTrail = 0
                nextNode = null
                for all arcs connected to currentNode, except the one connected to  previousNode
                        if this arc's pheromone trail > greatestPheromoneTrail
                                greatestPheromoneTrail = this arc's pheromone trail
                        nextNode = node at the end of this arc
                        end if
                end for
                shortestPath(currentNode, nextNode, path)
        end if
end procedure
```

The above procedure is acceptable for the algorithm described so far when applied to simple graphs. We shall see shortly that some problems can occur with more complicated graphs. Note that the procedure is not guaranteed to return the shortest path; it is only the shortest path found so far according to the state of the pheromone trails in the graph. The trails will only determine the truly shortest path if the system has been sufficiently trained. Moreover, the S-ACO algorithm may be applied to NP-hard problems, for which there is no guarantee of finding a globally optimum route.

Table 1. Results on an artificial ant colony trained on the double bridge graph shown in Figure 1(a)

	Pheromone		
Arc	10 iterations	100 iterations	1000 iterations
1 → 2	0.225	0.875	2.825
2 → 3	0.275	0.875	2.825
1 → 3	0.950	21.000	238.210
% choosing shortest path (1→3)	65.00%	92.30%	97.68%

Table 2. Results on an artificial ant colony trained on graph shown in Figure 1(b) with 10 ants. Since there are two equally short paths, the percentage of ants choosing the correct path is the sum of the percentages taking the paths 1→6→5 and 1→7→5.

	Pheromone		
Arc	10 iterations	100 iterations	1000 iterations
1 → 2	0.1250	0.3500	2.0625
2 → 3	0.1375	0.3500	2.0625
3 → 4	0.1500	0.3500	2.0625
4 → 5	0.1625	0.3625	2.0625
1 → 6	0.1500	3.1000	34.9998
6 → 5	0.1500	3.1500	35.0248
1 → 7	0.1500	1.6083	17.3832
7 → 5	0.1500	1.2750	15.6499
7 → 8	0.1167	0.4333	1.8333
8 → 5	0.1167	0.4333	1.8333
% choosing shortest path (1→6→5)	35.29%	61.28%	64.28%
(1→7→5)	19.85%	23.73%	28.58%
Total	**55.14%**	**85.02%**	**92.86%**

Experiments

The algorithm described so far is sufficient to learn short paths through some simple graphs, and we now present results for the example graphs shown in Figure (1). In each of the experiments, one ant was spawned on the first iteration, and one additional ant was spawned on each successive iteration, up to a maximum of 10 ants. Initially, all arcs had a pheromone value of 0.1. The η parameter was set to 0.05, and the pheromone deposit was according to equation (3). For the double-bridge problem, as in Figure 1(a), good results are achieved after as few as 10 iterations, and these are shown in Table 1.

The results show very fast convergence to the shortest path; however, this is a very trivial problem to solve. The graph in Figure 1(b) presents a slightly more challenging problem, since there are five possible paths to take, two of which are equally short paths: $1 \rightarrow 6 \rightarrow 5$ and $1 \rightarrow 7 \rightarrow 5$. The results of that experiment are shown below in Table 2 (10 ants) and Table 3 (50 ants).

Even with only 10 ants, the shortest path has been found after only 10 iterations, with over 50% of ants choosing one of the two shortest paths. Increasing the number of ants to 50 marginally increases the confidence with which the shortest path can be found. The path $1 \rightarrow 6 \rightarrow 5$ was favoured over $1 \rightarrow 7 \rightarrow 5$ after 100 iterations in this particular simulation, although in some other runs of the simulation, path $1 \rightarrow 7 \rightarrow 5$

Table 3. Results on an artificial ant colony trained on graph shown in Figure 1(a) with 50 ants

Arc	Pheromone	
	100 iterations	1000 iterations
$1 \rightarrow 2$	1.2375	1.6125
$2 \rightarrow 3$	1.2500	1.6125
$3 \rightarrow 4$	1.2875	1.6125
$4 \rightarrow 5$	1.3000	1.6125
$1 \rightarrow 6$	14.1749	173.7440
$6 \rightarrow 5$	14.3249	173.9190
$1 \rightarrow 7$	3.7416	110.7550
$7 \rightarrow 5$	2.9750	99.4288
$7 \rightarrow 8$	0.9167	11.5667
$8 \rightarrow 5$	0.9167	11.5667
% choosing shortest path ($1 \rightarrow 6 \rightarrow 5$)	74.00%	60.73%
($1 \rightarrow 7 \rightarrow 5$)	14.93%	34.68%
Total	**88.93%**	**95.40%**

was favoured. Note that the path $1\rightarrow7\rightarrow8\rightarrow5$, while not being the shortest path, has significantly higher pheromone levels than $1\rightarrow2\rightarrow3\rightarrow4\rightarrow5$, showing that it is closer to the shortest path. Figure 3 shows the effect of using different numbers of ants in the simulation. The graph clearly shows that using more ants gives a greater degree of confidence in finding the shortest path, as does training for more iterations.

Improvements to the S-ACO Algorithm

Dead Ends and Loops

The graphs used so far have served to introduce the S-ACO algorithm, although they represent very trivial problems in terms of finding the shortest path. The graph shown in Figure 4 is a more difficult problem because it has dead-end nodes, and more significantly, *loops*. It is possible for ants to take a longer path than necessary, perhaps including dead ends and loops, and then deposit pheromone on these unnecessary parts of their journey, which in turn leads other ants along these inefficient routes. Of course, the pheromone trails on dead-end subpaths will eventually lose their significance as shorter paths are discovered and more pheromone is left on those shorter routes; however, the situation is worse with loops. Arcs that are part of loops may have more pheromone deposited on them than the other arcs in the route, and this reinforces these inefficient subpaths. These complications have a profound effect on the time required to converge to the shortest path and can even prevent convergence.

Figure 3. Graph showing the percentage of ants choosing a shortest path against the number of training iterations

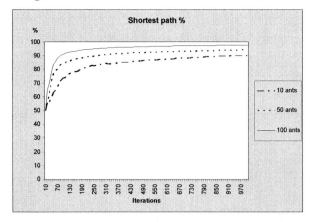

It was stated earlier in this chapter that the neighbourhood set N_i^k of a node i should include all other nodes that the node i is directly connected to by arcs, *except* the last node visited by an ant k. However, when an ant arrives at a dead-end node, the set N_i^k *must* include the previous node visited. In fact, the previous node will be the only element in the set N_i^k. This is a special case, as normally N_i^k does *not* include the last node visited.

Removal of Loops

Normally, when an ant arrives at a food source, it will simply retrace its steps back to the nest, depositing pheromone on the way. Loops can be removed from the path

Figure 4. A graph containing loops and dead ends

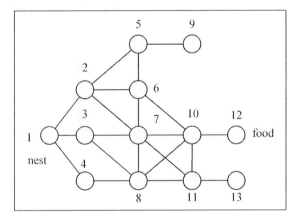

Figure 5. The path nest→a→b→c→a→d→e→f→g→h→c→food contains the loops a→b→c→a and c→a→d→e→f→g→h→c, which are staggered

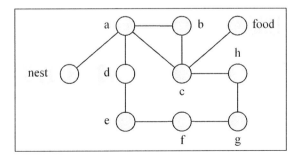

that is retraced by identifying nodes that were visited more than once. A path can contain multiple loops, and these can be nested. For example, consider the path $1\rightarrow 2\rightarrow 6\rightarrow 10\rightarrow 8\rightarrow 7\rightarrow 10\rightarrow 11\rightarrow 7\rightarrow 6\rightarrow 10\rightarrow 12$ from the graph in Figure 4. This path contains the loop $6\rightarrow 10\rightarrow 8\rightarrow 7\rightarrow 10\rightarrow 11\rightarrow 7\rightarrow 6$, which also contains loops within it, $10\rightarrow 8\rightarrow 7\rightarrow 10$ and $7\rightarrow 10\rightarrow 11\rightarrow 7$. By removing the outer loop, the inner loops are also eliminated. This is only true when the shorter loop is contained entirely within the larger loop. However, consider the situation where the loops are staggered, for example, the path nest$\rightarrow$a$\rightarrow$b$\rightarrow$c$\rightarrow$a$\rightarrow$d$\rightarrow$e$\rightarrow$f$\rightarrow$g$\rightarrow$h$\rightarrow$i$\rightarrow$c$\rightarrow$food on in Figure 5. This path contains two loops, a$\rightarrow$b$\rightarrow$c$\rightarrow$a and c$\rightarrow$a$\rightarrow$d$\rightarrow$e$\rightarrow$f$\rightarrow$g$\rightarrow$h$\rightarrow$c, but the smaller loop is not entirely contained by the larger loop. If the loop a$\rightarrow$b$\rightarrow$c$\rightarrow$a is eliminated, the path will be nest$\rightarrow$a$\rightarrow$d$\rightarrow$e$\rightarrow$f$\rightarrow$g$\rightarrow$h$\rightarrow$c$\rightarrow$ food, which contains no loops. Since the first visit to node c has been eliminated, the longer loop no longer exists. It would therefore be better to remove the loop c$\rightarrow$a$\rightarrow$d$\rightarrow$e$\rightarrow$f$\rightarrow$g$\rightarrow$h$\rightarrow$c instead, which would result in the final path nest$\rightarrow$ a$\rightarrow$b$\rightarrow$c$\rightarrow$food.

Figure 6 outlines a recursive algorithm for removing loops in largest-first order. The algorithm will remove all loops, starting with the largest, and will reduce any path to its shortest equivalent path without loops.

Pheromone Evaporation

The S-ACO algorithm as described so far can be applied to many static problems. However, what if the environment were to change over time, such as arcs of the

Figure 6. Pseudo-code for a procedure to remove all loops from a path, from largest to smallest

```
procedure removeLargestLoop(in/out: path)
        int loop_length = 0
        int loop_start;
        int loop_end;
        for i=first to last node in path
                for j= last node in path to i+1+loop_length /* descending */
                        if position i and position j of path are same node
                                loop_length=j-i;
                                loop_start = i
                                loop_end = j;
                        end if
                end for
        end for
        /* if a loop was found, remove it, and search for more loops */
        if (loop_length>0)
                remove nodes from i+1 to j
                removeLargestLoop(path);
        end if
end procedure
```

graph being removed, new arcs being added, or moving/removing food sources and/or nests? In that case, we would have a significant problem because once a path has been identified by a trail of pheromone it will never be removed. The solution is to allow pheromone trails to *evaporate*.

The trail pheromone that is deposited by real ants evaporates, and if a trail ceases to be followed by a significant number of ants, then the trail will gradually vanish. The rate at which the trail evaporates affects the 'memory' of the ant colony. Suppose, for example, that a rich food source was found by foraging ants, and a strong trail of pheromone was laid as a result, but after some time the food source was exhausted. Many ants would still follow the trail but find no food at the end of it. On return to the nest, they would not deposit the strong pheromone scent that they formerly did, and the trail would slowly evaporate. If the trail pheromone did not evaporate, then the ants would indefinitely continue to attempt to forage food from the exhausted food source.

Dynamic environments are common in computer games, and it is therefore desirable that game AI should adapt to changes in the game environment. We therefore add an evaporation term to the algorithm, which reduces the amount of pheromone on all arcs in the graph. In order to avoid arcs having zero probability of being followed by ants in the future (according to equation (1)), the amount of pheromone on each arc is constrained so that its minimum value is α, the term used for the initial pheromone level. Without this constraint, the values τ_{ij} would asymptote to zero for some of the arcs, making it impossible for the simulated colony to explore new areas of the graph. This is summarised in equation (4) below, where ρ is the *evaporation rate* parameter, and A is the set of all arcs in the graph,

$$\tau_{ij}(t+1) = \max((1-\rho)\tau_{ij}(t),\alpha), \forall (i,j) \in A \qquad (4)$$

This step is carried out for all arcs of the graph regardless of whether they have been visited by any ants. It works well when performed during every iteration of the algorithm, although it is also perfectly acceptable to perform this step less often, say every 20 iterations. Performing pheromone evaporation less often can reduce the computational cost of the S-ACO algorithm, making it more suitable in situations where processing resources for AI are scarce, which is often the case with video games. In the experiments presented in this chapter, the evaporation rate parameter was assigned a value of 0.01, and the evaporation was simulated on every iteration. If the evaporation were to be performed less often, the evaporation parameter, ρ, should be adjusted accordingly. The ρ parameter was assigned a value of 0.05.

The effectiveness of pheromone evaporation can be demonstrated by a simple path-finding problem where the environment changes over time. In the following scenario, a simulation was run on a graph that initially had one nest and two food sources, one closer to the nest than the other. After 1000 iterations of the algorithm, the closer of the two food sources was removed, and after a further 1000 iterations, it was replenished again. If the S-ACO algorithm is able to adapt to these changing circumstances, then the pheromone trails should initially converge to a path leading to the food source that is closest to the nest. When that source is exhausted, a new trail should be found, leading to the secondary food source. When the closer food source is replenished, the trail leading to it should be rediscovered. Figure 7 shows the graph that was used.

The S-ACO algorithm was run on the above graph for a total 3000 iterations, and the amount on pheromone on two arcs was sampled throughout the simulation. Figure 8 shows a plot of pheromone on the arcs nest→1 and nest→2 (which lead to food

Figure 8. Graph with one nest and two food sources

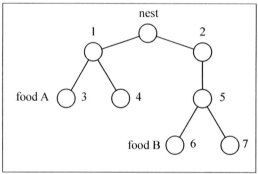

Figure 8. Pheromone levels on the paths leading to two different food sources. Food source 1 was removed after 1000 iterations, and replenished again after 2000 iterations.

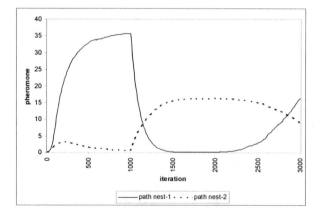

sources A and B respectively) over the 3000 iterations for which the simulation was run. Early in the experiment, source A is quickly established as the favoured food source. When food source A is exhausted after 1000 iterations, there is a rapid drop in the level of pheromone on the arc nest→1, and the other arc gains pheromone. At this point, no pheromone is being deposited on nest→1, since the arc leads to a dead end with no food. Any ants that follow this arc will be forced to travel back to the nest node and continue their search for food. The removal of loops ensures that they do not lay more pheromone on the trail that led them to the exhausted food source. After 2000 iterations, food source A is replenished, but source B remains available, albeit it is further from the nest than source A. There is a change in the pheromone trails, but it is more gradual than the previous change. The distribution of pheromone, combined with the fact that there are two plentiful food sources, mean that ants are unlikely to explore the arc nest→1. However, an initially small number of ants do explore the arc nest→1 and rediscover food source A, relaying the trail to this newly rediscovered source. After around 800 further iterations, food source A regains its status as the favoured food source.

We can conclude, therefore, that simulating evaporation of pheromone allows the S-ACO algorithm to learn and relearn shortest paths in a dynamic environment. In the following section, the algorithm is used as part of the AI for a computer game, although the food source *and* the nest will be allowed to move around the graph.

Case Study: S-ACO and Combat

The video game Combat was originally released by Coleco in 1977 in the form of a dedicated video game console. It was later reintroduced in 1982 as a cartridge for the Atari 2600 (originally known as the Atari 'Video Computer System' [VCS]) console. Atari sold the game bundled with their games console, and Combat became widely familiar and popular.

Overview of the Game Combat

The basic idea of the game is that two players each control a vehicle and attempt to shoot the opposing player's vehicle while avoiding shots aimed at their own vehicle. This is a classic gaming scenario that is still massively popular in online action games, particularly in the first-person shooter (FPS) genre. In the Atari 2600 cartridge version of the game, 27 different variations of the game were offered featuring three games types using tanks, biplanes, and jet fighters. This case study will focus on the variations of the game that used tanks, and so the remaining description of the game refers exclusively to this mode. Tanks can move around the playing arena or they can brake and remain stationary. They can also shoot, but only in the direction in which they are facing, that is, no rotating gun turrets. Some levels have walls that tanks cannot move through, and bullets cannot penetrate the walls. The gaming arena is viewed top-down, that is, from an aerial perspective. Some game modes feature bouncing bullets so that players can aim their shots to rebound off walls and into their opponent's vehicle. For the purposes of this case study, we will not consider bouncing bullets.

Despite Combat being such a dated game, it features the basic elements of strategic path finding, which permeates the majority of action-based video games, even today. The 1982 edition of the game did not feature any AI; the game was simply played by two human players. In this section, we will show how the S-ACO algorithm can be used for path finding in the control of an AI player in the game of Combat. In a scenario such as the one shown in Figure 9, for one player to shoot at their opponent, the tank must be moved around the obstacles, so that a straight line of fire can be established. Both players are able to move their tanks, so the AI player must be able to find shortest paths to a *moving* target. Our goal is to find a method that will allow the opposing player to be found in *any* design of level, unlike some of the more ad hoc approaches to path finding. Note that path finding is only one component of the AI; a full AI implementation would include evading the opponent's shots and determining lines of attack for firing shots.

In the 1980s, it was common for games to have very crude path-finding AI, which would simply move the AI player in the direction of its target. If a barrier prevented

Figure 9. Mock-up of the game Combat released in 1982 for the Atari 2600 games console

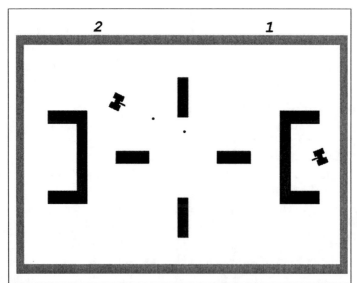

the player from moving further, then the AI player would be able to move no further. (For example, this behaviour was present in the 80s games Head Over Heels by Ocean Software and Avenger: Way of the Tiger II by Gremlin.) With modern games, players expect to see computer controlled game objects with more convincing intelligence. (McLean, 2004)

Before proceeding, it should be noted that there are numerous existing solutions to the problem of path finding in dynamic environments, and while we shall show that the S-ACO algorithm can be used to solve the path-finding problem, it is by no means the only solution or even the best solution; it is simply one of a number of algorithms that game developers may use, including the D* algorithm (Stentz, 1994). The often used A* algorithm is not a particularly good solution in this case, since it is not designed for dynamically changing environments.

Applying S-ACO to the Game

For the sake of simplicity and computational tractability, the playing arena can be represented as a discrete set of nodes, similar to the graphs that we have dealt with already in this chapter. Figure 10 shows a playing arena based on one of the levels from the Atari 2600 version of Combat, with 60 nodes defined. Arcs exist between nodes that are immediately adjacent vertically, horizontally, and diagonally, except where a barrier blocks a straight line being drawn between the two nodes. For example, the tank indicated by the square in Figure 10 can move up, down, right, or

Figure 10. The graph for a level of combat

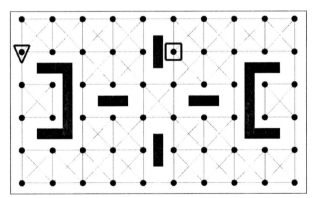

Note. Black dots indicate the nodes; the triangle indicates the position of the computer-controlled player, and the square indicates the position of the human player. Thin lines are used to show the arcs on which pheromone may be deposited. Players are unable to move through or shoot through the walls shown as thick black lines.

along either of the two diagonal arcs to its right, but not left or diagonally left due to the barrier to its left. Of course, this graph should be invisible to the player, and tanks should be able to move into the space between nodes, as with the original version of the game. Similarly, the game implementation should ensure that the AI moves in a realistic fashion using the nodes and arcs only as guides for targeting destinations.

Up until now in this chapter, all arcs have been treated the same, having equal cost associated with them. In this scenario, however, diagonal arcs must be treated differently from horizontal and vertical arcs, since they represent longer distances in the game arena. Therefore, each arc connecting two nodes i and j has a weight w_{ij}; vertical and horizontal arcs have a weight of 1, and diagonal arcs have a weight of $\sqrt{2}$.

Pheromone is now deposited using a modified version of equation (3):

$$\Delta\tau_{ij}^k = \eta\frac{w_{ij}}{L^k} \tag{5}$$

The probability of an ant k following an arc ij is redefined as:

$$p_{ij}^k = \frac{\tau_{ij}/w_{ij}}{\sum_{l\in N_i^k}\tau_{il}/w_{il}}, \text{ if } j \in N_i^k \tag{6}$$

Using these simple rules, a simulation was conducted where the computer-controlled player's position on the graph determined the position of the nest of the artificial ant colony, and the human player was treated as a food source. The nest (AI player) can be moved by selecting the arc connected to the nest's node, which has the most pheromone on it. As the human player moves around the playing arena, the AI player (i.e., the nest) is moved, and the AI player chases the human player. Figure 11 shows an example of the pheromone trails that are laid, leading to the human player.

Clearly, the AI has found the shortest path to the human player. There are actually three equally short paths, but one has been favoured over the other two, and this is expected due to continued reinforcement of the initial slight favouring of one of the paths. The simulation was continued. The human player anticipated that the AI player would move around the top-right of the barrier, and the human evaded the attack by moving the player around the bottom of the barrier. (Note that in these simulations, the human player was allowed to move faster than the AI player. In a fair implementation of the game of Combat, this would not be allowed, although in this case it has helped to demonstrate the effectiveness of the AI search mechanism.)

Figure 11. Pheromone trails leading the computer player to the human player

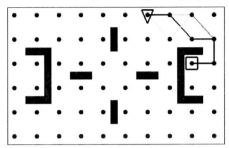

Note. Darker lines indicate arcs with stronger trails of pheromone. The triangle indicates the position of the computer-controlled player, and the square indicates the position of the human player.

Figure 12. Pheromone trails after the human player has evaded the computer player's attack around the top-right of the barrier

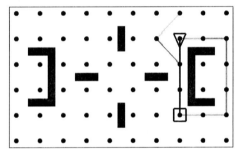

Figure 13. Pheromone trails after the human player further evades the AI player's attack

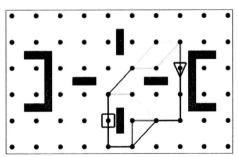

Figure 12 shows the state of play after the evasion of the AI attack. The AI player has adapted to the human player's movements, and has now found the path anticlockwise around the barrier. The figure shows a position where the computer may fire at its opponent and have a chance of scoring a point. The pheromone trail for the AI player's former (clockwise) route of pursuit still exists, and the clockwise trail now leads all the way to the human player, albeit it is not the strongest trail.

The human player further evaded attack by moving into another position so that two barriers are between the players. Very quickly, the AI has found paths to the human player. However, the shortest path (starting to the left of the AI player) is fainter than the path that it has followed, that is, straight down initially. At first, it may seem like the AI player has made a poor choice, although this can be explained by the fact that for the human player to move into its current position, it had to move across the bottom of the arena, and the computer player already chose the downward path as the shortest route to the human player at that time.

Defensive Play

Most people who play Combat use a combination of offensive and defensive tactics. If an AI player were to constantly attack, with no defensive play, then it would make an unconvincing opponent. It is common for AI bots in FPS games to use a combination of attacking and retreating, and the selected mode is often determined by the health levels of the players. If the AI player's health is low, the player may retreat, and the primary objective is to collect more health points. When the player's health is later restored, the player will resume to the offensive mode. The Atari 2600 version of Combat had no 'health' levels; players were simply killed whenever they were hit by a single shot from their opponent, so it may seem pointless to make the AI retreat. However, producing realistic retreating behaviour can make the AI more human-like, and retreating is still an interesting feature that is relevant in many other game scenarios.

A simple rule reversal in the method described so far will produce a convincing evasive strategy. When a new target node needs to be chosen for the nest to move to, select the arc that has the least pheromone on it. The player will then move away from its opponent, and will tend to move behind walls, using them as a defensive barrier. This behaviour is shown in Figures 13 and 14, which were taken from a simulation where the AI was in the retreat mode. If the simulation is allowed to continue without the human player (the square) moving, the AI continues to retreat further to the bottom-left corner of the arena. Pheromone trails build up on both routes around the barrier, and the AI player has effectively evaded the attack using the walls as a shield. If the human then pursues the computer player around one side of the barrier, the pheromone trail on the opposite side will weaken, and the computer player retreats towards the weak trail.

Figure 14. The human player (square) is in pursuit of the AI player (triangle)

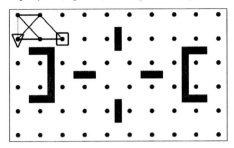

Figure 15. The AI player retreats from the human player, using the wall as a defensive barrier

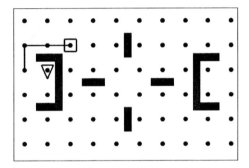

A combination of the two approaches can make a convincing strategy, for example, if the AI pursues its opponent, fires some shots, and then retreats. The AI could also sense when it is in danger of being shot, and go into retreat mode when necessary.

Summary

The previous sections have explained how the S-ACO algorithm has been inspired by the behaviour of biological ants, and how their collective intelligence emerges as a result of simple processing in each ant. Shortest paths can be found in graph structures by the S-ACO algorithm, and this can be applied to path-finding in computer games. We have seen how the method can be applied to the game of Combat and effective behaviour was produced that could form *part* of the AI mechanism for a computer player. The results have shown that the AI is able to move the tank towards the opposing player and can adapt to changes in the environment, including the evasive moves of the human player, and can also retreat when deemed appropriate.

Clearly, the S-ACO algorithm has been successful in finding shortest paths to the opponent in a dynamic environment. We can conclude that the S-ACO algorithm is therefore a viable option for a path-finding algorithm that can be used by game developers in dynamically changing scenarios.

Of course, there are other game genres that could have the S-ACO algorithm applied to them. Most real-time strategy (RTS) games involve the use of simple units that explore the surroundings and gather useful materials. Human players control these units using a point-and-click interface, but AI players could use the S-ACO algorithm to lay trails to resourceful parts of the environment, and this could allow the AI to perform well in truly dynamic environments with the programmer requiring no previous knowledge of the game levels to which the AI is applied.

Further Reading

SimAnt, designed by the legendary Will Wright and developed and published by Maxis/Electronic Arts, is a simulation game which puts the player in the role of a single ant in a colony. The goals of this game are for you to help lead your colonies to success in domination over a garden by gathering food, distributing eggs, and avoiding spiders and eliminating rival colonies. This game is of interest due to its implementation of pheromone trails; once one ant has left the nest and found food, it can follow its own trail back to the nest and then other ants can follow the food trail. The game also features comprehensive notes, and a 'laboratory' mode where environments can be modified so that players or students can then see how ants behave in the set-up environment.

References

Benzatti, D (2006). *Emergent intelligence*. Retrieved August 20, 2006, from http://ai-depot.com/CollectiveIntelligence/Ant-Colony.html

Deneubourg, J.L., Aron, S., Goss, S., & Pasteels, J.M. (1990). The self-organizing exploratory pattern of the Argentine ant. *Journal of Insect Behaviour, 3(1)*, 159-168.

Dorigo, M., & Stützle, T. (2004). *Ant colony optimization.* Cambridge, MA: MIT Press.

Goss, S., Aron, S., Deneubourg, J. L., & Pasteels, J. M. (1989). Self-organized shortcuts in the Argentine ant. *Naturwissenschaften, 76(12)*, 579-581.

McLean, A. (2004) Hunting down the player in a convincing manner. In S. Rabin (Ed.), *AI Game Programming Wisdom 2* (pp. 151-159). Hingham, MA: Charles River Media

Moyson, F., & Manderick, B. (1988) *The collective behaviour of ants: An example of self-organization in massive parallelism.* Paper presented at the AAAI Spring Symposium on Parallel Models of Intelligence, Stanford, California.

Stentz, A. (1994). *Optimal and efficient path planning for partially-known environments.* Paper presented at the IEEE International Conference on Robotics and Automation (pp. 3310-3317), San Diego, California. IEEE

Chapter XII

Reinforcement Learning

Introduction

Just as there are many different types of supervised and unsupervised learning, so there are many different types of reinforcement learning. Reinforcement learning is appropriate for an AI or agent which is actively exploring its environment and also actively exploring what actions are best to take in different situations. Reinforcement learning is so-called because, when an AI performs a beneficial action, it receives some reward which reinforces its tendency to perform that beneficial action again. An excellent overview of reinforcement learning (on which this brief chapter is based) is by Sutton and Barto (1998).

There are two main characteristics of reinforcement learning:

1. **Trial-and-error search.** The AI performs actions appropriate to a given situation without being given instructions as to what actions are best. Only subsequently will the AI learn if the actions taken were beneficial or not.

2.   **Reward for beneficial actions.** This reward may be delayed because the action, though leading to a reward (the AI wins the game), may not be (and typically is not) awarded an immediate reward.

Thus the AI is assumed to have some goal which in the context of games is liable to be: win the game, drive the car as fast as possible, defeat the aliens, find the best route, and so on. Since the AI has a defined goal, as it plays, it will learn that some actions are more beneficial than others in a specific situation. However this raises the exploitation/exploration dilemma: Should the AI continue to use a particular action in a specific situation or should it try out a new action in the hope of doing even better? Clearly the AI would prefer to use the best action it knows about for responding to a specific situation but it does not know whether this action is actually optimal unless it has tried every possible action when it is in that situation. This dilemma is sometimes solved by using ε-greedy policies which stick with the currently optimal actions with probability 1-ε but investigate an alternative action with probability ε.

Henceforth we will call the situation presented to the AI: the state of the environment. Note that this state includes not only the passive environment itself but also any changes which may be wrought by other agencies (either other AIs or humans) acting upon the environment. This is sometimes described as the environment starts where the direct action of the AI stops, that is, it is everything which the AI cannot directly control. Every state has a value associated with it. This value is a function of the reward which the AI gets from being in that state but also takes into account any future rewards which it may expect to get from its actions in moving from that state to other states which have their own associated rewards. We also create a value function for each action taken in each state.

In the next section, we will formally define the main elements of a reinforcement learning system.

The Main Elements

Formally, we can identify four main elements of a reinforcement learning system (Sutton & Barto, 1998):

1.   **A policy:** This determines what action the agent can take in each state. It provides a mapping from the perceived state of the environment to actions which can be taken in that state. It may be deterministic such as a simple look-up table or it may be stochastic and associate probabilities with actions which can be taken in that state.

2. **A reward function:** This defines the goal of the system by providing a reward (usually a floating point number) given to the AI for being in each state. Note that rewards can be positive or negative (i.e., penalties) and so define good and bad events for the AI. The AI's task is to maximise its rewards (over the whole game). The reward function is external to the AI; the AI cannot change the reward function during play but will instead change its policies in order to maximise its long term rewards.

3. **A value function:** This indicates the *long term value* of a state when operating under the current policy. Thus, for state s, when operating under policy π, and using $E_\pi\{.\}$ to indicate expected value when using policy π, we have a value function:

$$V^\pi(s) = E_\pi\{R_t \mid s_t = s\} = E_\pi\{\sum_{k=0}^{\infty} \gamma^k r_{t+k+1} \mid s_t = s\} \tag{1}$$

which is giving the long term value of the state in terms of the discounted rewards which can be expected when using this policy. Since the discount rate, $\gamma < 1$, the value of the rewards at time t decreases the further into the future they are given. $V^\pi(s)$ is called the *state-value function for policy* π. We also have an *action value function*:

$$Q^\pi(s,a) = E_\pi\{R_t \mid s_t = s, a_t = a\} = E_\pi\{\sum_{k=0}^{\infty} \gamma^k r_{t+k+1} \mid s_t = s, a_t = a\} \tag{2}$$

which measures the expected return from taking action a in state s. A greedy policy would always take the action which had the greatest state-action value. Note that whereas the rewards are immediate (associated with each state), the values take into account long-term success or failure and are predictions rather than immediate rewards. The AI will know precisely the reward/penalty for being in the current state but will use the value functions to predict or estimate the future rewards. Note that if $\gamma = 0$, we are simply taking the reward for moving under that policy to the next state, an extremely myopic reward function:

$$Q^\pi(s,a) = E_\pi\{R_t \mid s_t = s, a_t = a\} = E_\pi\{r_{t+1} \mid s_t = s, a_t = a\} \tag{3}$$

At the other extreme, we may have $\gamma = 1$ and perform no discounting at all which is usually only useful if we have a limited time span so that:

$$Q^\pi(s,a) = E_\pi\{R_t \mid s_t = s, a_t = a\} = E_\pi\{\sum_{k=0}^{K} r_{t+k+1} \mid s_t = s, a_t = a\}. \tag{4}$$

4.   **A model of the environment:** Not all reinforcement learning methods require such a model but those that do use these models for planning. The model is required to capture some essence of the environment so that it can be used to predict the next state of the environment given its current state and the AI's action. For a reinforcement method without such a model, every action is a trial-and-error action.

These are the bare essentials of a reinforcement learning system. The central importance of the reward functions must be emphasised. Note also the double uncertainty associated with the reward functions. Not only are they stochastic in that they are attempting to predict future rewards but we are often, while learning, having to estimate the functions themselves. This gives central importance to finding ways of accurately and efficiently estimating the correct values associated with specific policies.

Finding the Best Policy

There are a number of different ways of finding the optimal policy. We start with the simplest, the action-value methods, before discussing more sophisticated methods under the headings Dynamic Programming, Monte Carlo methods and Q-learning.

Action-Value Methods

Let the true value of an action, a, be $Q^*(a)$ while its estimated value at time t is $Q_t(a)$.
Then, if action a has been chosen k times prior to t resulting in rewards $r_1, r_2, ...,r_k$,
then $Q_t(a) = \dfrac{r_1 + r_2 + ... + r_k}{k}$, the average reward each time it has been performed.
It is possible to show that $Q_t(a) \to Q^*(a)$, as $k \to \infty$. A totally greedy rule would select the action, a^*, for which $Q_t(a^*) = \max_a Q_t(a)$, the action with the greatest perceived pay-off. However we wish all actions to be sampled and so we have to create a nonzero probability that all nonoptimal actions will be used at some stage. The three most common approaches are:

1.   Use an ε-greedy method. Select a random action with probability ε and the currently optimal action with probability $1-$ ε. Thus for an infinite learning process, each action will be sampled infinitely often and its reward can be calculated.

2. Select each action with probability $\dfrac{\exp(Q_t(a)/\tau)}{\sum\limits_b \exp(Q_t(b)/\tau)}$ which is known as Soft-max action selection.

3. Make an optimistic assessment of the value of each action at the start of the simulation. Any reward received will be less than this and so more exploration will be carried out.

The first method has the disadvantage that the second most optimal action has the same probability of being selected as the worst action, whereas the second method chooses actions proportional to the exponent of their perceived rewards. The third method is only used for stationary problems in which we use an update method which washes out the original estimate of the value. This is not the case for nonstationary problems for which we use a constant update rate (see below).

We note that we may incrementally update the values since,

$$Q_{k+1} = \frac{1}{k+1}\sum_{i=1}^{k+1} r_i = \frac{1}{k+1}\left(r_{k+1} + \sum_{i=1}^{k} r_i\right) = \frac{1}{k+1}(r_{k+1} + kQ_k) = Q_k + \frac{1}{k+1}(r_{k+1} - Q_k)$$

(5)

In this form, we can see that we are adjusting the estimated value incrementally to make it more like the current reward. For a nonstationary reward, we may decide to keep the step size constant to give $Q_{k+1} = Q_k + \alpha(r_{k+1} - Q_k)$ which will continue to track the changing values. One disadvantage of this is that the original value estimated at the start of the simulation remains as a bias in the estimated value after training, since,

$$Q_{k+1} = Q_k + \alpha(r_{k+1} - Q_k) = \alpha r_{k+1} + (1-\alpha)Q_k = \alpha r_{k+1} + (1-\alpha)r_k + (1-\alpha)^2 Q_{k-1}$$

$$= \sum_{i=1}^{k+1} \alpha(1-\alpha)^{k+1-i} r_i + (1-\alpha)^{k+1} Q_0$$

(6)

which is a weighted sum of the rewards but also the bias caused by the original estimate of the value of the action.

Dynamic Programming

Dynamic programming is a set of algorithms that can find optimal policies if they are given an accurate model of the environment. They typically iterate between:

1. **Policy evaluation:** Let $\pi(s,a)$ be the probability of performing action a when in state s, and let $P^a_{ss'}$ be the probability that we transit from state s to state s' after performing action a. Then the value for state s can be calculated from the values of all other states s' using a set of updates derived from the Bellman equations:

$$V_{k+1}(s) = E_\pi\{r_{t+1} + \gamma V_k(s_{t+1}) \mid s_t = s\} = \sum_a \pi(s,a) \sum_{s'} P^a_{ss'}\{R^a_{ss'} + \gamma V_k(s')\} \tag{7}$$

This is iterated over all states so that we are evaluating the policy as a whole while keeping the policy fixed.

2. **Policy improvement:** Now we know how good the current policy is, we can attempt to improve it. Thus we may select one action which is different from the current policy *and then subsequently revert to the original policy.* If we find that the new policy (the existing policy plus the change) is better than the existing policy, we accept the new policy. This is a greedy method.

$$\pi'(s) = \arg\max_a Q^\pi(s,a) = \arg\max_a E\{r_{k+1} + \gamma V^\pi(s_{k+1}) \mid s_k = s, a_k = a\}$$
$$= \arg\max_a \sum P^a_{ss'}\{R^a_{ss'} + \gamma V^\pi(s')\} \tag{8}$$

It can be shown that these two iterations will converge to the optimal policy. Sutton and Barto make a distinction between the algorithm above and that in which we perform several sweeps through the first (policy evaluation) stage. However it seems to be the case that there is no general rule as to which method is best; it is dependent on the particular problem we are dealing with. Indeed, in the policy evaluation part of the program, we may either have all policies evaluated dependent on the values of the other policies at the start of the sweep or we may use each newly evaluated policy to update all the others as we come to them. The latter method tends to be slightly faster as we might have guessed.

Example

We illustrate this method with an example from Sutton and Barto (1998). A gambler is betting against the house and will stop when money has run out or $100 is reached. At each moment in time, the gambler holds $\$x$ and so may bet any amount of money between 0 and the minimum of $\$x$ and $\$(100 - x)$. Thus the state is the gambler's capital, $\{1,2,\dots99\}$, and the gambler's actions are to bet $\{1,2,\dots \min(x,100 - x)\}$. The optimal policy should maximise the probability of getting to $100. If the probability of success on any one gamble, $p = 0.4$, is known, we may solve this problem with the above algorithm. We set an initial value of the state 100 at 1; all other states have initial value of 0. The results are shown below.

In Figures 1 through 3, we see that the rewards are gradually being backed up from the final most rewarded state of having \$100. Note that Figure 4 has the final policy which is very strict; it says bet as little as you need to do to reach the next jump state when you should bet all your money on one gamble.

Figure 1. The estimated values of each state after the first iteration

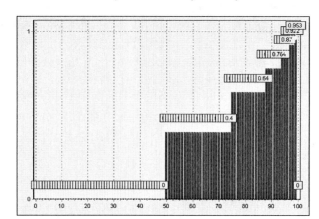

Figure 2. The estimated value of each state after only 2 iterations

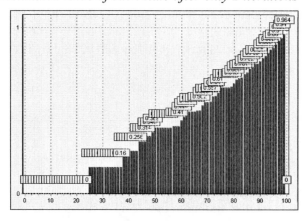

Figure 3. The final estimated values of each state

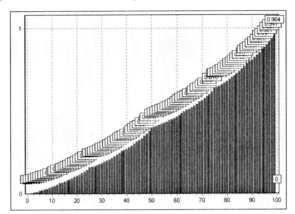

Figure 4. The final actions taken in each state. The height of the column represents the amount of the bet undertaken in the state.

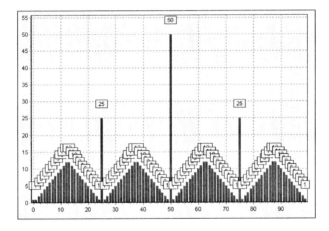

Monte Carlo Methods

Dynamic programming methods assume we have an accurate model of the environment. Monte Carlo methods make no such assumption but rather they learn from experiencing the environment and average the sample returns which they get from their experiences. Since we cannot investigate infinitely long sets of experiences, we assume that experiences occur in episodes which means we can always calculate returns and update policies and values when the episode completes. Having said that, we will see that there is a great deal of similarity between Monte Carlo methods and dynamic programming.

The simplest Monte Carlo method can be used for policy evaluation. It initialises the policy, π, for evaluation, and begins with a random state-value function and an empty list of returns for all states in S. Of course some states may not be known at the start of play so when a new state is encountered it initially has an empty list of returns. Then we iterate (forever):

1. Generate an episode using π
2. For each state s appearing in the episode:
    a. $R \leftarrow$ return following first occurrence of s
    b. Append R to the set of returns for s
    c. Value of s, $V(s)$ = average of the list of returns

An alternative is to find R for every occasion s is visited.

Note first that we did not require $P_{ss'}^a$ or $R_{ss'}^a$, which is necessary for the dynamic programming methods. We are letting the episode of data speak for itself. Note also that the estimate for one state does not build upon the estimate of any other state and so, unlike dynamic programming, the computational expense of the method is independent of the number of states.

However it is actions on which we really wish to be focussed and which we really wish to optimise. One assumption which the Monte Carlo method employs is that every state-action pair has a nonzero probability of being the starting point of an episode. However, the method has the same elements as before; the policy is evaluated and then, using the current evaluation, the policy is optimised. Thus the method is

1. Initialise for all s, a
    a. $Q(s,a)$ randomly
    b. $\Pi(s)$ randomly
    c. Returns$(s,a) \leftarrow$ empty list
2. Repeat (forever)
    a. Generate an episode using π
    b. For each state-action pair, s-a, appearing in the episode
        i. $R \leftarrow$ return following first occurrence of s,a
        ii. Append R to the set of Returns(s,a)
        iii. Value of s, $V(s)$ = average of the list of returns
    c. For each s in the episode, $\pi(s) = \arg \max_a Q(s,a)$

However, it is particularly important in Monte Carlo methods that we continue to explore the environment. Thus one version of Monte Carlo control uses an exploratory policy to generate episodes (the behaviour policy) while optimising the estimation policy. This is known as off-policy Monte Carlo control whereas the above algorithm uses on-policy control (we are generating episodes from the policy we are optimising). Off-policy control requires that every state-action pair which appears in the estimation policy has a nonzero probability of appearing in the behaviour policy. Also the updates to the estimation policy require taking into account the relative rate of appearances in each of the policies. See Sutton and Barto's (1998) work for details.

Temporal Difference Learning

Temporal difference (TD) learning is central to most modern reinforcement learning. It attempts to marry the best bits of dynamic programming—the updates to the values of policies being immediate—with the best of Monte Carlo methods—the updates being model-free and totally dependent on the experiences created by the current policies. Thus TD-learning is a bootstrapping method (like dynamic programming) in that it updates value estimates based on existing estimates of values,

$$V_{k+1}(s_t) \leftarrow V_k(s_t) + \alpha\{r_{t+1} + \gamma V_k(s_{t+1}) - V_k(s_t)\}.$$

Note the double estimation present in this. Instead of the expected value, it uses the value of a sample of the next state and also this value is itself used to bootstrap the estimation. Despite this double estimation, the TD method has been found to converge faster than Monte Carlo methods on stochastic tasks (which most interesting games are). To see why this is, Sutton and Barto (1998, p. 143) give a nice argument which we repeat here. Let us imagine you observe the following eight episodes:

A,0   B,0   B,1   B,1   B,1   B,1   B,1   B,1   B,0

The first episode starts in state A transits to B with a reward of 0 and terminates there with a reward of 0. The next six episodes all start at B and then terminate with a reward of 1. The final episode starts at B and immediately terminates with a reward of 0. We might agree that the value of B is 0.75 since that is the average return from B. TD learning would then say that on the one instance A was observed, it immediately moved to state B (with no reward) and so A's value should be the same as that of B, 0.75. However a Monte Carlo simulation would say that, in the single episode in which A was observed, the total reward was 0 and so A's value is 0. Thus Monte Carlo methods tend to fit the observed data very well but may be lacking in generalisation.

As with Monte Carlo methods, we can identify two types of TD control: on-policy and off-policy. On-policy TD control considers the transitions from one state-value pair to the next using $Q(s_t,a_t) \leftarrow Q(s_t,a_t) + \alpha[r_{t+1} + \gamma Q(s_{t+1},a_{t+1}) - Q(s_t,a_t)]$ after every transition. If s_{t+1} is terminal, $Q(s_{t+1},a_{t+1}) = 0$. This method is also known as Sarsa since it concentrates on the quintuple $(s_{t+1}, a_{t+1}, r_{t+1}, s_{t+1}, a_{t+1})$.

The off-policy TD control is also known as Q-learning and uses,

$$Q(s_t,a_t) \leftarrow Q(s_t,a_t) + \alpha[r_{t+1} + \gamma \max_a Q(s_{t+1},a) - Q(s_t,a_t)],$$

that is, regardless of the actual action taken during the episode, it uses the maximum possible value from the next state-action pair in its target.

Simulations

We illustrate the method with a route-finding task. The challenge is to find routes from anywhere on the square $[0,9] \times [0,9]$ to the point $(9,9)$, the goal. In Figures 5 and 6, we show examples of learned routes from three random starting locations. In training, each episode had a maximum of 1,000 states, each move gained a reward of -1 with a move off the board at the bottom or left being awarded -100 and a move off the other two sides being awarded -10. In both of the former cases, the

Figure 5. The routes found by Q-learning

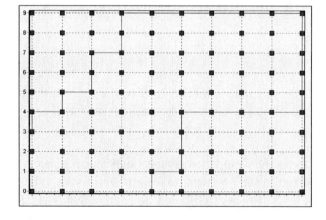

route is reinitialised to (0,0) while in the latter cases, the move is disallowed. The negative reward/penalty was to encourage a fast route to the goal. We see that both have found routes but of a different nature: Q-learning tends to go to one edge of the map and then follow it to the goal while Sarsa goes straight up the middle. These types of interesting divergences mean that both types of learning will form part of the arsenal of learning methods used by modern computational intelligence.

TD(λ) Methods

The above methods are actually known as TD(λ) methods. They change the valuation by looking one step ahead in the episode whereas Monte Carlo methods look ahead to the end of the episode before changing the valuation. This suggests that we might consider re-evaluations on the fly taking into account the states most recently met. One way to do this is keep a note of the trace of the states met and use it in the learning rule. Of course the trace itself needs to decay in time which is where the λ is used. An algorithm for TD(λ) is to generate an action and change state from s_t to s_{t+1} to get reward r_{t+1} and then calculate,

$$\delta \leftarrow r_{t+1} + \gamma V_k(s_{t+1}) - V_k(s_t)$$
$$e(s_t) \leftarrow e(s_t) + 1$$
$$\forall s$$
$$V(s) \leftarrow V(s) + \alpha \delta e(s)$$
$$e(s) \leftarrow \gamma \lambda e(s)$$

Figure 6. The solutions found by Sarsa learning

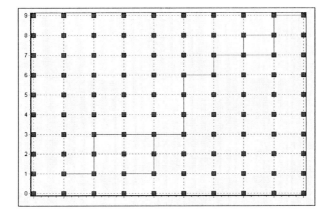

The $e(s)$ are known as memory traces and are integral to rewarding states which appeared in a successful episode. Note that the change to values and traces occurs for all states.

Simulations

We repeat the goal finding experiment with Sarsa(λ) with $\lambda = 0.8$, $\gamma = 0.9$ and $\alpha = 0.01$. Resulting routes from three initial starting points are shown in Figure 7. The additional computational overhead of this method was alleviated by training for only 10,000 iterations.

Continuous State Spaces

The methods discussed so far in this chapter have been useful for problems in which there are a relatively small number of states and similarly a relatively small number of actions. In many situations, this is not appropriate. For example, the path finding examples we used above were based on positions at 100 grid points and the only actions allowed were to move up, down, left, or right. However in many computer games, we wish to have fully continuous spaces, that is, the position of the AI at any

Figure 7. The route found by Sarsa(lambda) with lambda=0.8, gamma=0.9 and alpha=0.01

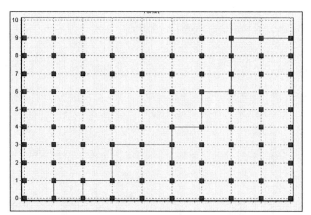

Note that all three starting points quickly converged to the same route but one has experimented (unsuccessfully) with a different route at the point (7,9).

time is a two or three dimensional vector of floating point values and the actions are to take a move which has both distance and direction.

In this situation, what we require is a way to define the mapping from the state-action pairs to an associated value. This is simply a function approximation problem which may be solved by the methods of supervised learning such as the multilayered perceptron or the radial basis network. The underlying rationale is that, even though only a finite number of data points are seen in training, the supervised learning method is sufficiently powerful that it can generalise to state-action pairs which are not seen during training. We illustrate the basic idea in Figure 8. We create a radial basis network which has centres at x-coordinate, y-coordinate, and action values where each x-coordinate and y-coordinate takes the integer values $0,\ldots,9$ and action takes the values $0,1,2,3$ corresponding to up, right, down, and left respectively. The radial basis network learns to output the $Q(s,a)$ values and we can then use its generalisation properties to generalise to state-action values not seen in training. The figure shows three sample routes from three random starting points. Success in training is getting to the square in which $x >= 9, y >= 9$. We see that in testing, two of the routes go to the square $8 < x < 9, y > 9$ which would have been faulted in the training phase since we require both criteria ($x >= 9, y >= 9$) to be satisfied simultaneously, however the RBF network has smoothed over this in testing and given a route to the success-giving square.

Thus, the greedy policy is found by getting the maximum response of the radial basis network to (x, y, θ) where (x,y) defines the state of the route (the current position) and θ ($= \pi/2, \pi, 3\pi/2,$ or $2\pi = 0$) is the action taken. At any one time, the maximum value of the radial basis function's output defines the best value of θ, the action taken in that state. Thus the standard learning rule $Q(s_t,a_t) \leftarrow Q(s_t,a_t) + \alpha[r_{t+1} + \gamma Q(s_{t+1},a_{t+1}) - Q(s_t,a_t)]$ is replaced by,

$$Q_t = V_t \phi(x_t, y_t, \theta_t)$$
$$\Delta Q_t = \alpha(r_{t+1} + \gamma Q_{t+1} - Q_t),$$

where the first line denotes the radial basis function's current output in response to the current state-action pair and the second line gives the change in the value function. Then $Q_t + \Delta Q_t$ becomes the target for training the radial basis network.

However, the above method really only enables us to have a continuous state space, not a continuous action space (we see that we are still moving right or up in the test cases, rather than moving diagonally). Figure 9 shows the results from a simulation in which the θ_t values were integer values $1,\ldots,8$ while the radial basis centres remained at $\theta = \pi/2, \pi, 3\pi/2,$ and $2\pi = 0$. We see that diagonal routes are possible but at the expense of some less-than-perfect routes in the top right corner. Now we are still using a quantisation of the action space but one which is more fine-grained than before.

Figure 8. The paths found when a radial basis network learns the state-action value function

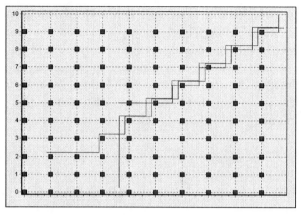

Figure 9. Sample paths when the training and testing actions are different from the RBF centres

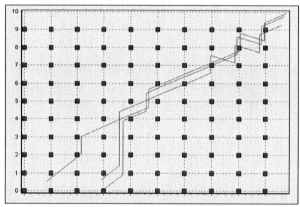

Figure 10. A second simulation with the same parameters

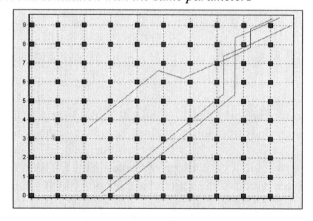

The routes found are a function of those data samples seen in training; a second simulation of the same type is illustrated in Figure 10. This time the path found is close to optimal except for a section in the top path around the point (5,6). For this simulation, there is strong gradient towards the diagonal route towards the goal.

Ideally we would like to find the θ_i corresponding to the maximum value of state-action value function, however this is, in general, a difficult optimisation problem and one which is generating a great deal of current research. One possibility for radial basis functions is to smooth the estimate, x, of the direction to take using a weighted sum of estimates, given the radial basis function's response to the current state-action pairs:

$$x = \frac{\sum w_i \varphi(-\gamma(x - \theta_i)^2)\theta_i}{\sum w_i \varphi(-\gamma(x - \theta_i)^2)}.$$

However a more principled method uses a memory of the effect of the individual parameters. The methods discussed above for the continuous space do not use memory traces at all which have important advantages in speeding up simulations. We may incorporate these methods into our continuous space methods as follows:

$\theta_{t+1} = \theta_t + \alpha(v_t - Q_t)\nabla_{\theta_t} Q_t$ where we have used v_t as the expected reward from subsequent actions and ∇ defines the gradient of Q with respect to the parameters. We may then use,

$$\theta_{t+1} = \theta_t + \alpha\delta_t e_t,$$

where

$$\delta_t = r_{t+1} + \gamma Q_t(s_{t+1}, a_{t+1}) - Q_t(s_t, a_t)$$
$$e_t = \gamma\lambda e_{t-1} + \nabla_{\theta_t} Q_t(s_t, a_t)$$

This is known as gradient descent Sarsa(λ), but note that it is a little different from standard Sarsa(λ) in that there is one trace, $(e_i)_t$, for each parameter in θ. Note also that it does not give an answer to the central problem: how to find an optimal action in a continuous space of actions. It does, however, lead to very fast convergence. In Figure 11, we show the route found by a simulation which learned on only 1,000 episodes.

It is however, entirely possible to combine this with standard gradient descent on the RBF weights. This is shown in Figure 12. We see that, whereas in Figure 11,

Figure 11. Test routes found by gradient descent Sarsa(lambda) after 1,000 episodes

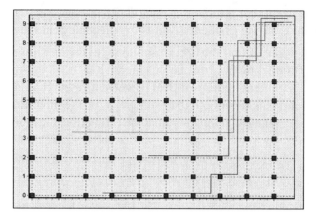

the route-finding strategy is very much to go right till around $x = 8$ and then go up, with the combined method, the diagonal route—which intuitively seems somewhat more robust—predominates. However whether used alone or with the standard radial basis learning of weights, the number of episodes required is only 1,000. Standard radial basis learning alone cannot match this speed of learning.

Immediate Rewards

The reinforce (Williams, 1992; Williams & Peng, 1991) algorithm is a reinforcement learning algorithm based on the concept that each node in, for example, a connec-

Figure 12. Routes found by gradient descent Sarsa(lambda) after only 1,000 episodes

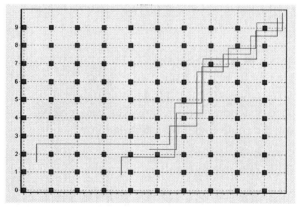

tionist network, can act like a reinforcement learning agent and try to maximise its *immediate* reward. The essential exploration part of reinforcement learning is provided by introducing randomness in the output response to any input and the exploitation part of reinforcement learning is provided by means of maintaining a probabilistic model of the optimum response of the learner. This has been used for clustering by Likas (1999). We first apply the method in that paper to the same basic model as the GTM and then extend the type of learner and show how a second topology preserving algorithm can be derived.

Let the output of the ith learner be 1 with probability p_i, where p_i is a function of the current input, x, and some parameters, w_i. Then the learner will provide an output y with probability p_i to gain immediate reward, r. The core result from Williams (1992) is that the update rule,

$$\Delta w_{ij} = \alpha_{ij}(r - b_{ij})\frac{\partial \ln p_i}{\partial w_{ij}},$$

where b_{ij} is a reinforcement baseline, will change the weights to maximise the expected reward (Williams, 1992, Theorem 1). Three special cases of this rule will be discussed below. These use respectively the Bernoulli distribution, the Gaussian distribution, and the multinomial distribution. The first two will be used to find topology preserving maps of a data set while the last will be used in a simple game.

The Bernoulli Learner

Bernoulli learners were introduced by Williams (1992) and Williams and Peng (1991) in a rather general setting. We will consider a Bernoulli learner who will learn to identify a specific cluster. It will fire +1 if a data point is in the cluster and 0 otherwise. The ith Bernoulli learner has a set of parameters, m_i, which enables it to identify the cluster and it will output 1 if a data point presented to the learner is identified as belonging to the cluster and 0 otherwise. Crucially, this is done in a probabilistic manner which is what maintains the exploration in the method.

Let $s_i = f(m_i, x)$ be a measure of how close the data point is to the cluster. Then $p_i = 2(1 - \frac{1}{1 + \exp(-s_i)})$ determines the probability that the data point is recognised by the ith Bernoulli learner. This learner will output a value y_i with probability p_i to indicate that the ith Bernoulli learner accepts this point in the cluster. Williams (1992) and Williams and Peng (1991) shows that the probabilities should be adjusted using $\Delta p_i = \alpha_i(r - \bar{r})(y_i - p_i)$ where r is the reward for taking the decision yi, $\bar{r}$ is the average reward to the learner for all its decisions, and α is the learning rate. Likas (1999) uses this method in the context of cluster formation by identifying learner i^* with greatest probability and giving it a reward of +1 if it decides correctly (y_{i^*} =1) that the point is part of the cluster and -1 ($y_{i^*} = 0$) if it errs. The learning rule from Williams (1992) is developed as,

$$\Delta m_i = \alpha_i r(y_i - p_i)\frac{\partial s_i}{\partial m_i},$$

where $s_i = \|x - m_i\|$, the Euclidean distance between the data point and the parameter, m_i, which determines the current centre of the cluster. We can use this with the underlying GTM model (Bishop, Svensen, & Williams, 1998) which has also been used in ToPoE and HaToM (Fyfe, 2007).

This model envisages points in a latent space generating the points we actually see in data space. The task of learning is to change the parameters of the model to make the data as likely as possible under the model. Let $t_1, t_2, t_3, \ldots, t_K$ be the points in latent space. These are then passed through a set of nonlinear basis functions, $f_1(), f_2(), \ldots, f_M()$ which create a set of points in an intermediate feature space. This gives us a matrix Φ (K by M), where $\varphi_{km} = f_m(t_k)$, the projections of the latent points to feature space. These points are then mapped using a matrix, W (which is M by D), so that ΦW maps latent points to data space, that is, each $t_k \to m_k$.

We therefore have one more derivative to take into account, $\dfrac{\partial m_k}{\partial w_{ij}} = \phi_j(t_k)$. In this context, the operation of our Bernoulli learner is:

1. Input a new data point, x.

2. Find the closest centre, $i^* = \arg\min_i s_i = \arg\min_i \|x - m_i\|$ which will also identify the learner which accords the highest probability to the data point. Set $p_i = 2(1 - \dfrac{1}{1 + \exp(-s_i)})$.

3. Generate y_{i^*} from this distribution. Update weights according to $\Delta w_{ij} = \sum_k \alpha r(y_{i^*} - p_{i^*,j})\phi_{jk}$ where we have used i^* to identify the winning node and have summed over all basis functions.

4. Recalculate m_i for all latent points, $m_i = W\phi_i$. We may optionally use a decay term here $m_i = \gamma m_i$, with $\gamma < 1$, which is said to encourage exploration (Williams & Peng, 1991).

Results from a two dimensional data set are shown in Figure 13.

Figure 13. A two dimensional data set and a one dimensional manifold found by the reinforce clustering method

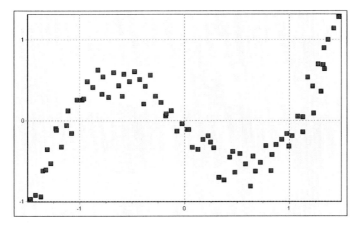

The probabilities of the trained map are shown in Figure 14 in which we have arranged the data points in increasing order of their x-coordinate. We see the local adaptation of probabilities which we might have expected.

The Gaussian Learner

The ith Gaussian learner has a set of parameters, m_i, which are the centres of the Gaussian learner and β_i which are the variances associated with the ith Gaussian learner. Williams (1992) shows that these may be adjusted using:

$$\Delta m = \alpha_m (r - \bar{r}) \frac{y - m}{\beta^2}$$

$$\Delta \beta = \alpha_\beta (r - \bar{r}) \frac{(y - m)^2 - \beta^2}{\beta^3},$$

Therefore the algorithm is:

1.   Input a new data point, x.
2.   Find the closest centre, $i^* = \arg\min_i s_i = \arg\min_i \|x - m_i\|$ which will also identify the learner which accords the highest probability to the data point. Set $r_{i*}(x) = \exp(-\|x - m_{i*}\|^2)$ and calculate the average reward to i^* over all times it has won the competition.

Figure 14. The probability each latent point associates with each data point

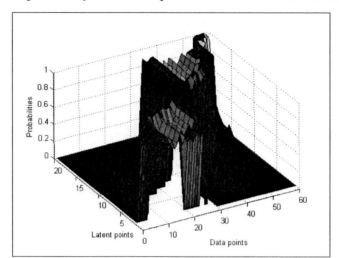

3. Generate y_{i*} from this Gaussian distribution, $N(m_{i*}, \beta_{i*})$. Find what reward would have accrued to the agent from y using $r_{i*}(x) = \exp(-\|x - m_{i*}\|^2)$ and calculate the squared distance between y and the mean, m_{i*} $d = \|(y - x)\|^2$.

4. Update weights according to $\Delta w_{ij} = \alpha(r_{y_{i*}}(x) - \bar{r}_{i*})(y_{i*j} - m_{i*,i})\phi_{i*j} / \beta_{i*}^2$ where we have summed over all basis functions.

5. We may optionally also update the width of each Gaussian using
$$\Delta\beta_{i*} = \alpha_\beta (r_{y_{i*}}(x) - \bar{r}_{i*}) \frac{d - \beta_{i*}^2}{\beta_{i*}^3}.$$

6. Recalculate $\boldsymbol{m}_i$ for all latent points, $m_i = W\phi_i$. We may optionally use a decay term here $m_i = \gamma m_i$, with $\gamma < 1$ (Sutton & Barto, 1998).

Note the effects of the learning rules on the Gaussian parameters. If a value y is chosen which leads to a better reward than has typically been achieved in the past, the change in the mean is towards y; if the reward is less than the previous average, change is away from y. Also, if the reward is greater than the previous average, the variance will decrease if $(y - m)^2 > \beta^2$, that is, narrowing the search while it will increase if $(y - m)^2 > \beta^2$, thus widening the search volume. We have found that it is best to update the variances more slowly than the means.

Results are similar to those above. We also illustrate the final variances in Figure 15 in which we show circles of radius one standard deviation (β_i) centred on the means, m_i.

Figure 15. Each circle has a radius one standard deviation (β) centred on the means, m.

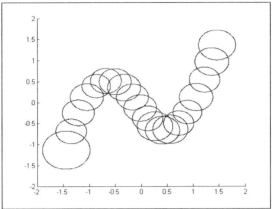

Application to Games

We consider an artificial game straight out of the game theory books. We wish to investigate whether our AIs can cooperate with each other. To do this, we create a typical game situation where we have three AIs each with slightly different interests. Let us have the AIs labelled *A*, *B*, and *C* and let the possible strategies be labelled 1, 2, and 3. The game consists of each of the AIs choosing a strategy and the strategy with the highest number of votes wins. If no strategy has a higher number of votes than any other, A wins by default. The payoff functions are:

- $\mu_A(1) = \mu_B(2) = \mu_C(3) = 2$
- $\mu_B(1) = \mu_C(2) = \mu_A(3) = 1$
- $\mu_C(1) = \mu_A(2) = \mu_B(3) = 0$

where we are using $\mu_i(X)$ as the payoff for AI$_i$ on strategy X. At each stage, we give the AIs no global information; we merely select from each population of strategies separately a strategy which gives that particular AI the best payoff at that stage in the simulation. The AIs learn using,

$$\Delta w_{id} = \alpha(r_{id} - \overline{r_i}),$$

where *d* is the winning choice and *i* identifies the AI.

This is then used to estimate the probabilities that the ith AI will select strategy j in future using,

$$p_{ij} = \frac{w_{ij}}{\sum_k w_{ik}}.$$

In one typical simulation, the average rewards were $A = 1.61$, $B = 0.43$, and $C = 0.96$. This is achieved by A playing 1 most of the time but giving B an occasional 2 which gives the AI enough reward not to play 3 (which would suit C since C would get 2 rather than the 1 received by cooperating with A) so that C accepts the second best reward by cooperating with A.

Comparison with Other Methods

Evolutionary algorithms are sometimes described as a type of reinforcement learning system but there are major differences between these methods and those described in this chapter. It is true that evolution works by trial and error, however, an evolutionary algorithm need not have a specific value function and in addition the fitness of a policy is directly assessed. Reinforcement learning is usually defined as learning while interacting with the environment which is different from the usual evolutionary algorithm. Many reinforcement learning methods take account of the states the AI enters throughout the game or its actions in those states whereas evolutionary methods ignore such information.

We might also compare these methods with traditional minimax methods which at each round of a game will attempt to maximise the reward under the expectation that the opponent will play optimally in order to minimise the AI's reward. Notice the weakness in this: the assumption that the opponent will play optimally. This method will always avoid a game state from which it could lose *even if it actually always won* from this state because the opponent always played suboptimally. Because reinforcement learning methods learn policies during play, a policy which leads to a win will be detected even when the opponent could beat that policy by playing differently. Also reinforcement learning can track opponent's behaviour just as a human would during play which leads to much more satisfactory games than simply playing to a fixed policy each time.

Finally we may compare these methods with supervised learning. The first and most obvious difference is that learning occurs based on the AI's interaction with the environment and no supervisory signal as to what to learn is given. Sutton and Barto (1998) calls the feedback from the environment 'evaluative feedback' since it evaluates what actions have been taken. This is compared to the 'instructive feedback' given in supervised learning in which the AI is given an indication of what action should be taken. The former comes after the action has been taken while the latter may be given in advance of any action and, even when given after the action has been taken ('you should have done this') is independent of the action actually taken and is only a function of the action the instructor believes should have been taken.

Conclusion

Reinforcement learning should be thought of as a group of methods rather than a single method. These methods are intended to search a problem space, exploiting information as it becomes available to the AI. However there always remains an element of exploration in the method which is useful in that the AI can never be sure that its current strategy is optimal at the current time. This mimics how a human would play computer games.

These methods are very useful complements to the other methods discussed in this book but have so far been found most useful in situations in which the state-action space is discrete and finite. There is still much on-going research into those problems in which the state-action space is continuous.

Further Reading

Temporal difference learning with a multilayer perceptron network was used in a seminal paper by Tesauro (1995). In this work, which used a form of TD(λ) learning, MLP networks with random initial weights were able to develop strong backgammon play.

Successful multiagent reinforcement learning has been demonstrated by Bradley and Hayes (2005), using standard Sarsa(λ) learning with utility functions that calculate utility on the basis of *teams*. The team utility function itself is an extension of the notion of group-utility functions (Wolpert & Lawson, 2002).

References

Bishop, C. M., Svensen, M., & Williams, C. K. I. (1998) The GTM: The generative topographic mapping. *Neural Computation, 10*(1), 215-234.

Bradley, J., & Hayes, G. (2005, April). Adapting reinforcement learning for computer games: Using group utility functions. In *Proceedings of the IEEE 2005 Symposium on Computational Intelligence and Games*, Essex University, Colchester, Essex, U.K.

Fyfe, C. (2007). Two topographic maps for data visualization. *Data Mining and Knowledge Discovery, 14*(2), 207-224.

Likas, A. (1999). A reinforcement learning approach to on-line clustering. *Neural Computation, 11*, 1915-1932.

Sutton, R.S., & Barto, A. G. (1998). *Reinforcement learning: An introduction.* Cambridge, MA: MIT Press.

Tesauro, G. (1995). Temporal difference learning and TD-gammon. *Communications of the ACM, 38*(3).

Williams, R. J. (1992) Simple statistical gradient-following algorithms for connectionist reinforcement learning. *Machine Learning, 8*, 229-256.

Williams, R. J., & Peng, J. (1991). Function optimization using connectionist reinforcement learning networks. *Connection Science, 3*(3), 241-268.

Wolpert, D. H., & Lawson, J. W. (2002, July). Designing agent collectives for systems with Markovian dynamics. In *Proceedings of the First International Joint Conference on Autonomous Agents and Multi-Agent Systems*, Bologna, Italy.

Chapter XIII

Adaptivity within Games

Introduction

This book centres on biologically inspired machine learning algorithms for use in computer and video game technology. One of the important reasons for employing learning in computer games is that there is a strong desire by many developers and publishers within the industry to make games adaptive. For example, Manslow (2002) states, 'The widespread adoption of learning in games will be one of the most important advances ever to be made in game AI. Genuinely adaptive AIs will change the way in which games are played by forcing each player to continually search for new strategies to defeat the AI, rather than perfecting a single technique.' However, the majority of learning techniques to date that have been used in commercial games have employed an offline learning process, that is, the algorithms are trained during the development process and not during the gameplay sessions after the release of the game. Online learning—that is, learning processes that occur during actual gameplay—has been used in only a handful of commercial games, for example, Black and White, but the use of learning online within games is intrinsically linked to adaptivity and the use of the algorithms in this way needs to be explored more fully.

All game players are different. Each has a different preference for the pace and style of gameplay within a game, and the range of game playing capabilities between players can vary widely. Even players with a similar level of game playing ability will often find separate aspects of a game to be more difficult to them individually and the techniques that each player focuses on to complete separate challenges can also be very different. This is at the core of our reasoning that adaptive game technology can have an important role to play in next-generation games. There are a range of ways in which adaptivity can be advantageous, for example, modifying the difficulty levels, in helping players avoid getting stuck, adapting the gameplay more to the player's preference/taste, improving replay value of the game, or perhaps detecting exploitative player behaviour and modifying the game in response. What we mean by exploitative player behaviour is, for example, when a player uses or abuses an oversight in the game design to an advantage. Often this means that the player finds it easier to succeed in the game but the enjoyment of the game is lessened because the challenge that is face is reduced and the player finds it unnecessary to explore the full features of the game. That is, players will often repeat a successful strategy over and over again because it leads to a predictable win, even if it is boring and ruins the game somewhat. This happens frequently in real-time strategy games such as Warcraft or Command and Conquer. Bungie, the creators of Halo—a game much praised for its AI—acknowledged the importance of dealing with this issue when they reported at the Game Developers Conference in 2002 that they deliberately designed the AI to prevent players from using 'boring' tactics and the game positively rewarded players when they used imaginative or adventurous tactics (Butcher & Griesemer, 2002).

Important issues such as the serious deficiency of game completions by players, teaching players effectively, the problem of 'beginning' (Poole, 2004), as well as the niche quality to current games and their lack of accessibility to a wider group of people (Redeye, 2004) are relatively well known both within the games industry and the games research community. However, this issue is only beginning to be addressed properly and it is especially rare to see the use of dynamic technology within games that is responsive to individual players. One quite well-known and straightforward attempt at this type of technology is 'auto-dynamic difficulty' as realised in Max Payne (Miller, 2004). In this game the difficulty level is altered by increasing the numbers of enemies in a room (or their difficulty to be killed) by observing features of the player's game playing. Statistics on a player's average health, shot accuracy, number of times shot, numbers of times died, and so forth may be recorded to help make a decision in-game as to how difficult the game should be for the player. While this was undoubtedly successful for many players of the game it was least successful in cases were the player knew or worked out that this form of adaptivity was occurring. When players discovered the technology they often abused it by deliberately playing poorly in order to make the challenge particularly easy. This seems to be a common facet of human behaviour when it comes to game playing. While most players seem to prefer to start a game on normal or hard settings, it is not unusual for a player to attempt to discover the easiest path through a game. This is one of the factors that need to be addressed when designing adaptive game technology.

Existing Approaches to Adaptivity in Games

ost of the existing methods used in commercial games to help a player play are more straightforward help mechanisms, for example in the Crash Bandicoot series if a player repeatedly fails at the same point in the game then a mask is provided to the player character which acts as a shield. This essentially allows the player to make one mistake and still be able to progress; for example, the character may hit a land mine once without losing a life. In the racing game Mario Kart, a player who is performing well will not receive the best power-ups or weapon bonuses while a player who is struggling will gain a lot of help through a discreet speed up or by receiving more powerful item drops. In Mario Kart the help/hinder system is very obvious and so it can cause quite a controversy among players. Players are aware of the technology and so they often try to use (or abuse?) it by deliberately staying behind the leader until very close to the end of the race, saving their powerful weapons to help them win at the last moment. We can see that the game is designed to respond to the capability of players and one outcome from this is an emergence in the gameplay; the responsive game technology causes players to play in a new way. In the case of Mario Kart it could be argued that it enhances the overall gameplay by introducing another set of complex strategies to choose from. However, in some games the adaptation could result in a game that is very different from the one intended. This is perhaps an inevitable consequence of introducing this type of technology and is another important issue to be aware of.

Adaptive Technologies

Though there is little use of adaptive technologies in current commercial games and game research, successful research in other areas demonstrates the potential of this technology. In particular, research on intelligent interfaces (Livingstone & Charles, 2004) and user centred educational software (Beal, Beck, Westbrook, Atkin, & Cohen, 2002). A long history of research can be drawn from the user modelling community, such as on adaptive intelligent tutoring systems (e.g., Brown, Burton, & Bell, 1975). By considering this research, the structure of modern commercial games and the variable requirements of players we suggest an approach similar to the framework illustrated in Figure 1.

There are three key facets to this approach:

1. Profiling or modelling a player.
2. Adapting to a player.
3. Monitoring the effectiveness or appropriateness of adaptation.

We need to monitor the adaptation effects on the player. Because adaptation occurs to enhance the playing experience of the player then we should check if this is in fact the case. The effects of adaptation on the player can be monitored quite easily by observing game data, checking how easily a player is progressing, monitoring the length of gameplay sessions, and other similar in-game data. However, we believe that this form of data may not be satisfactory by itself and that it may also be useful to monitor player emotions (Sykes & Brown, 2003), such as frustration levels (Gilleade & Dix, 2004), by taking measurements from game control pads (Sykes & Brown, 2003) or more advanced sensors. Of course, this is not easy because game playing is an inherently emotional experience and so information obtained may be corrupted by interaction stress.

There are two main reasons for modelling players in games. First, in order to create realistic nonplayer characters by observing and modelling real player behaviour in a game. Second, so that we can recognise the distinctive characteristics of players as they play so that the game may be adapted to suit the needs of individual play-

Figure 1. A potential framework for an adaptive game system

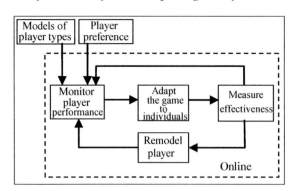

Figure 2. A factorial approach to player modelling

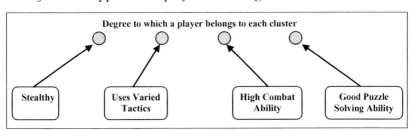

ers. Most existing approaches to player modelling is based in working out how the player should be modelled using in-game variables and then developing the model by observing and recording data from these variables for each player, for example, in Max Payne as we explained earlier. Houlette (2004) describes a similar approach but also goes on to discuss the difference between data variables that inform us about player habits and preferences as opposed to knowledge and proficiency. The autodynamic difficulty technology of Max Payne is based on the first of these and this type of data is easier to access and process for an appropriate dynamic game change. Factors such as knowledge and proficiency are much harder to model as we require a better understanding of player behaviour and more care needs to be taken in preconstructing the framework for the model. The model for these types of player characteristics is more complex and we may not be able to construct a model by observing simple statistics in the data. However, models with this sort of higher order player profiling are more useful for ensuring a more appropriate adaptation to individuals. One effective approach for forming a more complex or higher order profile of a player is a factorial model such as the one shown in Figure 2.

In this way we may manually partition data space to attach different meanings to various aspects of the data, perhaps using trait based models. In the example illustrated above, each player would have a four variable profile with four real numbers that uniquely identify each player's playing characteristics. For example, a player with a numerical profile of (0.8, 0.2, 0.4, 0.7) may tend to prefer to play a game by avoiding direct, close-up conflict. Of course, there some difficulties with setting up this sort of model. Working out which game variables to use and how to partition them so as to useful in identifying separate traits of player behaviour can be tricky. An experienced game designer may be able to work this out manually by using trial and error. However, it is also possible to use data mining tools or unsupervised statistical techniques such as factor analysis to identify correlations between the variables and then we can attach a meaning to them. This could require an observation and recording of player data while playing an almost completed game (note that this implies a two phase approach to the game development); the creation of the game and then the implementation of the player modelling and adaptive technology. A second issue with factorial approach shown in Figure 2 is that we must put an interpretation on the combinatorial patterns of the game playing factors for each player. We could use trial and error coupled with a crude rule based system to attach meaning to certain numerical profiles. However, using clustering techniques to partition the output space before attaching a meaning to groups of profiles would be more efficient and effective, although, again this implies a two phase approach to the game development. Inevitably, all of this implies a hierarchical approach to the modelling of players such as the one illustrated in Figure 3.

A further issue that needs to be dealt with in the modelling of players for adaptive games is concept drift (Tsymbal, 2004). Naturally, players will learn and adapt to the game as they play. Some players will learn faster than others and additionally various players tend to excel in different aspects of the game. Each player plays and progresses in a unique way. Therefore, the models that we use at the beginning of the game may no longer be entirely appropriate as the game develops. Perhaps the reclassification of a player will suffice in some cases; however it would be better to account for a concept drift in our original classification by updating our models on the basis of new data. In many cases the drift may be slight, however, this can still have a significant impact on the response of the game to the player, especially if the drift continues over a long period of time.

Once we have recognised the need to adapt a game on the basis of recognising a player type and the current game state we then need to decide which aspects of the game to adapt. In general we can identify three main aspects of a typical game that may be adapted: nonplayer characters or opponents in the game, the game envi-

Figure 3. An example of a hierarchical player model (Adapted from Houlette 2004)

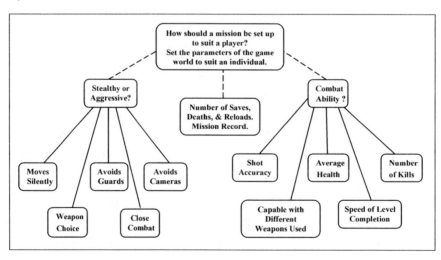

ronment or game state, or player's character. The last of these is perhaps the most interesting because an alteration of the player character in this way can lead to a greater sense of embodiment. Although it does not quite relate to adaptation, Poole (2005) provides an example from Metal Gear Solid 3: Snake Eater to illustrate how a player's actions can alter the state of the player's character and thus how the player plays. If the play gets hurt (or smokes too much) there is a consequence to the player character's wellbeing and the gameplay; if the player has been injured then progress is hindered until the injury is treated. This feedback loop of action-consequence-action can instil a great sense of embodiment that increases the sense of immersion in the game. The use of player modelling and adaptation may lead to the same sort of sense of embodiment if the adaptation directly affects the player character. The most obvious way to adapt a game is in changing the difficulty level of nonplayer character opponents, but the behaviour of friendly nonplayer characters may also be modified depending on the type of game. Nonplayer characters can used to provide clues or support to a player according to needs and playing preferences. In fact, there are a host of imaginative ways in which a variety of nonplayer characters can be used to affect the choices open to the player and even altering the game narrative. The game environment can also be modified in response to the player. This can be anything from increasing the number of items that can be picked up, for example, heath, bullets, and so forth through to the actual landscape of the world changing. The designers of the RPG Fable set out to create a game world where the game landscape would change in response to a player's evolved character and the actions that they performed. If they create an evil character then the world would respond dynamically to reflect the actions and personality of the player's character. In the end most of the more ambitious aspects of this technology were not realised in Fable, but the principle was sound. Players can enjoy a heightened sense of immersion and enjoyment in playing a game if they feel that the game is responsive to them as an individual. We believe that the combination of player modelling and adaptive technology can take this principle forward.

Adaptivity will be an important technology in some future commercial games but we address a few of the more serious criticisms or concerns. The first relates to the concern that players may not approve of the technology because when adaptive technology is in use then the game experience is different for each player and therefore it is not as easy for players to compare experiences and/or brag about their successes. This is true to some extent, however, we believe that there are two opposing desires in players that we need to take into account:

1.   The desire of a player to learn the rules so as to master the game.
2.   The avoidances of 'sameness' or lack of variety of gameplay.

Not all games suit or require adaptive technology, and in fact it may be useful to allow a player to choose to turn the technology on or off, but we believe that the benefits to the majority of players in terms of tailoring an appropriate level of challenge and gameplay style for a player—not to mention replay value——outweighs the drawbacks. It also should be mentioned that players already modify their own gameplay through cheats, guides, walkthroughs, and modifying games (Kuecklich, 2004) in order to enhance the game experience and so there is a precedent for the use of adaptive technology for a similar purpose. It should be pointed also that multiplayer games are adaptive in nature by virtue of the fact than humans are playing humans. Multiplayer games are popular because playing against other real people is generally more interesting and complex in current games than against computer controlled characters, and part of the reason for this is than people adapt to a dynamic environment and come up with novel strategies. Above all we wish to keep a player playing and enjoying the game and not abandoning the game because of lack of understanding of gameplay, inappropriate levels of challenge, unsuitable progressive difficulty, uninteresting gameplay, lack of variety, or gameplay bugs. Intelligently designed adaptive game technology can help with all of these factors.

A second concern relates more to the profiling and modelling aspects of the technology. The modelling approach assumes that a particular game save will always be used by a single person, and while this generally is the case with PC games it is often not the case with console games where the playing of a game (on a particular game save) may be shared by several friends or family. It may be possible to design technology that recognises a switch in user but this would not be easy. Play on a PC tends to be more solitary except where people are playing online. Typically a person will have to log on to a PC and also to an online game server and so there is much less doubt that the individual who is currently playing is the owner of the profile or game save. Also, on a PC where different players are sharing a game they will tend to use their own game save even if they log on as the same user. Microsoft already has a similar system on their Xbox 360 console and use a limited form of player profiling on their Xbox Live network for 'player-matching'; however, there is much more scope in this technology for accurately tailoring the gameplay experience to the player and finding appropriate players to play with or against through more advanced player models and profiles.

Developing Adaptive Solutions

A third concern relates to the difficulty in testing adaptive products and the extra time that is required in development. Using adaptive technology, particularly with machine learning, in game inevitably means that the game can not be tested for the majority of game possibilities. Many game publishers require a guarantee that a game has a very low percentage of game bugs and that they do not significantly impact the key aspects of the gameplay. If adaptive technology is responsible for introducing an unforeseen but significant game bugs, then players could be entitled to a refund and this would be serious issue for both the publisher and the game developer. As an example of this (nonadaptive) we can recall what happened with the game Little Computer People (1985) which resembles an older version of the The Sims. After release it was discovered that if a player let a 'little person' die then a player could not continue to play the game nor restart it. This had not been discovered during testing and so new disks had to be sent out to players who had let their person die, difficult as this was to do.

This third concern is related to the debate on emergent gameplay. In the purest sense emergence may be considered as the 'the movement from low-level rules to higher-level sophistication' (Johnson, 2001) and so 'the interaction of simple rules may lead to surprisingly complex outcomes' (Laramée, 2002, p. 62). As far as emergent gameplay is concerned most game designers generally seem prefer to clearly define and control the exposure of game elements to the player so that the player is encouraged to play in a manner as defined by the designer. This is not unexpected nor is it unreasonable as both publisher and developer prefer to thoroughly play test the product for their targeted potential player group and a product with emergent properties is hard to test and quality control. Players, nevertheless, often desire to play games in a way that differs from the published game format and they often discover or devise original gameplay through cheats, mods, or simply playing in a way that was not considered by the designer. One of the most well known examples of emergent gameplay that was not foreseen by the designer was in the arcade game Centipede. As arcade players played the game over and over they uncovered patterns in the predesigned game logic (Rouse, 2001, Chapter VII). It is well known by players of the game that a build up of mushrooms is not conducive to a long game and that fleas drop mushrooms, however, the presence of fleas is actually triggered by the absence of mushrooms in the bottom row. Once this was realised then the 'blob' strategy was adopted by knowing players so that after the first wave of attacks—fleas do not appear in the first wave—mushrooms were allowed to accumulate only on the bottom-right quadrant of the screen. This simplified the game considerably for the player because mushrooms were no longer dropped and thus the result was longer playing sessions and so higher scores. Game players tend to look for strategies to make a game easier or to make them more successful in the game. It is human nature. In the Centipede, this strategy lengthened their game session (and cost them less money) enabling them to achieve record scores and we could praise the game design because it was flexible enough to allow players to develop their own gameplay style or strategy through the imaginative combination of the gameplay elements; the game demonstrates an example of emergent gameplay. On the other hand we must consider whether the discovery of this feature has been responsible for a breaking of the optimal gameplay and that as a result the game becomes less challenging and enjoyable. The conflict between designer directed and player effected gameplay is one that we must often address when refering to game design and it is a particularly important issue in relation to adaptive game.

Emergent Gameplay

The game designer Eric Zimmerman believes in the intentional design of a game to encourage emergent gameplay: 'One of the pleasures of what I do is that you get to see a player take what you have designed and use it in completely unexpected ways' (Johnson, 2001). The PC game Gearheads, which was released in 1996, was deliberately designed to comprise a simple set of game elements (wind up toys) which although individually had straightforward behaviours, when used in combination, complex and unpredictable outcomes emerged. It is quite rare for games to be designed with this purer sense of emergence in mind, however, the principle designing a game so that the player has a range of choices in how to proceed through the game is not unusual. For example, in a typical MMORPG game players generally have a choice of character races (e.g., Orc, Elf, etc.) that they can play as a class (e.g., Druid, Mage, and Warrior) and profession (e.g., fishing and mining). The idea being that a player can tailor a character exactly as they prefer and thus they have some control over how they play the game because each tailored character will have different requirements and somewhat different quests to fulfil as they progress through the game. Emergent gameplay styles can develop in MMORPG games due to the high level of permutations of combinations of game elements and player styles. The developer by observing the evolution in gameplay can alter the game design in response to the needs of the players, either by reinforcing positive in-game (or out-of-game) gameplay or discouraging disruptive behaviour and aspects that degenerate the gameplay.

The emergent or unpredictable properties of adaptive technology make the design of a game more challenging but this should not prevent us from being adventurous because the rewards are potentially great. If the adaptive technology is restricted by architectural design as it is for the learning of the creature in Black and White, then problems can be constrained and controlled so that gameplay can only be altered in restricted ways and within predetermined boundaries.

Conclusion

Until recently, the major approach to adaptivity in commercial games has been to limit it or prevent it altogether. The last decade has seen increasing amounts of experimentation, with a few key titles demonstrating that adaptive AI and commercial success are not necessarily mutually exclusive. We argue that, indeed, there is a great deal of untapped potential in making games more adaptive.

References

Beal, C., Beck, J., Westbrook, D., Atkin, M., & Cohen, P., (2002). *Intelligent modeling of the user in interactive entertainment.* Paper presented at the AAAI Spring Symposium on Artificial Intelligence and Interactive Entertainment (pp. 8-12), Stanford.

Brown, J.S., Burton, R.R., & Bell, A.G. (1975). SOPHIE: A step towards a reactive learning environment. *International Journal of Man-Machine Studies, 7*, 675-696.

Butcher, C., & Griesemer, J. (2002, March 21-23). *The illusion of intelligence: The integration of AI and level design in Halo.* Paper presented at the Game Developers Conference, San Jose, California.

Gilleade, K., & Dix, A. (2004, June). Using frustration in the design of adaptive videogames. In *Proceedings of ACE 2004, Advances in Computer Entertainment Technology.* ACM Press.

Houlette, R. (2004). Player modeling for adaptive games. In S. Rabin (Ed.), *AI game programming wisdom 2.* Hingham, MA: Charles River Media, Inc.

Johnson, S. (2001). *Emergence.* Penguin Science.

Kuecklich, J. (2004, December). *Other playings: Cheating in computer games.* Paper presented at the Others Players Conference, IT University of Copenhagen, Denmark. Retrieved March 2005, from http://itu.dk/op/proceedings.htm

Laramée, F.D. (Ed.). *Game design perspectives.* Hingham, MA: Charles River Media.

Livingstone, D., & Charles, D. (2004, July 25-26). *Intelligent interfaces for digital games.* Paper presented at the AAAI-04 Workshop on Challenges in Game AI.

Manslow, J. (2002), Learning and adaptation in games. In S. Rabin (Ed.), *AI game programming wisdom* (pp. 557-566). Hingham, MA: Charles River Media.

Miller, S. (2004). *Auto-dynamic difficulty (Website forum debate).* Retrieved February 22, 2006, from http://dukenukem.typepad.com/game_matters/2004/01/auto-adjusting_g.html

Poole, S. (2004, August). On beginnings. *Edge Magazine, 139*, 24. U.K.: Future Publishing.

Poole, S. (2005, March). Snake in the grass. *Edge Magazine 147*, 120. U.K.: Future Publishing.

Redeye. (2004, August). Content with the playgrounds. *Edge Magazine, 139*, 22. U.K.: Future Publishing.

Rouse, R., III (2001). *Game design: Theory and practice*. Wordware Publishing.

Sykes, J., & Brown, S., (2003). Affective gaming: Measuring emotion through the gamepad. Human Factors in Computing, pp 732-733 CHI 2003.

Tsymbal, A. (2004). *The problem of concept drift: Definitions and related work* (Tech. Rep. TCD-CS-2004-15). Trinity College Dublin, Department of Computer Science, Ireland.

Chapter XIV

Turing's Test
and Believable AI

Introduction: Contemporary Game AI

It is very evident that current progress in developing realistic and believable game AI lags behind that in developing realistic graphical and physical models. For example, in the years between the development of Neverwinter Nights by Bioware and the release of its sequel Neverwinter Nights 2 by Obsidian in collaboration with Bioware there were obvious and significant advances in the graphics. The character models in the first game are decidedly angular, the result of having limited resources to expend on the polygons required for simulating the appearance of natural curves and body shapes. No such problems now. A few years, and the difference is remarkable.

But how much has the AI progressed over the same time?

In both games the player controls one character through adventures while the computer AI controls the player's companions. Playing the first game, it was observed that the AI did not always help in the most natural manner. For example, companions would be prone to running off to fight enemies that were still outside of the view of the player. Or perhaps ignore a fight in progress to disarm a trap instead, which clearly could wait until the current combat is completed.

There appears to have been limited progress in developing more realistic AI in the sequel, however. Companions still leave fights in progress to disarm traps. More distressingly, on occasion companions join fights when their path is partially obstructed, leaving them as ineffectual observers lurking behind a barrel while a vicious fight to the death occurs just yards away.

These two examples are from highly successful and polished games. Many more, often humorous, stories of obviously flawed game AI found in leading games have been collected by Baylor Wetzel (2004).

Given that current game AI often struggles with simple tasks, and often falls over in obvious ways, it may seem inappropriate to question whether game AI can pass the Turing Test. But in this chapter we present a review of the Turing Test and some of its key criticisms and variants. We then consider whether some form of the Turing Test might prove useful in the development and assessment of game AI.

To aid in this we also consider the practice of *believability testing*, what it means, how believability can be assessed, and some of the problems and issues that appear when one tries to determine whether or not a character or creature in a game is exhibiting convincing and natural life-like behaviour.

The Popular Turing Test

In popular conception, the Turing Test challenges an interrogator with the task of determining whether a correspondent—communicating via typed conversation on a computer terminal—is a human or a machine. The correspondents are located in another room and the only evidence the interrogator has, on which to make judgements, is the typed conversation itself. The typical view of this is that if the interrogator is unable to tell them apart, then the machine has beaten the test. For some, any AI that succeeds in beating the test must then be considered intelligent.

An annual competition for the Loebner prize is run along these lines. Each year several judges gather to converse with contestants and human confederates via computer terminals, and attempt to rate each conversation partner according to 'human' they believe then to be. So far no program entered has succeeded in fooling the judges. And yet Turing himself predicted that by the year 2000 computers would be sufficiently capable of passing the test to succeed in about a third of trials:

I believe that in about fifty years it will be possible to programme computers... to make them play the imitation game so well that an average interrogator will not have more than 70 per cent chance of making the right identification after five minutes of questioning. (Turing, 1950)

There has been little significant improvement in performance of the best programs since Krol (1999) reported on the 1998 competition in which the top scoring computer scored close to, but below, the lowest scoring human confederate. This was despite evidence that some of the human confederates appeared to be trying—and failing—to fool judges into thinking that they were machines. And two years later, judges were able to successfully distinguish human and machine with 91% success within five minutes of starting a conversation (Ackman & Blackburn, 2000).

Despite the apparent difficulty facing the programs submitted in successfully fooling the judges, the requirements for winning the Loebner prize were recently revised to require that the program significantly exceed Turing's original challenge, with a 'grand prize' winner now required to be able to respond in a human like way to submitted images and videos (more details are available at http://www.loebner. net/Prizef/loebner-prize.html). It will clearly now be many years before a machine can claim the grand prize.

Recent competitions have seen the winning programs (the program that scores the highest is always selected as a winner, with the grand prize being reserved for the first program to convince judges that it is human) score points that place it in the range of *probably* being a computer program down to being evaluated as *definitely* being a computer program. Human confederates generally rank in the range between *undecided* and *probably human*. This perhaps says something about how the limitations of the Turing Test affect our ability to recognise intelligence when we encounter it.

Despite this, it would appear that the challenge that Turing set is much more difficult than he expected. And even when the challenge is eventually passed, there remain strong arguments that this does not indicate the existence of 'intelligence' in the computer. The most famous argument here is Searle's (1980) 'Chinese Room Argument'.

The basis of the Chinese Room Argument is that the test can be reduced to a problem of outputting a sentence, a string of symbols, for each string of symbols input. Searle reimagines the test as a room in which a person sits with a book of Chinese symbols. Every time a piece of paper with a symbol on it is passed in, the person looks up the book to find the page with the symbol on it, and copies out the symbol on the facing page onto a second sheet of paper. This second sheet is then passed out. Thus, the problem can potentially be solved without any understanding or intelligence being required by the program.

The Real Turing Test?

Turing himself called his test the 'Imitation Game.' Reading Turing's 1950 article, a number of differences between the popular conception of the test and Turing's original are apparent. Turing starts by proposing a game in which an interrogator puts questions to a male and a female contestant via teletype. Based on the responses, the interrogator has to judge which is female with the male contestant trying to fool the judge. From this, Turing proposes replacing the female contestant with a machine. Thus it appears that Turing's game is played by a machine and a male contestant, the computer trying to score as well as the man at convincing the judge that it is in fact female. While in the Loebner competition all judges know that they are interrogating a mixture of human collaborators and machine, in Turing's description it is not made clear whether the judges are to be aware of the possibility that a contestant is not in fact human. Hayes and Ford (1995) consider the significance of the differences between this 'gender test' and the conventional Turing Test and also argue that the Turing Test in its popular form does not provide a useful goal for AI research.

They are not alone amongst AI academics in rejecting the Turing Test as a goal for modern AI research, a move which has seen the development of a new set of grand challenges for AI. The new 'grand challenges,' which tend to focus on tasks embodied in the real world, consist not only of some final test or objective, but also provide incremental goals, and it is the incremental goals that enable systematic progress to be made, where the Turing Test is an 'all or nothing' test (Cohen, 2004).

The key surviving feature of the Turing Test in these new challenges is the focus on the ability of machines to undertake tasks which demonstrate intelligence rather than on developing machines which are 'provably' intelligent. Indeed, Turing saw that it would be troublesome in the extreme to develop a formal definition of intelligence that would be sufficient for *proving* whether or not a machine was intelligent. Instead, he formulated a different problem. So instead, the machine has to convince an interrogator that it is human by means of a test which explicitly disallows any inspection of the machine itself. The test does not just prevent interrogators from seeing the machine, it explicitly prevents any consideration of how it works. The Chinese Room argument shows, however, that the set-up of the test itself prevents it from being sufficient for judging intelligence.

This, and the recognition within the academic world that there is more to intelligence that symbolic reasoning has led to robot football and other embodied tasks being considered more promising challenges (e.g., Brooks, 1991; Cohen, 2004). In part this is because academics are more interested in being able to replicate, or at least *understand* intelligent behaviour and intelligence. But this is not a driver for game developers. In games, the *appearance* of intelligence is what counts, not the substance behind it. Believability is more important than truth.

Playing the Turing Test

Some suggest that the Turing Test is more successful as a means of provoking thought about the nature of human intelligence, that it is as a useful measure of machine intelligence: 'We suspect that Turing chose this topic because he wanted the test to be about what it really means to be human' (Hayes & Ford, 1995).

The idea of using machine intelligence as a means to frame questions about human nature and intelligence was developed as a literary device employed by the science-fiction author Philip K. Dick (1968), most famously in his book *Do Androids Dream of Electric Sheep?*. In the book, as in the film adaptation *Bladerunner* (Dick, Fancher, Peoples, & Scott, 1982), the only reliable way to determine if someone is a human or android—a machine with human like intelligence and appearance—is by means of a Turing Test analogue: the Voight-Kampff Test.

An adventure game was later made based on the film, and shares its title of *Bladerunner* (Westwood, 1998). While the game does not feature any AI of note, the Voight-Kampff test does make an appearance. The human player is able to direct a character while performing a Voight-Kampff test on one of the other characters in the game. Thus, in the game the player is acting as an interrogator in some imitation of the original imitation game, trying to determine which other characters are machines. The catch here is, of course, that this is a computer game. They are *all* machine.

This, however, is merely an aside. In practical terms the application of the Turing Test to games more widely relates to the ability of developers to create AI characters and opponents that act truly intelligent. To understand how this might apply in the constrained domain of a computer game, we first need to generalise the test away from the specific conditions Turing set for it.

Generalising the Turing Test

The reason for generalising the Turing Test is to remove the inherent restrictions and requirements of games which feature typed conversation as the only possible interaction between players and other agents are far from the norm. A useful article which generalises the Turing Test, and which considers the implications of different versions of the test, was written by Harnad (2000). Harnad elaborates the test and proposes a hierarchy of variants. Each variant is accompanied by goals against which that particular variant is to be tested. Harnad's hierarchy reaches from subtotal or 'toy' tests, 't1', up to machines which are indistinguishable from humans by any empirical or testable means, '*T5*.' The original 'pen-pal' Turing Test (a version of the conventional Turing Test but where the game can be played over a lifetime rather than in a simple five minute session) sits low in this hierarchy, just one level above the 'toy' level, at level '*T2*.'

Harnad focuses in his article on the higher levels of the hierarchy and the related philosophical implications. However, it is the lowest level, '*t1*', which is of most interest in the development of computer and video games. Here '*t*' stands not for 'Turing' but for 'toy.' Harnad argues that toy models of intelligence are those which replicate some subtotal fragment of human functional capacity, whether arbitrary fragments or self-sufficient modules.

While at the higher levels the machine must surpass the ability to pass as human at a conventional Turing Test and be able to interact with the world at large in a convincing manner, at the lowest level the ability to converse in type is not a requirement at all. Any aspect of human intelligent behaviour can be selected for testing. But to pass even a reduced 'toy' test, it is not a requirement for the machine to be able to beat or necessarily equal human capacities but to be able to imitate them convincingly. For example, beating a grand-master at chess does *not* mean that a computer has passed the *t*1 test for chess. If, however, the opponent player and expert observers, watching the movement of pieces on the board and the strategies employed, are fooled into thinking that a human was playing *then* the conditions for passing the *t*1 test might have been met. Some years ago Deep Blue defeated the world chess champion Gary Kasparov, leading to some speculation as to whether the Turing Test had been passed. However, it was not Deep Blue's victory that created controversy. Rather it was Kasparov, and other chess experts, questioning whether or not he had been playing a computer throughout the game that raised the issue of whether the Test had been passed (Krol, 1999).

What games require is certainly not unbeatable AI, but believable AI.

Believable AI?

What remains to be done is determine whether or not some AI is 'believable.' For this we need some idea of what believable is and some means of testing it. Philosophical arguments over whether a machine that fools a human is or is not intelligent can be forgotten. All that matters is that it some sense it can.

So what does it actually mean to say that some game AI is 'believable'? It turns out that the answer to this question depends heavily on the context: the game being played and the role taken by the AI. For example, consider two different games set in some fictional or historical war.

Consider a first-person shooter (FPS) game where the players look through the eyes of their characters and control their avatars as they walk and run around the virtual battleground. Other avatars—opponents and/or compatriots—might be controlled by other players or by computer programs. Success for the computer programs could be said to have occurred in any game where the majority of players are unable to tell which of the other avatars are human and which are machine operated.

But is this the correct goal? In a historical setting, the challenge might be to make the AI avatars to convincingly act like the soldiers they are supposed to represent by performing individually and together to imitate the training, tactics, and combat styles of the historical combatants. This goal is actually more in keeping with the original Imitation Game: challenge human and machine controllers to see which is better at role-playing the historical combatant. Modifications to the imitation game to have the computer take on different roles have previously been explored in several works (Colby, 1981; Hayes & Ford, 1995).

Similarly, if instead of FPS, we have a strategy game, which places the player in the role of a general able to command a large army, we could pose the same question. Should we be testing whether the AI plays like another contemporary human or whether it uses strategies and tactics that are historically accurate and representative of the behaviour of generals from the period in question?

There would likely be significant differences between these two alternate challenges. Indeed, winning strategies in many computer games are often ones which might unlikely be used in the real world.

Further, these two examples both place the AI in the role of a surrogate human player. But AI is employed to control not just opponent or allied computer game players, but to give 'life' to vast arrays of nonplayer characters (NPCs). In a typical real-time strategy (RTS) game the computer controls not just players but the individual units—soldiers and vehicles—which each are given their own limited autonomy to react to threats as they occur. It makes no sense to whether the individual units are being played by humans or by machines, so what goal should AI have to meet to declare it to be 'believable'?

So there is clearly a distinction to be made between 'player AI' and 'NPC AI.' Issues relating to both of these will be explored after we consider how believability might best be measured.

Measuring Believability

Depending as it does on how observers or interrogators perceive the behaviour of an AI, judging believability is clearly a subjective process. Some of the questions raised by this, and some means to limit the subjectivity, have been considered by Mac Namee (2004, Chapter VI).

As the task of judging the degree of believability depends on the perception of people playing or watching games, the most obvious tests of believability are those based on gathering feedback from observers and participants, such as by questionairres (e.g., Laird & Duchi, 2000, see below). Mac Namee (2004) notes that the answer to the question whether something is 'believable' is highly subjective. Scoring it according to some scale (Laird & Duchi 2000) is just as subjective. But some degree of objectivity is desirable, and this Mac Namee is able to achieve by asking a subtly different question.

Rather than present different AI's and asking subjects to rate how believable they are, he presents different versions of some AI in pairs, each time asking users which of the pair is *more* believable, requesting comments on any perceived differences. It is hoped that the comparison reduces the effects of different ideas of how variations in behaviour map to points on any scale used, and result instead in definitive notions of how an AI might be improved.

Mac Namee's own test show, however, that even this is not sufficient to remove subjectivity from the results, and further that results can be subject to cultural effects. One interesting result came from a test which populated a virtual bar with AI agents, each of which would order drinks from the bar, sit at tables, and make occasional trips to the toilets. In one version, the AI agents would sit preferentially at tables occupied by 'friends,' and had behaviour governed by a goal-driven approach. In another version their actions were more random, with new goals being randomly picked every time an action is completed. Both versions were presented side by side, and test subjects were asked to rate which was more believable. While almost all subjects felt that the nonrandom variant was the more believable, one felt otherwise. To this one subject, a native Italian, the observation that agents returned to sit at the same table time after time was unrealistic, although the other (Irish) subjects all felt this more believable of the behaviours.

It would be interesting to try further tests to find where there are culturally significant differences in the perception of believability, for though such tests are yet to be carried out, the possibility of finding them does appear quite real.

A further difference in assessment by subjects was noticed by Mac Namee between those made by game-playing novices and veterans (Mac Namee, 2004, Section 6.5.2). Novices were sufficiently inexperienced at playing games that they would in many cases fail to notice significant differences between multiple versions of an AI, even though the differences might be readily and almost instantly apparent to anyone with even a moderate amount of experience in playing modern computer games. Current work on believability testing appears to be limited to rather small numbers of test subjects, certainly insufficient in both number and coverage of distinct user groups to draw out the impact of cultural factors and experience from the results.

Commercially, there is also some interest in creating believable NPCs for games, and there are some examples where game AI has been tested against the perception of players. Most notably, the value of believability testing has been demonstrated with work on highly the successful game, Halo (Butcher & Griesemer, 2002). When developing Halo different versions of the opponent AI were shown to testers. Perhaps the most interesting result of this work was the finding that AI behaviours needed exaggerated animations, expressions, and visible effects for them to be at all noticeable to players. The contrary implication of this is that in order to improve believability, it may be required to give characters unrealistically over-emotive reactions and actions. This may be because the players are too busy playing to notice subtle effects and reactions, and testing could avoid this effect by having observers rather than players rate the AI. But this would seem somewhat against the whole point of believability testing in games, of providing more immersive and realistic experiences to players.

Despite this work on Halo, current games still frequently include large numbers of NPCs which loiter lifelessly when not directly set to perform some scripted on programmed action (Neverwinter Nights 2, mentioned above, is just one example that comes readily to mind). The unnatural lack of emotion, thought, or action is increasingly at odds with the ever greater graphical fidelity, forming an uneasy 'uncanny valley' (MacDorman & Ishiguro, 2006).

Believable Computer Players

Computer games may enable players to compete and cooperate in a variety of ways, whether as allied and opposing generals, in teams of opposing foot-soldiers, or as allied combatants facing vast armies of computer controlled units. Where we ask the computer to take on the role of a human player, the applicability of Harnad's Turing Test hierarchy is clear. The AI should play the game in such a way that other human players or observers find it difficult to distinguish machine from human players. In Harnad's hierarchy this would appear to be a '$t1$' challenge or a simple 'toy' test of intelligence. In fact, in some games, it could be argued that the challenge may be equivalent or even greater than that posed by the traditional Turing Test. Aha (2005) does just this, outlining how the many varied challenges inherent in RTS games make solving such games a more involving and difficult arena for AI research than many traditional AI problems from the continuous and real-time nature of the problem, with terrain, resources, strategies, and tactics all needing considerable AI analysis and decision making. Other game AI tasks would seem to be more easily categorised at '$t1$' challenges; controlling an avatar in a typical FPS game makes less strategic demands, for example. Our next example reviews how believability testing was conducted for evaluating an AI player developed for such a game, and includes comments on the evaluation findings.

The Soar Quakebot: Almost Like Human

Laird and Duchi (2000) note that human players can be so involved in playing a game that they may not be able to devote much time to close observation of other players or characters (as may have affected the evaluation of AI in Halo, above). Additionally, they may be limited to seeing the other avatars for only short periods of time, revealing only small portions of their behaviour. In FPS games in particular, the amount of time another specific player is actually in view might form a very small portion of the game time. Thus, a human player may be in a poor position to judge a Turing-type test. On the other hand, strategy games where the players are able to interact over longer periods of time, with a slower pace of play, may better allow players to judge their opponents on the basis of their strategies and play styles.

With the limitations on player-judges in mind, Laird and Duchi (2000) used video footage of already completed games shown to observers for judging instead of having the judges play games themselves. The AI that Laird and Duchi evaluate is the Soar Quakebot (Laird & van Lent, 1999), an AI bot for the Quake II FPS game. For the trials, a range of two-player deathmatch Quake II games were recorded. These included five human players of differing degrees of experience playing against an expert, and a further 11 games of the expert playing the Soar Quakebot. For each game in which it participated, the Soar Quakebot had its parameter settings adjusted to modify its behaviour in play. Each judge was then shown videos of games in which every case they were asked to rank, for skill and degree of 'humanness,' only the nonexpert player. Judges were not informed in advance whether the video showed a human or computer controlled avatar.

Some promising results were obtained from this work. Bots with human-like decision times were rated as more human than bots with slower or faster decision times. However, no bot scored as high as any of the human players. Bots with more tactical reasoning were similarly rated more human-like, while bots with very high aiming skills were rejected as being too competent to be human. Thus, bots with poorer aim were rated as more human. Despite the noted preliminary nature of this work, a few design principles that can be drawn from this work are noted by the authors.

1. The AI should have human like reaction and decision times (from 1/20 to 1/10 of a second).

2. The AI should not be given any superhuman abilities (e.g., overly precise aiming).

3.   The AI should include some degree of tactical or strategic reasoning so that it is not a purely reactive agent.

Human-Like Behaviour by Imitating Humans

We have also conducted some studies on the believability of AI players (McGlinchey & Livingstone, 2004). The first of these is quite a bit simpler than a Quakebot and involves testing the human-like qualities of AI Pong players. While seemingly trivial it has been seen that the AI used (as described in Chapter V), trained on human data, is able to replicate the distinct quirks and behaviours of different players with some degree of fidelity.

A number of games of Pong were recorded and played back to test subjects. Noting the previously mentions principles for reducing subjectivity in judgements of believability, the test subjects were not asked to rate believability. Just eight games were recorded and shown to judges. In four of these games, a human was playing against a trained AI player (as described in Chapter V). Two further games were played between pairs of AI players, one between a pair of human players ,and a final game pitted a human player against a hard-coded computer controlled bat.

The hard-coded AI used the very simple approach of projecting the point at which the ball will intersect with the bat's vertical line of movement. A short delay to simulate human reaction time was applied, and then the bat would move gradually to the intersection point, its speed controlled by a limiting weight parameter. A small random value was added to the target position to introduce a small degree of fallibility.

Judges were asked to simply declare whether they thought, for each game, whether the left bat, right bat, both bats, or neither was controlled by a human player. An additional question asked what evidence, if any, had led the judges to making their decisions. Observers were allowed to stop viewing a particular game once a decision had been reached, and most observers took this opportunity to quit games before they reached the end of the recording.

The decision to attempt these tests was made because although the AI had already been shown to successfully imitate the distinct play-styles peculiar to different human players (McGlinchey, 2003, and Chapter V in this book), it was not known whether the imitation was accurate enough to fool human observers. This additional testing had some interesting results which not only highlight areas for improvement in the AI itself, but which also demonstrate the usefulness of believability testing and the are that needs taken in setting questions and reviewing results.

At first a review of the returns would seem to indicate that the trained AI performs well—being identified as human about as often as the human players are. With only a very limited aspect of human-controlled behaviour observable, it might seem that this 'toy' task is easily passed. However, a closer look at the results shows otherwise, and highlights limitations in judging success by the ability of some program to fool observers into rating some behaviour as being human like.

In the tests one judge correctly judged 14 out of 16 players. Another only managed to get 2 out of 16 correct. Most of the judges responses varied from chance significantly either getting almost all responses correct or almost all wrong. Thus, the judges were able to *distinguish* between human and machine controllers, although they were not necessarily very good at knowing which was which. Similarly, although the hard-coded AI was often misclassified, the results indicate that it was still visibly distinct from real human players.

The free-test question and answer, asking respondents to explain how they made their decisions, proved conclusive in this analysis. The answers here showed that many of the judges—both those who were most often correct and those most often wrong in their judgements—noticed that some bats moved with more jerky and sudden movements than others. Although some of the observers thought that this was a marker of human control, it was in fact a feature of the trained AI, due perhaps to insufficient smoothing being performed on the decisions made by the ANN.

Believable Characters

Different criteria and methods are required for judging the believability of NPC AI. NPCs in a game are generally not required nor expected to act like a player, but like and intelligent character or natural creature within the game world. In comparison with the work on developing opponent AI, research and development for character AI in games has been considerably more limited (Mac Namee 2005, p. 123).

Characters in games need not even be human, further removing testing from judgements of 'humanness' and evaluation of human-like behaviour. Does the Turing Test still apply at all? Harnad (2000, p. 432) notes that a Turing Hierarchy can be posited for any creature. Thus, there can be a '$t1$', 'toy', model for any creature we might wish to include in a game, from mouse to monkey.

To satisfy the $t1$ test, we could argue that it is sufficient to capture and replicate enough of the behaviour of the creature such that observers agree that it does indeed act and behave like a real creature would in situations similar to those simulated. For clearly fictional creatures and worlds (fantasy and science-fiction), the question could be restated as, 'Does the behaviour of the fictional creatures in the game seem believable and realistic in the context of the imagined setting?' As with the previous examples, testing could be conducted by letting judges watch or play sequences of games and completing questionnaires on the believability of what they observe.

The tests in Mac Namee (2004) are good examples of believability testing for character AI and, as reviewed earlier, discovered that while some judges are adept at noticing unrealistic character behaviour, other judges could be quite accepting. Yet although not all players are aware of what reasoning lies behind character actions (even when accompanied by somewhat exaggerated gestures and reactions, as seen by Butcher and Griesemer [2002]), for some players realistic and believable behaviours do seem to have a strong effect on the overall experience of playing the game.

Unbelievable Characters

If many players are oblivious to the reasoning behind AI, and fail to notice realistic AI behaviours when they occur, then why test believability at all? We opened this chapter with an example of an obvious AI failure, and a further example is presented here to highlight how in many cases unbelievable behaviour may cause players to drop suspension of disbelief, which can only serve to impair the enjoyment of playing the game. The first example comes from the game Fallout: Tactics, but the general nature of the failure—where NPC guards fail to react to obvious signs that something is amiss—is common to a large number of games (Wetzel, 2004).

Fallout: Tactics is a game which at many points challenges the player to get past guards unnoticed or to be able to eliminate them without any other guards noticing. At one point in the game, two guards can be found patrolling a wall. Both follow the same path as one another, starting at opposite ends and passing in the middle. It is possible to lay a mine at one of the end positions so that the first guard walks into it and dies messily and loudly. The other guard, less than one hundred yards away, continues his patrol oblivious. That guards do not notice loud noises more than a very short distance away is part of the game design, and though not realistic, is consistent throughout the game. But this is compounded by other clearly unrealistic behaviours. As the second guard continues his patrol, he crosses the passing point and fails to notice that his companion is suddenly missing. He continues his patrol, even walking through the bloodied remains of the other guard and back again without reaction. It is even possible to lay a mine on the now blood-stained wall, in the same position of the first, and the second guard will walk into it, his doom sealed by his complete failure to notice anything amiss.

The Embedded Turing Test

One AI challenge we have overlooked until now is the possibility of embedding the traditional Turing Test in a game. Many multiplayer games allow player to type and send messages to one another using the keyboard during play. With no limit on what may be typed, the Imitation Game could easily be embedded into such games. If the AI in an embedded Turing Test is also to play the game, then this forms a slightly extended T2 test, although the difficulty of playing the game in a convincingly human manner may be significantly simpler than that of passing the traditional Turing Test itself.

Admittedly, in many cases the chat in multiplayer games may be quite limited in range, consisting of little more that taunts and banter between players. To succeed here would not be particularly challenging for current AI techniques. Other games, such as online roleplaying games or strategy games, have more opportunities for extended chat between players. In many cases the conversation within the confines of such games may still be significantly more limited in topic and depth than allowed for in a more conventional Turing Test, but the challenge is likely to be similar. This remains to be formally shown, however. Some initial work along this direction is being taken by some residents (the preferred term instead of *players*, as it is not strictly a game) of Second Life where a small range of chat-bots, conversational AI characters, have been developed.

There is strong potential for extending this work. Some of the recent Loebner prize contestants develop and improve their programs with the help of Web-based chat between their programs and interested members of the public. As user-developed scripts in Second Life are able to communicate with Web-applications via HTTP, this might offer a good opportunity for bringing current leading chat-bot technology into a virtual world.

There is even room to argue that the Turing Test has already been passed by chat-bots in virtual worlds, as there are some reported cases of where people have been fooled by chat-bots. In text-based multiuser dungeons (MUDs) there have been some tales of individuals chatting to bots for significant amounts of time without realising that there was not another person involved (e.g., Humphrys, 1995). It these cases it would appear that individuals folders were unaware of even the possibility of chatting with a machine, but if they had they might have been harder to fool. While the conventional version of the Turing Test appears to include awareness that some of the conversational partners might be machines, Turing himself does not state clearly if interrogator should be aware that contestants might be nonhuman. Current, and imaginable future, conditions for the Loebner prize ensure that judges are well aware that some of the conversations held will be with machines, not humans. If we accept this is a condition of believability testing, then we can be confident that no program has yet passed the Turing Test.

Conclusion

As we have argued, game AI which succeeds at making players think it is another human player does not necessarily pass the Turing Test, simply because it is not taking part either in Turing's original or the conventional version of the Imitation Game. So there is some irony, then, that a machine playing Turing's game has the same basic goal of much of video game AI; that of fooling people into believing that there is a human mind at work where there is only a machine. Especially when Turing's game has been largely rejected by the modern mainstream of AI research.

We have seen that the idea that AI should be 'believable' gives a goal that is both nebulous and needing of careful definition for each context in which it is applied. The behaviours that the game AI should display will depend in great part of what precisely is imitated. We made a key distinction between AI which attempts to take on the role of another human player and that which attempts to give life-like behaviours to nonplayer characters in games. By making this distinction, the goals for the AI behaviours are made clearer, and allow believability testing to be extended to cases where the judges know in advance that it is machine intelligence that they are evaluating.

Defining a goal more tightly defined than 'believability' for game AI is likely to remain difficult. There is huge variation in the range of tasks that game AI has to perform and many games have only limited relationship with reality, with fantastic elements commonplace. And as AI itself becomes more sophisticated, then what is regarded as good AI also evolves. This and the knowledge that different players respond quite differently to game AI according to their level of experience and possibly due to cultural factors means that evaluating AI is likely to remain somewhat problematic.

We have seen that people who are relatively new to computer games have such limited experience of games themselves that they cannot be expected to be able to evaluate potentially subtle features of game AI. But by explicitly evaluating game AI as part of the quality assurance process—with evaluation by people who play games of the type under test—developers can identify strengths and weaknesses of their AI. Feedback from novices, while interesting and potentially useful for other reasons such as evaluating how accessible the game itself is to novices, will likely be less useful for evaluating the AI. As Baylor Wetzel (2004) notes, the first step in building better AI for future games is to document the failures and experienced game players are much more likely to notice failures in game AI when they see them.

Finally, in arguing that opinions and experiences of players need to be recorded and documented as an essential integral part of the process of improving the quality of game AI, we are in agreement with Sweeter and Drenna (2003) and Purdy and Thornton (2004) who argue this point for the evaluation of game design more generally.

Further Reading

An extension of this work, which includes a set of criteria for evaluating believable game AI, is presented by Livingstone (2006).

References

Aha, D. (2005, July). *TIELT: Testbed for entegrating and evaluating learning techniques*. Paper presented at the TIELT, AAAI'05 Intelligent Systems Demonstrations.

Akman, V., & Blackburn, P. (2000). Editorial: Alan Turing and artificial intelligence. *Journal of Logic, Language and Information, 9,* 391-395.

Brooks, R. A. (1991). Intelligence without representation. *Artificial Intelligence Journal, 47,* 139-159.

Butcher, C., & Griesemer, J. (2002, March 21-23). *The illusion of intelligence: The integration of AI and level design in Halo*. Paper presented at the Game Developers Conference, San Jose, California.

Charles, D. (2003, November 2-6). *Enhancing gameplay: Challenges for artificial intelligence in digital games*. Paper presented at the Level Up: Digital Games Research Conference, Utrecht.

Cohen, P. (2004, July 25-29). *If not the Turing test, then what?* Paper presented at the Nineteenth National Conference on Artificial Intelligence. American Association of Artificial Intelligence.

Colby, K. M. (1981). Modeling a paranoid mind. *Behavioral and Brain Sciences, 4,* 515-560.

Dick, P. K. (1968). *Do androids dream of electric sheep?*

Dick, P. K., Fancher H., Peoples, D., & Scott, R. (Director). (1982). *Blade runner* [Motion Picture]. Harnad, S. (2000). Minds, machines and Turing. *Journal of Logic, Language and Information, 9,* 425-445.

Hayes, P. J., & Ford, K. M. (1995). Turing test considered harmful. In *Proceedings of the International Joint Conference on Artificial Intelligence (IJCAI-95)*, Montreal.

Humphrys, M. (1995). *How my program passed the Turing Test*. Retrieved January 12, 2007, from http://www.computing.dcu.ie/~humphrys/eliza.html

Krol, M. (1999). Have we witnessed a real life Turing Test? *IEEE Computer,* (March), 27-30.

Laird, J. E., & Duchi, J. C. (2000, November 3-5). *Creating human-like synthetic characters with multiple skill levels: A case study using the Soar Quakebot.* Paper presented at the AAAI 2000 Fall Symposium: Simulating Human Agents, North Falmouth, Massachusetts.

Laird, J. E., & van Lent, M. (1999, November 3-5). Developing an artificial intelligence engine. In *Proceedings of the Game Developers Conference,* San Jose, California.

Livingstone, D. (2006). Turing's test and believable AI in games. *Computers in Entertainment*, 4(1). Retrieved March 2006, from http://www.acm.org/pubs/cie.html.

MacDorman, K. F., & Ishiguro, H. (2006). The uncanny advantage of using androids in social and cognitive science research. *Interaction Studies, 7*(3), 297-337.

Mac Namee, B. (2004). *Proactive persistent agents: Using situational intelligence to create support characters in character-centric computer games.* Unpublished doctoral thesis, University of Dublin, Department of Computer Science.

McGlinchey, S. (2003). *Learning of AI players from game pbservation data.* Paper presented at the Game-On 2003, 4th International Conference on Intelligent Games and Simulation, London.

McGlinchey, S., & Livingstone, D. (2004). *What believability testing can tell us.* Paper presented at CGAIDE, Microsoft Campus, Reading.

Purdy, J. H., & Thornton, J. S. (2004, August). *What effects should a game have on brain & body to be successful?* Paper presented at the Game Developers Conference Europe, London.

Searle, J. R. (1980). Minds, brains and programs. *Behavioral and Brain Sciences, 3*, 417-424.

Sweetser, P., & Drenna, P. (2003, November 20). *User-centred design in games.* Paper presented at the Australian Game Developers Conference Academic Summit, Melbourne, Australia.

Turing, A. M. (1950). Computing machinery and intelligence. *Mind, LIX*(236), 433-460.

Westwood. (1998). *Blade Runner* (PC CD-Rom).

Wetzel, B. (2004, July). *Step one: Document the problem.* Paper presented at AAAI Workshop on Challenges in Game AI, San Jose, California.

About the Contributors

Colin Fyfe is an active researcher in artificial neural networks, genetic algorithms, artificial immune systems, and artificial life having written over 250 refereed papers, several book chapters, and two books. He is a member of the editorial board of the *International Journal of Knowledge-Based Intelligent Engineering Systems* and an associate editor of *International Journal of Neural Systems*. He currently supervises six PhD students and has been director of studies for 16 PhDs since 1998. He is a member of the academic advisory board of the International Computer Science Conventions group and a committee member of the European Network of Excellence on Intelligent Technologies for Smart Adaptive Systems (EUNITE). He has been a visiting researcher at the University of Strathclyde, Riken Institute in Tokyo, Chinese University of Hong Kong, and a visiting professor at the University of Vigo, University of Burgos, and University of Salamanca, all in Spain.

Darryl Charles graduated from Queens University Belfast with a degree in electrical and electronic engineering (Hons) in 1988. After qualifying as a teacher at Stranmillis College, Belfast, he taught technology and design at Portadown College until 1995 and during this spell completed a MSc in microelectronics and microcomputer applications. He then spent a year as head of IT at Cox Green School in Maidenhead before going back into higher education to study for a PhD at the University of Paisley, Scotland. After completing a PhD in unsupervised neural networks in 1999, he was appointed as a lecturer then as a senior lecturer in computing at Paisley. In 2001, he returned to Northern Ireland to take up a lecturing post at the University of Ulster where his teaching and research specialism is now within the realm of computer games and in particular adaptation.

Stephen McGlinchey received a BSc (Hons) in computing science from the University of Paisley in 1996, and went on to do a PhD in neural networks, which was completed in 2000, also at Paisley. He now works as a lecturer at the University of Paisley, teaching computer games technology. He has published several research papers, mainly on neural networks and artificial intelligence for games. Recently, his research work has focussed on ant colony algorithms for path-finding in computer games, and automatic postprocessing of motion capture data.

Daniel Livingstone received a BSc (Hons) in computer and electronic engineering from the University of Strathclyde in 1993, an MSc with distinction in computer science (AI) from the University of Essex in 1995, and a PhD (modelling the evolution of human language and languages) from the University of Paisley in 2003. He currently lectures a range of classes related to computer game development, and his research interests range from AI and artificial life for computer games to the use of game technology in education. His current work is now focussing on the use of massively-multiplayer virtual worlds as learning platforms.

Index